Decent People

Decent People

Norman S. Care

ROWMAN & LITTLEFIELD PUBLISHERS, INC.
Lanham • Boulder • New York • Oxford

ROWMAN & LITTLEFIELD PUBLISHERS, INC.

Published in the United States of America
by Rowman & Littlefield Publishers, Inc.
4720 Boston Way, Lanham, Maryland 20706
http://www.rowmanlittlefield.com

12 Hid's Copse Road
Cumnor Hill, Oxford OX2 9JJ, England

British Library Cataloguing in Publication Information Available

Library of Congress Cataloging-in-Publication Data

Care, Norman S.
  Decent people / Norman S. Care.
    p. cm.
  Includes bibliographical references and index.
  ISBN 0-7425-0708-4 (alk. paper) — ISBN 0-7425-0709-2 (pbk. : alk. paper)
    1. Ethics. 2. Motivation (Psychology)—Moral and ethical aspects. I. Title.

BJ1031 .C35 2000
170—dc21   00-038737

©™ The paper used in this publication meets the minimum requirements of
American National Standard for Information Sciences—Permanence of
Paper for Printed Library Materials, ANSI/NISO Z39.48-1992.
Manufactured in the United States of America

For Barbara

Contents

Preface

Suppose—in imagination at least—you were today to set yourself the task of writing a letter to the children of your children's children. That is, you propose to write something to members of a "future generation"— a future generation whose existence you had a part in. Interestingly, you are part of their history, and, depending on circumstances and luck, they might know something of you. But you, now proposing to communicate to them, know nothing particular about them. They are not your children or your grandchildren, after all. They are pretty much beyond the range within which we can know others up close. You know that they "descend" from you, but you do not know whether they are tall or short or likable or dull or talented or bad-tempered and so forth.

You might, in your letter, tell them something of family history, I suppose—though it is worth noting that for some of us family history has its bits and pieces that one might not wish to pass along. But for the moment let us suppose that the letter is not confined to family history information. It is an opportunity for you to expand more broadly on your concerns— your concerns, in fact, about life and the human condition as you, now a grown adult, know them.

How would your letter go? Well, doubtless our letters would be different from one another in details. Here are some notes on how mine might go. I say "might go" here because the more I think about the task I have set, the less clear I become about what I would say. Overall, the letter to the future I thought might be fun to write soon goes gloomy.

I assume that at some point I must say to these future children that I live in the midst of issues, problems, and even crises. I am as aware as anyone that I do not know all I need to know about the dimensions and details of these various difficulties. They range from large-scale global environmental issues (almost too complicated to know well), to problems and crises in my nation and local communities, to difficulties in my personal life and my life with others. Some of these difficulties may be characterized as social; others are political, educational, economic, or concerned with health. Interestingly, all of them are moral in their respective and sometimes different ways. Some of them—large or small—are urgent. As I and the members of my generation conduct our lives, we in effect ship a number of crises forward to members of future generations.

I would have to notice in my letter that we are different in our fates with life's difficulties. These issues, problems, and crises are different in nature and in distribution. No one escapes them entirely, probably, but degree and seriousness of involvement can be different for different people. If crises are by definition challenges to life, the crises themselves can be different. Individuals in my day in Eastern Europe, the Mideast, and the new independent communities in the former Soviet Union all face problems and struggles relating to survival, but their challenges to responsibility, character, and value have content I do not face. However, as an American, marriage partner, parent, academician, and so on, I face other issues—some of them quite crisis-like—and these issues have content that challenges me in the matters of responsibility, character, and value. I live in my society—I am caught in it, so to speak, by history and contingency—and my society, which I care about, has not yet gotten past the racism, sexism, and violence embedded in its past. It is only now beginning to acknowledge its negative impact on its environment, as well as the plight of its uneducated young, the sorry state of its health care arrangements, and the abuse suffered by its current children and its elderly. All these things—and many things related to these things—impinge on my life and the lives of friends, enemies, colleagues, and associates in the current generation.

I wonder whether the future children I write to will live in a society like mine. I live in a society that is supposed to be materially affluent, is certainly preoccupied with sex, and seems filled on the surface with jokes and bright lights and pizza and bizarre media hype. Despite this bright and often silly veneer, I also know that beneath the surface some and even many current people are discontented, angry, and filled with resentment, and this negativity spills over into our streets and our popular culture. I am aware, too, that the anger, discontent, and resentment are not confined to those who express it by exploding federal buildings or playing at guerrilla militarism on weekends. I am saddened to have to report, to the future children I write to, that my society is difficult to live in: it is dangerous in many places and increasingly unkind and ungenerous in many others; it is tough and hard, and one must be very careful in it. If one is not very careful, one will get hurt. I hope the society of the future children will not be this way.

I have noticed again and again that challenges to responsibility present to us not only questions about principles and policies—for ourselves and our communities—but also questions about motivation to act. I have to report to my distant future children that for creatures like us, apparently, it is one thing to know the right thing to do in given circumstances but another thing to be moved to do the right thing in those circumstances. Sadly, to know the right is not automatically to be moved to do the right. And the human condition in my time is filled with challenges to responsibility wherein the motivational difficulty is at least as challenging as the knowledge difficulty.

When I stand back from my life and look out across the world community that I live in, I find that the first thing I notice is that over one-fifth of the people who are with me in the world community are, right now, *destitute* in some or many of the ways that jeopardize human life. These are human beings who are literally starving to death, or homeless, or suffering life-threatening political oppression, or so lacking in education that they have no ways of expressing themselves or living what anyone could call a decent life. When I understand that this is the character of the world I live in—a world brightened only a little by its snazzy gadgets and technology—I am more ashamed than I know how to say.

When I look out across the world community a second time, I find that the next thing I notice, alongside the absolute destitution, is such *disparity in the levels of life* available to people that I must fight back tears. The world is no extension of the affluence that shields a few of us; it is instead a sea of pain and despair, with only small and sometimes temporary islands of stability and prosperity here and there. Shall I write to my future children of the contrast between the level of life I have, and the life chances it gives me, and the life chances of one of the hundreds of thousands of youngsters or adults known to be living today in regions of famine or ethnic strife or, more specifically, in huge garbage dumps on the edges of polluted cities—cities that are, with today's forms of transportation, only a relatively short plane flight from my home? Shall I write of the contrast between my and their forms of housing, clothes, diet, educational opportunities, means of transportation, entertainment, equipment in homes, length of life, fullness of life, quality of life? The contrasts are hard to bear. Questions of fairness flood the mind.

I am sometimes outraged by the facts of destitution and disparity, and then I feel guilty over them, and then I simply want to turn away from them. I try now and then to be indignant and say the stereotypical me-first thing: "So what? It's all very sad, but it's nothing to me. I can't let such things bother me. I have my own life to live. I didn't make anyone starve." But I find that when I attempt this reply I am not able to sustain it. The facts of misfortune—especially when the facts could be remedied—are not easily dismissed, nor are they easily covered up by ultra-Right or ultra-Left ideologies. Certainly I find those with me in today's world who seem not to mind such facts—who consider themselves "winners" in life—to be either confused, ill, or, more hopefully, just pretending.

When I look across the world community a third time, I am ready to notice the environment more or less for its own sake. I can see how this matter of the environment might be very important to my future children—even more so, I assume (and even hope), than the other dismal facts and features of the human condition in my time. I know of no better words to express the results of this third viewing than those of the great forester and environmental ethicist, Aldo Leopold. Leopold writes that, for persons of ecological conscience, the environment is a "world of wounds."[1] The friends, associates, and strangers who make up humankind in today's world have, with me and with others before us, hurt the land; we have damaged the air and then tried to improve it, we have ruined small and large natural systems, we have made mighty rivers fail to reach the sea. And for Leopold, of course—as for Thoreau and perhaps even Jefferson before him—what we have wounded has positive value in its own right. The wounding we have done may also have hurt us—but the valuational damage is not exhausted in that fact. There is, as we are beginning to learn to say, intrinsic value in nature.

I am not clear about how I would end my letter to the children of my children's children. In a way the studies in this book are an attempt to explore some of what figures in the notes above being so gloomy. In what follows, then, I take up questions that concern ultimately what it is to be a good or decent person, where "good person" or "decent person" here has to do with what I call *moral-emotional nature* as well as *respect for principle*. The discussion centers primarily on what might be called "motivation issues" rather than questions about the content of moral principles or the grand imperatives that classical ethical theorists (e.g., Kant and Mill) called the "foundation" of morality. My view, put simply, is that decent people are constrained by moral-emotional nature so as to take certain things seriously, and this is part of what it is for them to have moral lives—moral lives that are, indeed, involved in the economic, political, family, and personal lives that constitute their lives as a whole. But these things that they take seriously are not just principles that they respect. Moral-emotional nature pressures us and makes demands on us, but this is not completely understood in terms that emphasize solely or even mainly what it is to respect principles.

I think of the chapters that make up the book as studies that are reasonably complete as essays but also connected to one another. I will explain toward the end of chapter 1 something more of the organization of the discussion. Here I will mention that the studies are organized by a familiar view of how we are relative to our responsibilities to and for other people.

Chapters 2, 3, and 4 concern moral-emotional nature regarding "self" and those we have, or wish to have, certain familiar sorts of relationships with. Thus these chapters deal conceptually with motivational issues located where most of us "live" most of the time, namely, in the immediacy of life with others.

Chapter 5 concerns moral-emotional nature regarding ourselves and "current others," when some (most, in fact) of the latter are distant geographically, and in some cases also distant culturally, yet we are aware of certain facts about them that seem normative in the ways they pressure us to respond to them, namely, serious basic human needs.

Chapter 6 concerns moral-emotional nature regarding ourselves and "future people," when all of the latter are so distant from us as to be identityless regarding particular facts that serve normally to distinguish people from one another.

Chapter 7 deals with a negative aspect of moral-emotional nature, namely, the aspect reflected in our occasional—and sometimes more than occasional—*indifference* to moral imperatives, and asks how we can be reconciled to our own nature in this connection. Just as a political philosophy might attempt to show how the principles of justice governing the basic structure of society can reconcile us as citizens in a nation-state to certain natural facts about the human condition,[2] and an ethical theory might illuminate how respect for certain moral principles in one's conduct might reconcile us to the unevenness of individual fates in the human condition,[3] so we need a theory that allows us to understand, and perhaps helps us to *live with*, our own episodic indifference to the demands of morality.

Beyond these studies, I include two appendixes. They concern mainly logical points about the ideas of *action* and *reasons*. These points operate in the background of the studies but are not required as a condition of understanding the studies.

My discussions here are "analytic" in part and "normative" in part, which is to say that they make conceptual claims but also, from time to time, take a stand on a substantive moral issue.

The writing that follows draws in places on earlier efforts, though the earlier pieces have been considerably revised and in some cases altered. Different parts of chapter 2 incorporate passages (slightly revised) from

my book *Living with One's Past: Personal Fates and Moral Pain* and also from
an essay titled "Moral Discourse" contributed to the (forthcoming, at this
writing) *Encyclopedia of Psychology*.[4] It also reflects a presentation I made
at a "grand-rounds" session for the Department of Psychology and the
Department of Bioethics at the Cleveland Clinic, Cleveland, Ohio, in April
1999. Chapter 3 derives from a presentation I made at the "Conversations
in Bioethics" series at the Center for Biomedical Ethics, Case Western
Reserve University School of Medicine, in March 1999. What I have written here will also appear in a volume (forthcoming) on "forgiveness" to
be edited by Sharon Lamb and Jeffrie G. Murphy. Chapter 5 draws not
only on the chapter titled "Career Choice" in my *On Sharing Fate* but also
on a lecture given at an eleven-state regional conference on public art in
Durham, North Carolina (published as "Public Art and Moral Responsibility" in *Public Art Dialogue: Southeast* [Durham, N.C.: Durham Arts
Council, 1989]), and another given at Cranbrook Art Academy in Michigan
in 1991. Chapter 6 draws on my future generations discussion in *On Sharing Fate* and my essay "Future Generations and the Motivation Problem"
in Jim Dator and Tae-Chang Kim's edited volume, *Creating a New History
for Future Generations* (Kyoto: Institute for the Integrated Study of Future
Generations, 1995). What I offer here is to appear in a (forthcoming) volume on energy being edited by Professor Robert Bent of Indiana University. The discussion of "mental illness" in Chapter 7 draws on my review
of Carl Elliott's *The Rules of Insanity: Moral Responsibility and the Mentally
Ill Offender* (Albany: State University of New York Press, 1996) in *Medical
Humanities Review* (11, no. 1 [spring 1997]). Appendix B contains some
passages from "On Avowing Reasons" (*Mind* 76 [April 1967]). The parts
of the preface that concern a "letter to the children of my children's children" draw on two earlier versions, one in the *Oberlin Alumni Magazine*
(fall 1998), the other in Oberlin College's *The Annual of the John Frederick
Oberlin Society* (vol. 2, 1998–99).

My thanks go to those who discussed with me the matters I write about
here. My departmental colleagues at Oberlin—Daniel D. Merrill, Robert
H. Grimm, Peter K. McInerney, Ira S. Steinberg, Alfred F. MacKay, and
Martin R. Jones—have always tolerated my idiosyncratic interests in philosophy and have been helpful in responding to my writing. I have discussed issues of moral psychology with David Love very often, and I have
benefited every time. Meaning-of-life conversations with Oberlin
colleagues and friends William E. Hood (art history) and Thomas Van
Nortwick (Classics) have been very helpful. Outside Oberlin, I have appreciated support from Claudia Card, Michael Stocker, Laurence Thomas,
and Jeffrie G. Murphy.

A Research Status Appointment from Oberlin College in 1998–99 made
it possible for me to complete this book. I am very grateful for this support.

My thanks, too, go to Karen H. Barnes of Oberlin College for help in the preparation of the manuscript and more generally for support of my teaching and writing.

Finally, I express my appreciation to Maureen MacGrogan (acquisitions editor), Dawn Stoltzfus (production editor), and Elisabeth Graves (copyeditor) at Rowman and Littlefield for their welcoming, efficient, and careful treatment of my manuscript.

1

✛

Motivation Issues

BEHIND MORAL ACTION

In this book I take seriously a distinction we make in our ways of understanding and conducting the moral life we share. I have in mind the distinction between what it is for actions to have or carry certain moral values and what it is that moves us to perform those actions. Thus, an action might be right in virtue, say, of it meeting the terms of a moral principle, but what moves us to perform that action may or may not be respect for the moral principle it meets. An action might be unkind in virtue of it violating certain principles of benevolence, but what moves us to perform that action may have little to do with negative attitudes toward those principles. This distinction is important, I think. To recognize it is to be led to see a certain complexity in human beings that has positive and negative aspects. If persons do not always do the thing that is right because it is right (or the thing that is wrong because it is wrong), then in some cases we may need to be on guard with them because their actions are not necessarily keys to their motives. In other cases we may need to be not so much on guard with others as simply aware of their vulnerability or frailty—for they (like us) may wish to do the things that are right but find sometimes or often that other motivations, impulses, or dispositions take them to other things.

Morality is confining for us, that is, it specifies conditions on our ways of coming to action that we do not always meet. It seems as if our rational thinking about others and ourselves sails along on one level of explanation and justification, assuming about people that they are unitary

1

agents pretty much in control of themselves and their actions, while we, that is, ourselves and others as actual real-life people, sometimes do and sometimes do not fit the course of life on that level. It is as if our rational thinking construes persons as agents living their lives on the basis of reasons in an explanatory and justificatory "straight line" from one point in their lives to the next; and, further, it is as if such thinking construes both movement along that line and departures from it as open to reason-giving accounts featuring coherence and an ordering of principles and policies (including weights placed on them) that can be transparent to all similarly positioned (in control) agents. I suspect, however, that our real-life course is, so to speak, crooked and meandering from point to point in our lives, sometimes coordinating with the straight-line course of life, sometimes coinciding with it, sometimes slightly or wildly off it, and so on.

The distinction in question allows us to suppose that there is no reason to think that when real people do what rational agents would do, they do so for the reasons the latter would have. (As such, the distinction is probably a condition of the possibility of the cynicism that seems so common these days.) It also may lead us to wonder whether what moves real people to do what they do is or can be known to them.[1] My views here are, I think, in line with some words from Kant's writings on ethics:

> It sometimes happens that in the most searching self-examination we can find nothing except the moral ground of duty which could have been powerful enough to move us to this or that good action and to such great sacrifice. But from this we cannot by any means conclude with certainty that a secret impulse of self-love, falsely appearing as the idea of duty, was not actually the true determining cause of the will. For we like to flatter ourselves with a pretended noble motive, while in fact even the strictest examination can never lead us entirely behind the secret incentives.[2]

I want to suggest, with Kant, that there is deep epistemological uncertainty about what moves us to action. I think, too, that in the rational thinking and moral judging we do as participants in ordinary life, we tend to forget, ignore, or suppress this unhappy fact about ourselves.

The distinction in question might be considered a "dark distinction" because it opens the door not only to uncertainty in our attempts to understand persons and what they do but also to unreliability in our thoughts about what people will do and to worries that what people do and why they do what they do are not always lined up in the ways morality may respect. But I should be careful to say that in what follows I do not attempt to deal with this distinction in the ways a psychologist or psychiatrist might. My writing about the distinction in question is conceptual and broadly analytic. It is sometimes normative, but I do not offer advice or counsel to individuals. It is not my aim, in general, to offer a program of therapy, or even propose a "recovery strategy" (the idea of which I discuss briefly in chapter 2 below), to those who think poorly of themselves or are simply baffled by themselves in their efforts to be conscientious moral agents.

On the conceptual front, one of my themes is that our forms of moral life carry with them (and radiate through them) conceptions of persons. The forms of moral life are in general sets or groups of attitudes and values that may be given different interpretations and different orderings or weights. When these forms of moral life are interpreted and their elements ordered, we then have what I call "moral conceptions," and I think of these conceptions as useful (when people choose to pay attention to them) in decision making and, hence, in the structuring of individual lives (when people are interested in being responsible agents). I do not mean anything especially technical, Wittgensteinian, or metaethical by the phrase "forms of moral life" beyond what I have just written. An important point for the moment is that these conceptual forms are not to be distinguished from one another just by their central principles, for example, the utilitarians' greatest happiness principle, or the Kantians' categorical imperative, or the Aristotelians' or Marxists' imperatives of self-realization. These forms of life have principles embedded in them, of course, but they also have in them views about human motivation, points about desirable sorts of character, and in some cases generalities about moral education, that is, about how persons are to be "prepared" for the moral life. These latter elements figure in the "conceptions of persons" I speak of, and they help distinguish the forms of moral life from one another. Whether one is to be utilitarian, Aristotelian, Kantian, Marxist, contractualist, or something else in one's life is not just a question of what principles one is to prize; it is also a question about what conception of person one can accept, tolerate, or embrace for oneself.

On the normative front, my discussion will issue more often in worries than in clean policy recommendations or solutions to moral dilemmas. I am moved, as many are, by some apparent facts about human nature and current social life that bear on our readiness to take morality seriously. From time to time we all experience a certain *indifference* to morality, and my perception is that this indifference is growing in the community I live in. It is said that America has suffered a loss of "consensus on values." A common response to questions of value in colleges and universities now is that such questions are really questions about "culture." And some who think in this way argue that the resolution of issues of value is essentially "political." There are even some views within ethical theory that, if taken seriously, tend to draw down or distort our motivation to do the right. (I mention possible examples of this briefly in the section titled "Indifference" below.) All this spins off "so what" or "it doesn't matter" or "anything goes" attitudes toward the imperative to do the right thing. My exploration of "conceptions of persons" in the studies that follow occurs in a context of worry or concern about this growing indifference. In the end, I want to claim, and argue, that the "choice problem" respecting these conceptions of persons is not a "subjectivist" or "relativist" matter. Arguments operate here. Some choices are better than others. The answer to the classical Socratic question, "What kind of person am I to be?" should not be today's increasingly heard, "Whatever."

ON MOTIVATION

There are values everywhere, and, as a result, problems of value are all over our lives. Some issues or problems of value are popularly thought to belong to individuals as matters of personal or private decision. Actually, there are few of these. In real life most of the important or interesting value issues involve moral choices of one sort or other, and these are rarely private or merely personal in any interesting sense. Insofar as value issues involve moral choices, they have cognitive dimensions and also self-regarding or other-regarding (or both) dimensions to them that block simple understandings of the words *private* or *personal*. Because these dimensions are involved, we can make *bad* or *mistaken* choices in our responses to these issues involving values. Morality may allow or even require us to think of ourselves as free, choosing beings, but the choices we make as moral agents are nevertheless vulnerable to being wrong, bad, or unwise.

In this discussion I am concerned with *motivational* aspects of our lives as moral agents. The general aim of my discussion in this chapter and those that follow is not so much to identify and argue for the principles that render our decisions right or permissible but, rather, to explore what it is that *moves* us both to figure out what "the right thing to do" is in some circumstances and also then to *do* the right thing once we have figured out what it is in those circumstances. My discussion, then, assumes and takes seriously the distinction indicated above that is familiar both in ordinary moral thought and in classical moral theory. This, again, is the distinction whereby human beings are viewed as capable of "knowing the right" but not in a way that guarantees or makes it even reliable that when they in fact know the right they are thereby "moved to do the right." In language from Kant's *Foundations of the Metaphysics of Morals*, "rational beings" (in contrast to "holy wills") are capable of discerning that certain principles have "objective necessity," that is, they are "valid for all rational beings," and hence rank as moral laws for most human beings; yet for human beings these moral laws are "subjectively contingent," that is, it remains a further question, once we have discerned the objective necessity of a principle, whether we will in fact obey that principle or (Kant's favorite metaphor) "rise to it."[3] In my discussion I assume that we experience the situation that Kant thought was relatively common, namely, the situation in which we are quite confident that a certain maxim for our conduct meets the conditions of objective necessity for principles and hence is an instance of a moral law, yet we are not much moved, or moved enough, by that fact to act in line with the principle in question. Our nature is such that we may know the right but not thereby do the right, even when we are not forced not to do the right. Knowing the right, on the part of human beings, does not immediately flow into doing the right. And if we in fact perform the action that is right, we may not do so because the action is right.

When in fact we face this situation, and then act in a way (if we act at all) that is not in line with the principle that specifies the right course of action, our choice is hardly consequence free. Depending on the details of the situation, our action leaves us vulnerable to *moral pain* of one sort or other, for example, we may (again, depending on details of the situation) experience guilt, or shame, or regret, or remorse, or resentment, or some other (as I will refer to them) of the "negative moral emotions." Interestingly, we may be vulnerable to this pain even if we do the right thing but for the wrong (or no) reasons. For most of us, negative moral-emotional experience is not unknown. I assume on the part of readers an acquaintance with negative moral emotion[4]—with, that is, what it "feels like" to know the right yet to end up doing something other than the right or end up doing the right "from" something other than its authorizing principle. And I further assume that negative moral emotion is experientially unwelcome, that is, it is not pleasurable or enjoyable. It is, in fact, a form of suffering. Some of us may claim not to care much about guilt or shame, but this seems to me largely pretense. For most of us, negative moral emotion is not sought, and, in fact, when we experience it we may find it to be motivational in its own right: it sometimes makes us resolve "never again" to do the sort of thing that brought its suffering to us.

In my discussion I propose not to simplify how the distinction in question is to be understood when we encounter it in real life. It is not so that all situations in which we know the right but end up doing something other than the right, or doing the right but for the wrong or no reasons, are cases in which we are "morally weak." Similarly, it is not so that all such situations involve our not *really* knowing the right, such that if we had known the right, we would not have done something other than the right. That is, the distinction in question, when it comes alive in real life, is not always either an instance of moral weakness or an instance of epistemological confusion. An especially intimidating situation exhibiting the distinction is the one in which an agent knows the right yet does not act from that knowledge, and the best that can be said is that the agent (neither morally weak nor epistemologically confused) is *indifferent* to the fact about the principle in the situation that it is "objectively necessary," that is, right. And I do not think that this indifference is the special mark of those around us whom we consider to be "alienated," psychopathic, or sociopathic. Most of us, I believe (as a matter of empirical observation), know "what it feels like" in certain cases to be indifferent to moral principle. Another situation in this difficult terrain is that in which one knows the right but finds that some other principle or policy—perhaps one concerning practical values (e.g., staying on a certain career path) or values of other sorts (e.g., aesthetic or religious values) or even one concerning the ultimate meaning of life—is so important as to render one's conduct out of line with the right.[5]

Of course, even if, as I am assuming here, there is no *tight* connection between understanding the principles that render action right and being moved to obey or rise to those principles, it does not follow that understanding those principles has no motivating power—no power in itself to move us into right action. But it does follow from the distinction between understanding principles and being moved to act in line with those principles that an account that shows what the principles of right action are, or even what morality more generally requires of us in some category of cases, does not thereby make clear (at least not directly) what moves people to act on those principles or all of what morality requires in that category of cases.

I should say that while I speak often enough of "motivation" in the pages that follow, it is not my aim in this book to develop a "theory of motivation." In particular, I bring no antecedently worked out account of human motivation to the discussion. Because one of my suspicions is that our ordinary "theoretical" thinking about motivation is simplistic, it would be highly artificial to approach my exploration of "what moves decent people" in different contexts and situations already equipped with a tidy account of how motivation is to be understood. My aim is to study what moves decent people *in* certain contexts or problematic situations, not from the vantage point of an assumed general account of motivation but simply from the pretty noncontroversial assumptions that we do not always act from respect for principle and that, even when we act in line with what moral principle requires, we may do so from other "considerations," some of which fuse cognitive, emotional, and other elements in ways that morality may countenance and even approve. At best, what I offer here may provide a sort of prolegomenon to a general theory of motivation.[6]

Even though it is not my aim to classify or botanize sorts of motivations, or develop a general theory of motivation, let me say something here—ahead of more detailed discussions—about certain forms of motivation that especially interest me.[7] Obviously, many factors of different kinds *move* people to do the things they do—and the things they thus do may include (on occasion) things that are required by the principles of right action. In the capital-letter terms sometimes used to mark central human "motives," Love, Hate, Fear, Sex, Ambition, Respect for Others, Money, Concern for Reputation, Power, Self-Respect, Self-Interest, Pity—all these would be on the list. And so would motivational factors of the quiet kind Hume enumerated so effectively: "Inward peace of mind, consciousness of integrity, a satisfactory review of our own conduct; these are . . . very requisite to happiness, and will be cherished and cultivated by every honest man, who feels the importance of them."[8] In more recent literature Bernard Williams has viewed "meaningful life," involving "ground projects," as based motivationally in "categorical desires" that "propel" persons forward in their lives.[9]

But, again, for my part I am not interested in cataloging in some general way all the sorts of motivations "available" to human beings. In what follows I sketch some features of motivation of the sort I am especially interested in. What guides my few remarks here is the notion that we have some idea of what motivationally constitutes a good or decent person. My thought is that even allowing for the "dark distinction" I refer to earlier, we do not restrict the motivations of good or decent people to "respect for principle." There is more to the "moral self" on the motivational front than this "respect for principle" that Kant called "self-wrought by a rational concept, and, therefore . . . specifically distinct from . . . inclination or fear."[10]

Consider the case in which it is true that a person, *J*, is moved by a motivational factor of the sort I have in mind to follow a certain policy—a policy that may in some cases reflect a principle of right action that *J* knows of. Let the policy be one that, when followed, tends to cut into *J*'s life, for example, it involves *J* in making what *J* regards as a sacrifice of something (perhaps time or resources) for the sake of certain other people. Thus, *J* may not want (*ceteris paribus*) to do the thing the policy calls for, but the principle of right action that *J* knows of calls for that thing to be done, and the motivational factor (something other than the principle per se) moves *J* to relevant action, that is, action that meets the terms of the policy. Then, among other things, the following several features obtain.

First, the "being-motivated" by the factor in question shows up in the fact that *J* makes the policy of sacrifice a *presumption for conduct*. That is, *J*, moved by this factor, resolves to act in line with the policy unless there is overriding reason not to. This is what it is for *J* to be motivated by this factor: the being-motivated is reflected by or exhibited in *J* making the policy of sacrifice a presumption for conduct.

Second, when *J* is moved by a factor of the sort I have in mind, that factor is itself viewed *by J* as "internal" rather than "external." *J* may experience the motivational factor as a pressure or demand of sorts—after all, it is moving *J* to do something she does not wish to do—but (in the cases I am interested in) it does not seem to *J* to "come from without," as, for example, in the manner of a threat of coercion.

Third, when *J* is moved by a motivational factor of the sort I have in mind, then that factor seems to *J not* to be the factor of "self-interest" as it is ordinarily and narrowly construed. That is, what moves *J* is not conscious attraction to something she understands to be "personal benefit" in the form of social or material advantage—though, indeed, the end result of *J*'s action (in line with the policy of sacrifice) may be, or turn out to be, something to her personal advantage in at least some cases.

Fourth, when *J* is moved by a factor of the sort I am interested in, it has certain *feeling tones* associated with it. There is, so to speak, an experiential side to the motivational factors I have in mind—enough so, at any rate, to make it seem plausible to suppose that one might be able to distinguish phenomenologically among such factors. There is a difference between, say, hate and pity or pity and sympathy—a difference that is beyond those differences in source, object, and rationality that may distinguish them; there are characteristic experiences or feelings associated with such motivational factors as they occur in human lives, and any account that leaves these out would appear to be incomplete.

Fifth (and less easy to express), when *J* is moved by a motivational factor of the relevant sort, then *J* "fits," either by comparison or contrast, whatever is the general conception of the *moral-emotional nature of a decent or good person* in the context provided by the case itself. We may recognize of course that the moral-emotional nature may not infallibly move one who has it to do what morality requires in particular cases. Thus, pity, for example, like compassion, can be "mistaken" and "lead us astray," as Sidgwick observes.[11] Even so, we still believe that the decent or good person can be moved by pity and compassion, and we desire to make this capacity to be moved by them a standing part of the moral-emotional nature of, say, our children as well as ourselves. But I say "comparison or contrast" just above, and by this I mean that the motivational factors of the sort I am interested in are not only the positive ones that belong to "decent" or "good" people; my attention goes to negative factors as well, that is, factors that, as it were, cause trouble (when they occur) for decent or good people, for example, impulsivity, self-centeredness, indifference, or even extreme shyness. Nevertheless, the latter motivational factors are understood by reference to their connections with positive moral-emotional nature, even if those connections are in some cases contrastive. The factors in question have a logical place in the moral framework.

ON DECENT PEOPLE

The last part of my sketch above of the sort of motivation that interests me raises questions. Does morality in fact go beyond "respect for principle" in what it requires of "moral-emotional nature"? Alternatively asked, do the moral forms of life (those elaborated in the general ethical theories of, say, Kant, Aristotle, and the utilitarians) specify anything for "moral-emotional nature" other than the capacity for respect for the principles and policies authorized by morality?

My thought is that morality as ordinarily understood and practiced does ask something more of moral-emotional nature than respect for principles. Michael Stocker suggests that this is so through a simple but powerful example.[12] Suppose *J* visits *S* in the hospital, does an effective job of cheering up *S* (who needs cheering up), and then prepares to depart. *S* offers thanks to *J* for the visit, remarking that *J*'s friendship is a great support for him. *J* responds (in effect) that she was visiting "from duty" and that she was thus meeting the terms of a universalizable moral rule that permits or even requires such visits to the sick by those who can manage them. (*J* adds that, in fact, she visits patients in this very hospital three evenings per week and thus meets her obligations under the principle in question.)

Stocker suggests that the point the example brings out is not that the *rule* that *J* obeyed was incorrect but that *J*'s motivation was, if not exactly wrong, then nevertheless somehow inappropriate in the context provided. In the situation in question, visiting "from duty" is a sort of moral shortfall. *J*'s visiting may have been an okay thing to do, but the "from duty" motivation behind it, at least in this case, robs the visiting of its full moral value. We want from *J* in this case something of moral-emotional nature that lies outside "respect for principle."

But the recognition of the shortfall in the Stocker example leads on to another question. Can morality require that we have (and "apply") the elements of moral-emotional nature that lie outside "respect for principle"? Can we judge, in the Stocker example, that *J* *ought* to have had certain feelings (of friendship or affection) behind or involved in the action of visiting *S* in the hospital, and can we say that if she did not have those feelings, then her action was less than fully morally valuable? Can

feelings be morally required, such that in their absence—even in a case
in which the right action is performed—the performing agent can be criticized?[13]

My initial thought is that morality does make demands on moral-emotional nature so that J's visit "from duty" is a shortfall or at any rate the
judgment that J's action was morally valuable is at least controversial. The
point is not merely that S finds J's visiting from duty disappointing. What
is at stake is whether morality is essentially a system of rules, which persons can obey for whatever reasons, or something that is broader in its
demands—a system that reaches to the ingredients of the characters or
personalities of those who obey its rules.

Aristotle claims early in *Nicomachean Ethics* that "it is no easy task to
be good."[14] The other general ethical theories I have in mind in this discussion, those of Kant and the utilitarians, would in fact agree. But the
account of why it is difficult to be good is rather different in the three theories. All three theories agree that there is a *cognitive* difficulty in being
good—though, again, the account to be given of this difficulty differs
among Aristotle, Kant, and, say, John Stuart Mill. Very briefly put, Aristotle
finds, in his analysis of virtue, that the cognitive difficulty is in one's ability
to perceive the "mean" between extremes as one struggles to reflect the
moral sensibility operative in one's community or, more exactly (for
Aristotle), the moral sensibility operative among those with "practical
wisdom" in one's community. The trouble here, for conscientious moral
agents, is that "in everything it is no easy task to find the middle," and
this renders judgment very particularized in actual situations.[15]

For Kant and Mill, the cognitive difficulty in the moral life is not located
in the notion that the "mean" floats between "extremes" from situation
to situation but, rather, in the task of applying their respective interpretations of the foundational principle of the moral system in particular
cases. What it is to apply the categorical imperative is elusive even after
Kant's discussion (several times) of four very different examples in *Foundations*.[16] And Mill would have to acknowledge that the difficulty of figuring out what is conducive to the greatest happiness of the greatest number is enormous—especially if figuring this out requires having some grip
on what is pleasurable and what is painful (and to what degree and to
what extent) to existing "sentient beings" in a "community" defined in
one way or other.[17]

Indeed, even as we tend to dwell on their many differences, these major theories have in common the view that the moral life is or can be difficult. But, interestingly, these theories tend to recognize as well, albeit in
different ways, that morality makes moral-emotional demands of human
beings beyond "respect for principle." For they recognize, alongside the

cognitive difficulties in being good, that there are motivational difficulties as well. For Aristotle, fully to live the moral life is not only to perceive the mean between extremes in particular cases that challenge responsible decision making; it is also to "feel rightly" in one's conduct of the moral life: "Fear and confidence and appetite and anger and pity and in general pleasure and pain may be felt both too much and too little, and in both cases not well; but to feel them at the right times, with reference to the right objects, towards the right people, with the right motive, and in the right way, is what is both intermediate and best, and this is characteristic of virtue."[18] For Kant, reason is expected to "constrain" inclination in the moral agent, and presumably one of the challenges of the moral life is the development of moral personality that, as it were, facilitates such constraint. There is no real moral agency, for Kant, in the absence of the experience of tension and conflict between the deliverances (imperatives) of reason and the promptings of inclination, that is, of emotion, impulse, and feeling.[19] Indeed, the being whom we imagine to experience no such tension in its nature is explicitly designated a "holy being," not a "rational being," by Kant.[20] Perhaps the most ambitious inclusion of moral-emotional demands on human nature in an account of moral sensibility is that of John Stuart Mill. For Mill's idea is that ordinary morality requires, as a condition of its possibility, beings capable of the other-regarding "sentiment of natural sympathy," that is, a sort of concern for the well-being of others as independent and elementary in the nature of the being as is its concern for its own well-being.[21] Indeed, a being who lacks natural sympathy is said by Mill to have a mind that is a "moral blank."[22]

This short discussion suggests that classical ethical theory, as well as ordinary moral experience, views morality as asking more of moral agents than "respect for principle." I will not try to develop this account further here. Examples of familiar motivational factors that figure in our idea of what constitutes a good or decent person, I think, are a person's love for another person, or pity for that person, or respect for that person—and, of course, love, pity, and respect are factors that may move one to do what morality requires in certain circumstances. Mill's "sentiment of natural sympathy," even if construed minimally as the fact about us that we are not indifferent to pain and suffering in others, may also be among the motivational factors I have in mind.[23] Something that does *not* fit the characterization is external coercion, even when it is filtered through the mind via, say, the emotions of fear, anger, or distrust. Thus, "fear of punishment" is not an example of the type of motivation I have in mind—though, obviously, fear of punishment may be motivating, albeit not in the "internalist" way I am interested in. When one is moved to do what morality requires by fear of punishment, one does not, I think, see either the punishment in prospect or the fear of it as "internal" to one. It seems, rather, pushed, intruded, or imposed on one from the outside. Nor does one see such a factor as a part of the positive nature of a decent or good human being. Rather, in the case of fear one seems to some degree *driven* to make a certain policy one's presumption of conduct, and one's recognition of this may lead one to resist following through.

In summary of this much, then, I mean for this book to be about what it is to be a decent person. But the book does not mean to be "preachy" or to be an exercise in pop psychology (or even "applied ethics"), and I certainly do not think of decent people as "unreal," "goody-goody," self-righteous, or stupid.[24] A decent person is simply a person under certain constraints—the constraints of moral-emotional nature. Moral-emotional nature includes "reason" of course—reason of both the Kantian and utilitarian kinds—but it involves much else, even something beyond the "perception" that Aristotle thought to be the result of proper moral education. I find the word *motivation* helpful as a word that points to the "something more." But I do not think of motivation as "one thing," located in some conceptual way "outside reason." As I said above, in what follows I do not apply an already worked out theory of motivation, nor do I end up with such a theory. (Sometimes I doubt that motivation is susceptible of a "general account.") At any rate, what I have to say about motivation I will say through explorations in topical contexts. The aim is to explore some motivational issues generated by taking seriously the demands of the moral life in such contexts.

There are minimal operating assumptions for me in what follows. The first is that moral-emotional nature is complex, so it is hard to specify what is within the range of "motivational factors" for an individual, and, too, it cannot be expected (in my view) that the motivational factors in a person all work in the same way. The second is that (as I hint above) the factors that move us to act are not cleanly divisible into separate departments of "cognition" and "affect." What moves us, I think, are "considerations" that *fuse* some elements that might, if they were separated out, be counted cognitive and others that might be counted something else (emotional, commitment-like, visceral, volitional, etc.). But, somehow, in real life, when we are moved by these factors, it is as if their pressure in us is something beyond the simple sum of such elements.

My effort to illuminate how moral-emotional nature in decent people works in certain topical contexts is ordered as follows. In chapter 2 I discuss what it is for a person to move from a moral-emotional low point, in which agency is reduced or nearly lost, toward the "recovery" of agency. My special interest in this subject here is the motivational role in such recovery played by what I call *meaningful-life platforms*, that is, the "operating systems" for human life that I suggest lie behind the moral aspirations of decent persons.[25] In chapter 3 I discuss another sort of factor that contributes, in some cases, to the restoration of full, effective moral agency, namely, *forgiveness* or, more exactly, our "participation" in the practices of other-forgiveness and self-forgiveness. These chapters are connected. The theme of "recovery of agency" introduced in chapter 2 is also a concern in chapter 3.

Chapter 4 explores *self-respect* as a motivational factor. I distinguish some different conceptions of self-respect, some of which seem to me more important than others. In chapter 5 I try to explain how it is that *others' needs* pressure us to respond in the ways we do or think we should. And in chapter 6 I explore what could move us to take seriously what morality requires of us (in the way of principles) to protect *future people*, that is, people who live in the very distant future, well beyond our children and their children; my special interest here is in the role of *novel ideas* in securing their protection.

INDIFFERENCE

There is a chapter 7 beyond those listed above. It is an inquiry into what might dramatically be called the "dark side" of human nature. But here I must be careful to say that my interest in this side of human nature will not carry me to much discussion of the extremes of the "psychopath" or "sociopath," or to "moral monsters," or even to figures filled with hate, aggression, or acquisitiveness.[26] I have in mind mainly the simple, more familiar *indifference* to moral pressure that is known surely to all decent people. We all know what it is to make a promise and then not get around to keeping it—not because of moral weakness or competing imperatives but just because we did not get to it. It seems a sort of unthinking rather than calculated omission of right action. This sort of indifference is not a principled rejection of morality, nor does it reflect a commitment to the stance and posture of a societal "outsider." It is something more primitive than any of those things. The indifference I have in mind is common, and it is not emotionally charged one way or other; it just is. It is also the case that when we think on it, and notice how and how often it figures in our lives, we (most of us) are pained by it.

In a remarkable set of pages from Walker Percy's novel *The Moviegoer*, there is an encounter between the young man who is the main character—a fellow named Binx, somewhat adrift in life—and his aunt. What has happened is that Binx has taken young suicidal Kate to Chicago for a weekend break from her troubles—but without letting the aunt know. The

aunt confronts Binx over this and in effect escalates an accusation of indifference into a character assassination:

> "First, is it not true that in all of past history people who found themselves
> in difficult situations behaved in certain familiar ways, well or badly, cou-
> rageously or cowardly, with distinction or mediocrity, with honor or dis-
> honor. They are recognizable. They display courage, pity, fear, embarrass-
> ment, joy, sorrow, and so on. Such anyhow has been the funded experience
> of the race for two or three thousand years, has it not? Your discovery, as
> best as I can determine, is that there is an alternative which no one has hit
> upon. It is that one finding oneself in one of life's critical situations need not
> after all respond in one of the traditional ways. No. One may simply default.
> Pass. Do as one pleases, shrug, turn on one's heel and leave. Exit. Why af-
> ter all need one act humanly? Like all great discoveries, it is breathtakingly
> simple." She smiles a quizzical-legal sort of smile. . . .
> "I am sorry that . . . you were not told of Kate's plans to go with me to
> Chicago. . . . I am sorry and I hope that your anger—"
> "Anger? You are mistaken. It was not anger. It was discovery."
> "Discovery of what?"
> "Discovery that someone in whom you had placed great hopes was sud-
> denly not there. It is like leaning on what seems to be a good stalwart shoul-
> der and feeling it go all mushy and queer. . . . I honestly don't believe it
> occurred to you to let us know that you and Kate were leaving, even though
> you knew how desperately sick she was. I truly do not think it ever occurred
> to you that you were abusing a sacred trust in carrying that poor child off
> on a fantastic trip like that or that you were betraying the great trust and
> affection she has for you. Well?" she asks when I do not reply.
> I try as best I can to appear as she would have me, as being, if not right,
> then wrong in a recognizable, a right form of wrongness. But I can think of
> nothing to say.
> "I did my best for you, son. I gave you all I had. More than anything I
> wanted to pass on to you . . . a certain quality of spirit, a gaiety, a sense of
> duty, a nobility worn lightly, a sweetness, a gentleness with women—the
> only good things the South ever had and the only things that really matter
> in this life. Ah well. Still you can tell me one thing. I know you're not a bad
> boy—I wish you were. But how did it happen that none of this ever meant
> anything to you? Clearly it did not. Would you please tell me? I am genu-
> inely curious."
> I shake my head. . . . I am silent. . . . I think of nothing in particular.[27]

Of course, indifference is not always of simply the episodic unthinking
omission sort (or of the episodic sort blown up to character trait, as in the
condemnation above). Other sorts of indifference can occur, perhaps bred
by very different kinds of phenomena. Thus, morality may be cheapened
by views that reduce it to "culture," and in real life this may foster a sort
of practical indifference to morality—or, anyway, "moral talk"—and in

extreme cases rejections of charges of responsibility as mere efforts to put one on a "guilt trip." Even sophisticated philosophical views can foster a kind of indifference: if act-utilitarianism, for example, really separates the "making" and "keeping" of promises as distinct acts, each of which is to be judged by the principle of utility, then the usual understanding of promise making as carrying with it commitments to promise keeping is cancelled or at least threatened. It might similarly be said that the analysis of valuational discourse that finds moral judgments and moral arguments to be "emotive" fosters ultimately an indifference to the demands and challenges of the moral life.[28]

Whatever its sources, the indifference we experience—occasionally or often, for short or long periods—challenges any positive conception we have of ourselves as conscientious moral agents. Even as we attempt to negotiate the moral life as responsible individuals, the indifference we experience is "there" as a fact—it cannot be, as it were, jettisoned from personality. If this is so, then how does one become "reconciled" to the facts that one sometimes or often will not do what one knows one ought to do and that one sometimes or often acts in this way from indifference. How, then, is one—a decent person, one who takes morality seriously— to live with the fact that from time to time one is indifferent to morality? That is the question I raise, and try to respond to, in chapter 7.

Let me end this introductory discussion with two quick caveats: (a) I have no particular religious orientation, so my discussion, despite the fact that some of the topics in it are treated by religion, is "secular" in nature; and (b) from time to time my writing runs the words *decent person* and *we* rather close together. This might give rise to the thought that I consider myself to be a decent person. Do I? Well, of course I do. But the moral-emotional nature of the "decent person" I write about here includes bouts of that "indifference" that gets discussed in chapter 7. Decent people are not "pure."[29]

2

✛

Moralized Suffering, Recovery, Meaningful Life

MORAL SENSIBILITY

The psychological low points that bring people to their friends, and sometimes to counseling and therapy, are typically experienced as negatively moralized. Thus, a person's bitterness over victimization, another's sense of loss from a broken relationship, another's resentment at the apparent onset of dementia in a parent, another's sensitivity to being "illegitimate," another's fear of professional success—all these might experientially be laced with the negative (and different) moral emotions of guilt, shame, remorse, or regret. As such, the negative moral emotions may have certain distinctive feeling tones, but they also have a cognitive core or base in perceived violations of moral principle. The negative moral feelings that constitute the emotional suffering that drains energy and diminishes agency have moral principles in the background. To experience them is to find one's view of oneself as a good or decent person to be suspect.

Decent people, moral philosophers, psychological theorists, and clinical practitioners can all have interests—albeit interests of different kinds—in "moral discourse" construed broadly as including moral judgments, moral principles, conceptions of moral agency, and the negative and positive moral emotions. At the most general level, *ethical theories* study moral discourse in an attempt to characterize and even systematize the structural features of human moral sensibility. The idea here is that just as human beings have certain capacities for intelligence, judgment, and

17

feeling that allow them to know the world and not just react to it, so they also have certain capacities (again, for intelligence, judgment, and feeling) relevant to valuational responses to the world, as reflected both in moral judgment and action and in the sort of appreciation we call "aesthetic." The task of the general ethical theories is to illuminate how these capacities work in the matter of moral judgment and action, and part of what there is to study in this connection is moral discourse.

The long-standing general theories that have been found to be important and insightful—for example, those of Aristotle, Kant, or the utilitarians—typically claim that moral sensibility has a distinctive sort of rationality to it, so that moral valuations are not merely "anything goes" expressions of personal subjectivity. The theories agree that positions on issues of value require defense and justification, even though the theories conflict in certain ways over how these rational processes are to be understood. Thus, if persons disagree in a matter of morality, then rational inquiry must persist, not terminate, and the business of a general ethical theory is to make clear what the logic of moral argumentation actually is, in contrast, say, to economic, political, or other sorts of argumentation.

Apart from their different accounts of moral argument, the main received theories may be seen to carry among their presuppositions certain conceptual images of what it is to be a moral agent. Thus, the Kantian theory prizes the "rational nature" in persons which is that juxtaposition of "reason" and "inclination" that provides the tension that gives rise to our interest in what we *ought* to do in certain cases, in contrast to what we could do in those cases as a matter of convenience, strong feeling, or self-interest. The utilitarian theory finds instead that morality prizes that form of existence for human beings (and sentient beings generally) that contains as much pleasure and as little pain as circumstances permit and then treats contribution to making that sort of existence as general as possible as a guideline for decision making between alternative policies or courses of action. Classical Aristotelian theory views persons as sets of dispositions forming "character" and urges the sort of moral education that helps individuals develop the "practical wisdom" that consists of good judgment within (and relative to) the communities in which they have their lives.

For many years in the middle of the twentieth century, professional philosophy seemed stalled in explorations of various reductionist theses about the nature of moral judgments, as if critical or positive moral judgments (even those reflecting acts of conscience related to principles) were somehow no more than expressions of emotion or manifestations of "intuitions" that might or might not be common in a community of individuals. During this period it appeared that professional philosophy mirrored popular culture in the notion that values are somehow noncognitive or "subjective." Fortunately, with the publication of John Rawls's *A Theory of Justice* in 1971,[1] this uninteresting period ended. Rawls shows how principles of justice for the basic structure of society have cognitive substance and are open to rational elucidation and critique. Under the pressures of the model provided by Rawls's achievement, philosophical theorists moved again into vigorous discussion of the alternative philosophical portrayals of the makeup of moral agency and the structure of moral sensibility—accompanied now, in fact, by a virtual industry of work in "applied" or "normative" ethics wherein topical policy issues (concerning, for example, abortion, capital punishment, physician-assisted suicide, etc.) are engaged.

The current discussion in both ethical theory and applied ethics features explorations of Kantian and utilitarian themes and is often critical of the latter. At the same time, there is clearly a resurgence of interest in Aristotelian "character ethics" or "virtue ethics," accompanied by increased attention to what contemporary philosophers call "moral psychology" and, thus, to the makeup of the moral self, especially its moral-emotional experience in the aftermath of moral action. In general, this latter resurgence may be represented as a shifting of attention away from the analysis and justification of candidate moral principles that are, in Kant's phrase, "valid for all rational beings" and toward recognition of the moral force of "particulars" involved in cases in which moral decisions are called for—particulars distinguishing moral agents from one another, such as the different relationships between people or the commitments they have to, say, careers or causes in which considerable emotional energy is invested. This shift in attention seems to suggest that morality itself is not just or only a system of principles, rules, and policies but, rather, countenances as well a whole range of other factors and elements in human lives that seem connected not so much to questions of right and wrong as to issues about *meaningfulness* in human lives.[2]

As a result, contemporary moral theory reflects renewed philosophical interest in classical questions about the "meaning of life" and "how to live," as well as interest in social, historical, and cultural aspects of the "moral self." Here we move closer to the moral phenomena that actually surface in the lives of real people in relationships with one another. Relationships—for example, among friends, enemies, family members, colleagues in the workplace—provide contexts that have their way of lifting important factors in the reality of individuals' lives into view and focusing attention on those "particulars," including the stresses and strains connected with them, without the philosophical theorist's preoccupations with generality and objectivity. But this is not to say that what takes place in these contexts proceeds independently of moral discourse.

ETHICAL THEORY AND RECOVERY

Imagine a situation in which two persons are in a relationship in which it makes sense for them to care about one another's well-being. Suppose *J* faces *S*, a friend suffering moral-emotional pain. The identity of this pain (is it guilt, or shame, or regret, or remorse, or resentment?) may be unclear to *S*, even though the pain itself is severe. *S*'s failure to understand the pain—its identity, its causes—may be as difficult for *S* to endure as the pain itself. And the failure to understand is not just painful to bear, for the identity of the moralized suffering bears on how it is to be responded to. If, for example, guilt (as classically understood) is the morally natural aftermath of violations of communitarian principles or rules, and shame is the analogous aftermath of failure to meet one's own standards of quality in some activity or relationship, then *how to proceed* in getting past the moralized suffering may be different in important respects. How one's pain is identified may guide one's recovery.

Apart from these cognitive issues, *S*'s suffering may be complex in further ways that require expression through the moral vocabulary. For it may seem uncontroversial to *S* that her pain is grounded in some wrong done to or by her or in her failure to perform an expected right action or meet the demands of a central self-defining relationship; and when this is so, the negatively moralized suffering involves for *S* the sense that her "control" has failed, sometimes through victimization and at other times simply gratuitously. The facts of the matter, for *S*, leave her confused, possibly in self-reproach, so that *autonomy* has been diminished and perhaps lost "for all practical purposes."

In these cases, the remote-seeming principles and conceptions of self that are targeted for attention by general ethical theories may seem to lack immediacy. *S* may be absorbed by negative evaluations of past actions and flooded by regret and remorse, and in some cases she may be experiencing despair as well as uncertainty about the future. In these circumstances, perhaps the flat languages of "rights" and "utility," so dominant in the Kantian and utilitarian theories, or even the language of "virtue" and "vice" from the Aristotelian account, may seem not to reach to the urgency of the particular case. But it is a distortion to suppose that moral discourse has been abandoned or left behind. Now the morally relevant features in particular cases—those features that generate moral-emotional pain and diminish prospects for the recovery of energy and self-esteem—are those features of commitment, concern, relationship, and responsibility that lie beneath the surface categories provided by the classical theories. Indeed, the questions for real people in ordinary life are not often of the form, "What principles do I apply here?" but instead of the form, "How can I go on from (get past, overcome) this disaster in my life?" In ordinary life, moral discourse is charged with meaning-of-life urgency and candidate how-to-live strategies. But the discourse in which such urgency and strategies are addressed is nevertheless moral discourse. The "ought" is as alive here as it is anywhere involving decisions and human flourishing, and the risks of bad or unwise choices and prolonged suffering make the rationality of such discourse a precious resource.[3] Moral reasoning, down on the ground where people are, can be intensely practical.

When a low point in one's life is morally negative, and accountability for it is painful to bear, or its identity is simply controversial, then one's self-conception is threatened. One seems now not to be what one had supposed oneself to be, and one may find oneself pained and confused by this "problematic" in one's life.[4] The experience of a person immersed in this negativity is unavoidably laced with negative moral emotion, and it seems plain that the responses of caring and responsible people to such a person cannot avoid engaging the normative vocabulary of morality. Indeed, to avoid that vocabulary, or attempt to set it aside in favor of chemicals, would be to ignore the sufferer.

Of course, when *J* and *S* work through *S*'s suffering, the aim is not to devise or establish a new ethical theory. It is rather, in general terms, to develop a recovery strategy for a real person who is suffering in a way that is conceptualized in important part in the vocabulary of morality. The philosopher's task of working out an ethical theory (an adequate form of utilitarianism, for example) is essentially a "timeless" activity, and when participating in it one's place in time or history does not matter much. The task of theory is governed by concerns for truth and coherence (among other things), and closure may not be urgent. But the development of an adequate strategy for "going on" for *this* individual is not similarly timeless in character. It is guided by concerns for the current health, energy, and functioning of the individual (this real person), and closure—or at least practicality—may be very important indeed. The difference in orientation is very great: ethical theory means to understand the moral vocabulary and ultimately the general features of moral sensibility; a recovery strategy means to use the moral vocabulary to move an individual beyond a low point toward "functionality."

But, of course, a "recovery strategy" will have a certain structure to it. First, it will recognize, and help the sufferer characterize, the identity of his or her negatively moralized suffering. This is the point of departure for anything worked out later in the way of a how-to-live strategy, and it is in that way the reason for the development of a strategy to be attempted. In the end it will also form a test of the strategy insofar as the amelioration of the suffering is what following the strategy is supposed to achieve. So, then, insofar as the suffering is itself conceptualized in the terms of, say, guilt, shame, remorse, or regret, the recovery enterprise begins with the power of the moral vocabulary to pick out and identify those aspects of the sufferer's condition that require change.

Second, *J* and *S* (friends) must work out an interpretation of what it would be to "detach" from one's life so that *S* can achieve some relief from the pain of the negatively moralized suffering—enough detachment, at any rate, to allow thought and reflection to occur. Somehow the recovery strategy in this intimate situation must provide *S* with the means of standing back from the interpretations of the past and present that are burdened with negative moral emotion. The realization of such detachment is essential if proposals for going on are to be considered genuinely available to choice—the sort of choice that involves deliberation—on the part of *S*.

A third element in the work of *J* and *S* will be the task of sharing a generalized understanding of the nature and makeup of the human condition *S* is enduring. This is, as it were, a metaphysical task embedded in the reasoning of *J* and *S* itself, and among its results, in fortunate cases, is the realization on the part of the sufferer that he or she is not "alone"—not "isolated"—in the troubling situation that generates the suffering.

A final part of the recovery effort of *J* and *S* will be straightforwardly normative and might even be expressed—implicitly if not explicitly—in a number of maxims or "policy directives" for *S*. That is, against the background of the interpretation of the moralized suffering worked out by *J* and *S* at the beginning, the detachment strategy worked out next, and the general understanding of the human condition that saves *S* from isolation, *J* and *S* work out a set of how-to-live prescriptions. The latter set may contain "exercises" of various sorts. Some of these may be quite concrete (bits of self-understanding writing to do, different sorts of relaxation techniques to practice); others may be general or abstract slogans or formulas to keep in mind, for example, principles that may seem platitudinous in themselves ("One day at a time," "Easy does it") but which come to be helpful or insightful in contexts that are disturbing relative to the moralized suffering in question in *S*'s case.

In general, then, the one-to-one work of *J* and *S* makes use of the vocabulary of morality—moral judgments, moral principles, conceptions of moral agency, interpretations of moral emotions—in an effort to move *S* toward an accommodation with the specific problematic in her life. The sketch above merely indicates a general structure within which, of course, different conceptual moves are made and various alternative prospective courses of action are considered.[5] What the process helps *S* do is (again, in the fortunate case) put together her own moral autonomy, that is, capacity for choice, with the givens of her physical, emotional, and mental being and all of these together with the contingent external factors in her life, so as to secure a level of functionality more adequate to the task of leading a life. Again, the aims are not those of ethical theory—truth and consistency—but instead those of the kind of personal reconciliation with the circumstances of one's life that in ordinary terms we call peace of mind.

PEACE OF MIND

In my view it is helpful to use the term *peace of mind* to identify the goal of the efforts of *J* and *S* to move *S* on from her moralized suffering. In fact, peace of mind is itself not just a sort of laid-back state of tranquility. It is a condition in which one is *morally* at ease with oneself—which is to say that it is itself a moralized state of a positive kind. An explanation of peace of mind would, philosophically, make reference to moral principles and respect for them and to conceptions of self that emphasize the autonomy that informs moral decision making. To have peace of mind is to have a sort of inner calm related importantly to integrity,[6] and it is this condition that is challenged or destroyed by the different sorts of life problems that many people bring to their relationships with others.

By this interpretation, moral life itself is no mere matter of helping a person "feel good" about him- or herself but, rather, a process whereby a person is helped to reach a level of understanding of self that allows peace of mind to occur. Within the structure given above, the ingredients of this process will be different from case to case. The loss of peace of mind in real people takes them down; that is, it results in diminished energy, loss of confidence, and a wariness or fear of decision making. Getting past such a loss need not require forgetting or ignoring the past or the events that generate the moralized suffering; it need not be "revisionist" regarding one's history; it need not involve the pretence that past wrongdoing did not occur or was not really wrongdoing. In the end, in fortunate cases, people can be helped to live *with* their pasts, without being blinkered in ways that land them in self-deception. Peace of mind is not the simple—and impossible—state that one gets to have only if one never did anything wrong ever and never had anything wrong done to one. It is instead a condition one may come to have if one gains a measure of humility, honesty, tolerance, patience, regard for others, and acceptance of human fragility. The moral dimensions of peace of mind are inescapable.

MEANINGFUL-LIFE ATTITUDES

The discussion above puts us in mind of cases in which individuals face what I call a "recovery problem." If one's suffering is "moralized suffering," and moralized suffering is pain of a certain sort (the sort that requires moral discourse to explicate), then, presuming one wants not to stay with such suffering, how does one move beyond it—without, of course, arrogance, dishonesty, self-deception, or fraudulence? Elsewhere I have discussed in a rather detailed way how Alcoholics Anonymous (AA) responds to this issue—at any rate, for the alcoholics in its membership who endure moralized suffering.[7] The AA response is given in its famous twelve-step program, worked through by the sufferer in the context of the AA fellowship itself. In the successful case the sufferer begins to develop a new "design for living," a way of life that incorporates not only abstinence but also some characterological conditions of the possibility of serenity and even of a certain down-to-earth form of spirituality.

I believe the AA twelve-step program exhibits the features of the "recovery strategy" that I outline above. Here, though, I do not want to review further the AA recovery strategy; I instead wish to discuss a motivational problem located logically "behind" the move from "suffering" to "recovery." It may be natural to suppose that the victim of moralized suffering will seek "a way out." But even this natural supposition takes for granted a more primitive motivational base in the sufferer. It takes for granted that, in an older vocabulary, the sufferer has "the will to live" and *thus* seeks a way out of the moralized suffering.[8]

In fact, there is interesting philosophical literature on how the will to live is to be conceptualized in the context I have provided for this discussion, that is, in cases in which individuals find themselves in moralized suffering. I wish to approach the discussion of certain of these conceptualizations by exploiting a metaphor from the computer world.[9] The computer world metaphor I have in mind is "platform." And by *platform* I refer to the things meant when we understand the computer we work with to run on an "operating system" that in effect makes certain things possible and other things impossible. A platform (e.g., Windows 95, 98, NT, or 2000; or the system associated with Macs) makes certain forms of action opportunities and disallows some other forms of action (all this in ways that sometimes please the user and sometimes irritate him or her to no end).

I propose to approach the issue of understanding the will to live that must mediate the move from moralized suffering to recovery as if what is at stake in the notion of "will to live" is, in part, a sort of attitudinal meaningful-life platform, that is, a sort of very basic operating system that must be in place (logically) before the content of a human life—even a new human life in the case of a person undertaking recovery—can be filled in. Here are some notes on what I will now call the "platform problem" relative to the moralized suffering that one might be enduring.

The first note is that the platform problem I have in mind is not simply the apparent choice problem one faces as one contemplates, with a certain degree of open-mindedness, the attractive parts of the characterizations of moral forms of life afforded by the different historically important general ethical theories. In fact, the so-called worldviews, including the conceptions of character, associated with Aristotelian ethics, or Kantian ethics, or utilitarian ethics are logically posterior to the solutions to the platform problem I have in mind. The will to live is logically prior to choices concerning what sort of person one is to be.

The second note is that the platform problem in question—the one that is thereby prior to the choice of ethical worldviews—is much more like a problem about whether life is to be meaningful, and if so what its meaningfulness is to consist in. This is to say—within the context I have provided—that the questions about life's significance, substance, or meaningfulness are logically more basic than the questions responded to in the competition among the main general ethical theories. I have in mind the kind of platform that provides at ground-floor level the energy, agency, and perhaps even measure of self-confidence that allows one to have, or even consider having, projects directed by one's intrinsic interests or to give allegiance to causes that political or other ideological conceptions give significance to. The platform is, as it were, a sort of open-ended attitudinal combination of energy and teleology that allows one to view certain things as opportunities and other things as simply not possibilities (no matter how logically conceivable they may be).[10] The attitudinal meaningful-life platform is what must be in place, in my view, for the classical Socratic issue of "what sort of person I am to be," construed as a question about moral character, to be, in fact, even a concern in one's life.

TWO EXAMPLES

Are there examples of basic meaningful-life platforms that can be laid out and philosophically examined? I can think of two fairly clear candidates for my discussion, though, of course, there are others.

Interestingly, the first example that comes to mind is one whose rhetoric appears to go against the notion that life has meaning at all at the level our problem suggests. I have in mind the "existential nihilism" of Albert Camus, as expressed, for example, in his book *The Myth of Sisyphus*, written in 1940, published in French in 1942, and published in English in 1955.[11]

The second example is that afforded by the meaning-of-life writings of the American psychologist and philosopher William James. I will call it by the term James suggests—*optimism*—though this term, in James's hands, is no throwaway reference to sentiment. James's work—in the volume titled *The Will to Believe* and the concluding chapter of *The Varieties of Religious Experience*[12]—is from very early in the twentieth century. Interestingly, it seems (to me) that James's view reflects an awareness of a view like the nihilism of Camus and is directed against it, though of course James had no chance to read Camus's words directly. It is worth mentioning that James's views were known to Bill Wilson, the cofounder of Alcoholics Anonymous, and were considered by Wilson to be inspiring.[13]

It is not necessary for my purposes here to offer a detailed account of the views of Camus and James. All I need for my later points is a sort of capsule summary of the meaning-of-life attitudinal imperatives characteristic of the two views.

Regarding Camus's view, then, its general structure seems to be that both ordinary experience and philosophical analysis show that human life itself is meaningless; and if life is meaningless—or the human condition "absurd," as Camus would say—it is natural for us to ask whether we should end it, either by committing physical suicide or by committing philosophical suicide, that is, in the latter case by disguising the true nature (the absurdity) of the human condition via acceptance of or adherence to a meaning-giving ideology of some sort, such as a religion, a cosmology, or even a generalized political view, for example, liberalism or Marxism. Camus insists that we should not commit either physical or philosophical suicide but should instead live so that we *persist in lucid awareness of absurdity*; that is, we are to go on with our lives but *without* interpreting them through the adoption of political, moral, religious, or metaphysical glosses on the world or our places within it. Life is indeed meaningless; however, we are enjoined by the prescription Camus offers not to end it but, rather, to live honestly regarding it, that is, in constant awareness of its absurd character. To live thus, in obedience to this maxim of persistence in lucidity, is in part, for Camus, to defy death: "It is essential," Camus writes, "to die unreconciled."[14]

James's view, needless to say, works in a different way. It also involves a "persistence" maxim, but the maxim characteristic of James's optimism is hardly the call to "lucid awareness of absurdity" that Camus proposes. In fact, James's view rests on a stubborn insistence that (most) human beings, beneath the layers of surface opinion and ideology, are of *optimistic natural temperament*, and this characterization of basic human nature helps support James's well-known appeals to the legitimacy of "passional nature" in serious life decisions when rationality is inconclusive.[15]

In brief, James sees no reason, philosophical or otherwise, for human beings to constrain their natural optimism in favor of the nihilism Camus favors. Of course, there are points at which James seems to allow that for some of us *natural* temperament might instead be pessimistic and thus carry with it the bleak moral psychology of what were for James the negativities of atheism, subjectivism, materialism, relativism, and nihilism.[16] But, overall, the agency celebrated in James's famous meaning-of-life essays is of the sort that *constitutes* life worth living. James insists further that this positive sort of agency—this optimistic natural temperament—is not itself a matter of dogma or definition. James does not begrudge one going beyond life-energizing agency to religious or theological doctrine, but he holds that the former does not require the latter to be effective and also that the latter must not declare anathema alternative doctrines.[17]

In James's own words, when rationality is inconclusive regarding certain views, including religious beliefs, then "passional nature" may govern sensibility, that is, "we have a right to supplement [the physical order] by an unseen spiritual order which we assume on trust, if only thereby life may seem to us better worth living again."[18] And to capture the sense that the "temperament" he speaks of is independent of ideologies or, say, denominational theologies, James adds,

> When I speak of trusting our religious demands, just what do I mean by "trusting"? Is the word to carry with it license to define in detail an invisible world, and to anathematize and excommunicate those whose trust is different? Certainly not! Our faculties of belief were not primarily given us to make orthodoxies and heresies withal; they were given us to live by. . . . It is a fact of human nature, that men can live and die by the help of a sort of faith that goes without a single dogma or definition. This bare assurance that this natural order is not ultimate but a mere sign or vision, the external staging of a many-storied universe, in which spiritual forces have the last word and are eternal—this bare assurance is to such men enough to make life seem worth living in spite of every contrary presumption suggested by its circumstances on the natural plane.[19]

In this account, then, we have two candidate attitudinal "platforms" whereby life can take on meaning in the ordinary sense, that is, the sense one has when one is immersed in one's activities and enterprises, and thereby open the door to the posterior choice problem of whether one, in one's moral life, is to be Kantian, Aristotelian, utilitarian, or something else—or, indeed, if one is to be somehow "indifferent" to moral values. For James the platform is "optimistic natural temperament," unfettered, as it were, by ideologies or cynicism. It seems to be a sort of life-affirming yea-saying attitudinal approach to daily life—one that tries not to beg any (or at least many) questions as regards theology or denominational religion. For Camus the platform is "existential nihilism," an attitudinal approach to life that obeys the maxim: persist in lucid awareness of the absurdity—the essential meaninglessness—of the human condition. Camus's maxim would be a difficult imperative to obey, especially if one carries it down through the surface layers to apply it to the real content of one's life. Nevertheless, and perhaps paradoxically, for Camus the meaning of life, at the most elemental level, is that life is meaningless, and while one is to live, one is to live honestly, with gaze fixed on that gloomy metaphysical fact.[20]

Curiously enough, the platforms of James and Camus, which seem so distant from one another, have some commonalities that are worth noting. For example, both platforms distance themselves from religion—though indeed James is open to religion as posterior "filler" for the faith he speaks of (but filler that is to be tolerant of the contents of others' faiths), while Camus is belligerently defiant toward it. Further, both find the human condition *in itself* to be meaningless—though indeed James wants us, as an act of will, to *constitute* it meaningful by optimistic natural temperament,[21] while Camus wants us to leave it meaningless and live every minute aware of its meaninglessness. Finally, both want not only to "propel" human beings on in life but also to do so in a way that "energizes" them,[22] that is, allows them what I can only think to call "zest" in living. And while James wants this done by releasing or unfettering temperament to pursue its natural optimism, Camus thinks (for some reason) that the living of life will be all the better upon the recognition of its essential absurdity.[23]

QUESTIONS RAISED

It is intellectual fun to compare and contrast the meaningful-life platforms of James and Camus, and it is intriguing to note their differences even though they have in common the aim of energizing human beings. Beyond that, I suspect that it is important for both individual ethics and ethical theory to realize that the attitudinal platform problem, as I have characterized it, is prior to the choice of ethical character involved in our moral lives. At one level this is simply to say that one must live before one lives in the way characterized by Aristotle, Kant, or the utilitarians. I admire the "first things first" efforts of Camus and James, even as I hope James wins in the competition between their views.

I recognize, too, that the platforms in question combine emotion, feeling, and reason in ways that would be challenging to sort out. James's optimism and Camus's nihilism are not just "gut reactions." They are attitudinal, certainly motivational, and laced with cognition—all at once. There are how-to-live imperatives involved in each view so that living Camus's way would be different from living James's way. In some cases (not all) there may be sameness in what is done in the world from their different imperatives, but in all cases (not merely some) there would be differences in, so to speak, tone and feeling in what is done in the world.

Many questions, then, arise from reflection on these philosophical efforts to sketch meaningful-life attitudinal platforms. For example, one wants philosophically to understand the background views and conceptions that yield the different meaningful-life maxims characteristic of these platforms and examine them for adequacy and consistency. Beyond that, one wants to ask whether either view can actually be *lived*, that is, be implemented *in* one's life. Could one raise children under the pressure of the nihilism Camus recommends in general for human life? Could a nihilist be a friend or sustain a commitment to a moral cause? Could one carry Jamesean optimism, even if natural, too far—and be foolish rather than vigorous? Perhaps more subtly, could one, struggling to realize the optimism that James thinks is natural, find that emotionally one cannot sustain the affirmative commitments that yield worthwhile life?

Beyond these questions about practicality or implementation, and with individual ethics more narrowly in mind, one wants to ask whether one of these views is more promising than the other regarding the development or cultivation of moral character. The meaningful-life platforms in question are thought of by their proponents as elemental or primitive in the order of things so far as moral personality is concerned. There may indeed be a moral-life form of the Socratic question about what sort of person one is to be: Am I to be Aristotelian, utilitarian, or Kantian in my efforts to do right in the world? (What shall I teach my children in this connection?) But according to the views in question there sits behind the moral-life question something even more basic: Am I to be Jamesean optimistic in natural temperament, or is temperament in my case going to reflect the nihilism of Camus—or, indeed, because these are doubtless not the only alternatives, is meaningful-life temperament to be structured in some other way? Offhand, it appears that Camus's view is not congenial to, or inviting of, the moral-life question. If the human condition is absurd in the way Camus has in mind, then the choice of moral character appears entirely gratuitous. One's choice of character in the form Aristotle or Kant or the utilitarians had in mind would be, as Camus himself says, a "whim."[24] If so, then of course this choice—whether made in this or that way or not made at all—does not matter. Offhand again, the Jamesean view might have ways of taking the question of moral character more seriously, but I do not myself see that it influences or limits responses to that question in any very specific ways. It is not clear that Jamesean optimism picks out or respects any particular moral orientation for character. In general, it may be that meaningful-life platforms of the sort Camus and James have in mind do not "point" one way or the other regarding what moral sort of person one is to be.

But here I run into a still deeper question—one that concerns not the consequences of the choice of nihilism or optimism as a meaningful-life platform but instead the status of such platforms as objects of choice. How far is the platform problem a *problem of choice* for an individual human being? Is the situation with natural temperament such that, as for James, I could (and ought to) choose "optimism"? Is it such that, as for Camus, I could (and ought to) choose nihilism? Or is it instead the case that natural temperament, perhaps structured one way for some and another way for others, is indeed natural and thus outside the reach of my will? Are the Jamesean optimists that way "by nature"? Are Camus's existential nihilists ultimately that way "by nature"? If I find myself to be too much the nihilist, can I go out and choose to be more the optimist? If I find myself to be too much the optimist, can I choose to be more the nihilist? What, if anything, establishes the structure of temperament at the basic level—and do I have any say in it coming to be something other than what it is?

It is one thing to see something prior to the choices one makes in the matter of one's moral-life persona, as I have suggested; it is another thing to figure out whether that prior thing—the platform for meaningful life—has an architecture that is within the power of the will. Is the platform itself an object of choice (as James and Camus suggest) and thus merely a contingent fact about the self—one that can be changed, as we say, "at will"? Or is it a "given" of one's nature, and thus one is stuck with it and able, at best, to effect slight but certainly not essential changes in it?

COMMENTS

While I cannot straightforwardly answer the basic question I have just asked, I will offer some notes about it.

First, I am not the only one puzzled by the question of whether structural features of personality, such as the "attitudinal platforms" I have been discussing, are or can be objects of choice. In a report titled "Personality and Personality Disorders" in *The Harvard Medical School Mental Health Letter*, the following negative response is indicated: "Many mental health professionals think that. . . . [p]ersonality is too pervasive and ingrained to change very much. It is also usually egosyntonic, that is, felt by the patient as natural and right, as the essence of what he or she is, rather than as a set of troubling symptoms. Patients may regard attempts to change it as brainwashing or punishment."[25]

A second note is that basic attitudes can of course *change* in persons, but what is at stake in my question is whether the changing can be achieved by an exercise of will on their part. Some forms of depression can be attacked, as it were, through the power of the will, but some other sorts cannot, as I understand the matter. Some forms of depression seem to be systemic—built into those who suffer them. Even these forms of depression can alter or "lift"; but such changes are not achieved through what is ordinarily thought of as exercises of will on the part of those who undergo them.

In this connection, I am struck by the following remarks about William James by Louis Menand:

> In his work, James can sometimes seem to be expounding, with a little too much bravado, a kind of can-do, self-help attitude toward life, to be suggesting that the answer to most of our problems is just to drop our philosophical worry-bones and get on with the business of making and doing. Many readers since James's time have complained that the pragmatism and pluralism he promoted are not enough, that life confronts us with some situations that call for a different sort of response. But no one knew this better than James. It is the poignancy of his life that he never found, for himself, that other sort of response. He created a philosophy of hope expressly premised on the understanding that there is, finally, no *reason* for hope. . . . James was too wise to believe that true melancholy can ever be overcome by a theory, and he was too honest to pretend to a spiritual satisfaction he was never able to feel.
>
> John Hay Chapman was one of the readers whom James's writings failed to inspire, but he loved James anyway, and in his memoir he put into words the quality others searched for: "there was, in spite of his playfulness, a deep sadness about James. You felt that he had just stepped out of this sadness in order to meet you, and was to go back into it the moment you left him." What lends authenticity to his philosophy is not its triumph over the unhappiness in his own life, but its failure.[26]

Third, I need to note that if certain basic attitudes are not objects of choice, and also, as may be true of Camus's prescription, they are incompatible with taking seriously what I have called "moral-life imperatives," such as the utilitarians' greatest happiness principle or the Kantians' categorical imperative, then the dark view that basic attitudes are not objects of choice has radical implications for our understanding of moral life and for our practices of holding others and ourselves morally accountable for what we do. It may be that some human beings, in virtue of their form of natural temperament, are in fact *unable* to take seriously the imperatives of the moral life, including its demands on character.

Finally, let me note that the issue of whether or not the basic attitudes are objects of choice may be importantly a socially contestable matter. This to say that the question of whether basic attitudes can be chosen may be deep enough to stand behind the ordinary empirical or experiential approaches to it, rather than be something that can be settled by empirical or experiential approaches. It may even be that responses to the matter are, in the fashionable jargon of today, "socially constructed." That is, one's view of whether basic attitudes can be chosen may be subject to influences not all of which are free of social, political, and cultural pressures.[27] I think, but am not sure, that a society through time may, for reasons that have to do with differences in these pressures, come to have different dominant opinions on such a matter.

I will not attempt to take this "postmodernist" thought further here. I will register again the notion that important matters, including how we think about moral responsibility, rest on how we think about whether basic attitudes can be chosen. I return to this subject in the different contexts provided by the discussion of forgiveness and the recovery of agency in chapter 3 and the discussion of indifference and reconciliation in chapter 7.

3

✛

Forgiveness and Effective Agency

In what follows I explore one of the main dimensions of the moral practice of forgiveness. My interest is in what might be called the forward-looking dimension of that complex practice. In this dimension what is at issue is not the backward-looking response to past wrongdoing involved in the victim's act of forgiveness but, rather, the possibility of "release" for the wrongdoer from the moral-emotional pain associated with the awareness of his or her wrongdoing, and thus the prospect of the renewal of energy for projects and the responsible conduct associated with effective human agency.

I assume that the practice of forgiveness has this forward-looking dimension. This assumption reflects my thought that our moral form of life wants full effective agency for, as it were, people of good will. So my discussion does not concern or rely on points made with moral monsters or other extreme figures in mind. Ordinary decent people—even very good people—make mistakes or commit wrongs from time to time, and in these cases the peace of mind and self-confidence needed for effective agency may be diminished or lost. Forgiveness—by others, by oneself—can help restore that peace of mind and self-confidence. It is in that way that the practice is forward looking relative to the one who makes mistakes or commits wrongdoing.

The backward-looking and forward-looking dimensions are uneasily related in the moral practice of forgiveness in ordinary life. The restoration of effective agency should not be cheapened by false or hollow expressions of forgiveness, and it should not be denied by self-centered refusals of forgiveness.[1] To some extent, it seems, our agency, when

33

diminished by our own recognition of our own wrongdoing, is harnessed to the capacity of others to "forgive and forget." Something similar may be true of our chances for self-respect: in certain contexts, for example, achievement-oriented sections of life, our self-respect may be more dependent than we wish on the views of others concerning our projects and conduct.[2]

Further, my discussion is preoccupied with the apparent logical fact about the practice of forgiveness that other-forgiveness is not sufficient for self-forgiveness. If you forgive me my past wrongdoing or corrupt attitudes and your forgiveness is sound, that is, you have good reasons for giving it, I have repented and (if possible) made amends,[3] and circumstances permit it without distortions in the judgments about wrongdoing or corruption involved, then presumably I may legitimately have the "release" thus offered by you. But our experience indicates that in some cases forgiveness by others, even when sound, is not enough for me to forgive myself. Self-forgiveness seems unavailable even when other-forgiveness is permitted and, in fact, given. How this complexity is to be understood, and whether, in particular, the failure of self-forgiveness may be legitimately remaindered beyond other-forgiveness (without becoming mere self-indulgence), will be explored—within, again, the main interest of the discussion in the forward-looking dimension of the practice of forgiveness.

THE PROBLEMATIC

The practical problem in the dimension of the practice of forgiveness I am interested in might be experienced as the problem of restoring agency—that agency that includes peace of mind and self-confidence when these have been, as it were, "challenged" by one's awareness of one's own serious mistakes or wrongdoing. Such awareness leaves a moral-emotional aftermath that diminishes or reduces agency by disrupting peace of mind and weakening self-confidence. Here are some notes and stipulations for my discussion of this familiar practical "problematic."

First, for this discussion I will consider the practice of forgiveness to be a possibility in the event of awareness of serious mistakes as well as recognized wrongdoing. Such mistakes might be those incurred when complicated procedures are in process, for example, in a medical setting; they might also be those involving problematic judgments made in the workplace when responses are surrounded by a penumbra involving urgency, pressures from colleagues, and uncertainty. Mistakes are not always moral wrongs, but they can be in some cases objects of forgiveness.

Second, I will not attempt to detail here the makeup of the practice of forgiveness. As a practice it has structure and rules giving context and meaning to gestures and phrases and emotional color to relationships. But I will not attempt to say how it differs from other nearby practices, such as pardoning or excusing. For this discussion it is more important to note that we are not all equally adept in participating in the practice of forgiveness. This is no surprise, of course. Something of the same is true for other practices, for example, the practices of promising and friendship (and pardoning and excusing). It is probably a general truth that if *P* is a practice, there will be people who are at different competence levels relative to *P*. Just as we are not all up to speed on being competent promisers, or on being friends, so we do not always give or receive forgiveness "rightly" (as Aristotle might say). Some of us do not have forgiveness know-how toward others or, indeed, ourselves.

In fact, there are some obvious hazards attending participation in the practice of forgiveness. I will assume here that as a decent person one wants in general to be a forgiving person, as one wants in general to be a courteous person, and to be capable of compassion in certain contexts as well. But there are episodic judgment pitfalls: just as one can go wrong in being courteous or in offering compassion, so one can be in certain cases too forgiving or too ready to forgive (call it "hasty forgiving"), or one can be excessively reluctant to forgive (call it "ungenerosity").

And, too, the lack of connection between other-forgiveness and self-forgiveness can be complicated in certain ways, as, for example, when the self-forgiveness that occurs when other-forgiveness is not justified is really arrogance. More salient for this discussion is the case in which other-forgiveness is justified, but self-forgiveness is still not available. After all, if you forgive me what I have done, presumably you have some reasons for doing so; and because reasons—or, anyhow, legitimate reasons—are (in a familiar view) considerations that a detached or objective person could have or recognize, I could have them, too. But, clearly, our experience is that the forgiveness that comes to us from others is not always "enough" for us to forgive ourselves. One explanation that comes to mind is that I am suspicious of your reasons, so that I think that the reasons on the basis of which you forgive me are essentially calculations of future benefits and have little or nothing to do with the substance of what I did, that is, that which makes a forgiveness problem arise in the first place. Another explanation comes to mind—one that brings estimates of self-worth into the picture: your forgiveness of me might be based on a washed-out view of yourself. You do not want me to be bothered by the terrible thing I did to you. You think (about yourself), "I'm not worth it."

Third, let me ask, is the "problem of the restoration of agency" something that *can* be discussed? After all, people may differ from one another on how internally strong they are, how they bear up under pressure, what it takes for something to get to them, and so on. Someone might think that these are matters for individuals to work out, not phenomena that can be captured in a theory or around which one can wrap a general account or a "policy" to be followed. My thought here is that doubtless there is something to individual differences in people; but these, I think, do not preclude learning something from engaging ethical issues in an orderly way. In any case, what is at stake here is not just "how one appears to others" on the confidence front (e.g., as the much admired or much hated "decisive surgeon") or even how one appears to oneself (one can deceive oneself as well as others). The issue here is ultimately the effectiveness of one's agency, that is, the effectiveness of one's capacity to control the content in one's life, including facing up to the next challenge that comes along in one's workplace or personal life. It concerns how far we can be, within realistic limits, masters of our fates and, when we cannot in certain circumstances be masters, how far we can be reasonable and constructive strategists when our circumstances go against us.

Finally, let me note that what can challenge effective agency (including, again, peace of mind and a measure of self-confidence) is not one or a small variety of things. There are many things that can "shake" a person (if not you, then another person) in a way that draws down and diminishes the elements of effective agency and thus makes it difficult for a person to move forward in ways that may be required in the workplace or personal life. The absence or withholding of forgiveness can be one of these challenges to agency. In *Letter to His Father*,[4] Franz Kafka makes clear that he does not—and cannot—forgive his father's treatment of him in childhood. One wonders how far this unforgiveness affected the father's life.[5] Mozart's father could not forgive Mozart for marrying Constanza— a woman "beneath him," according to the father. One wonders how far the unforgiveness diminished peace of mind for Mozart, despite his astonishing musical productivity. Rousseau, apparently, never could rid himself of the memory of his cruelty to a young servant girl, as recorded in *The Confessions* (written in order to get rid of it) and then returned to at the end of his life in *The Reveries of the Solitary Walker*.[6] One wonders again how in this case the self-unforgiveness affected agency—and, indeed, personality—in Rousseau's case.

Medical contexts provide settings for cases involving mistakes to which the possibility of forgiveness seems relevant but which are not aptly thought about as instances of moral wrongdoing.[7] For example, a physician botches a surgery and disfigures a person for life. Perhaps he or she amputates the wrong limb, but there are only procedural snafus in the background rather than violations of moral principle. Whatever the background, in such cases there is no genuine way to set things right. Apologies and money are hollow. The practice of forgiveness gets pushed to one of its limits. There are, after all, unforgivable acts—and genocide is not the only example.

In another case, a doctor in family practice sees an alcoholic through detoxification and then finds that no affordable follow-up treatment program is available (for insurance no longer covers one); but then the doctor must release the patient from the hospital, worried whether the patient will attempt recovery through Alcoholics Anonymous (AA) and, in general, uncertain about whether he or she has "done enough" to see to the patient's safety and health in a responsible way. In such cases there are very great risks of misjudgment. In the follow-up arena, when has one "done enough"? One can botch follow-up just as one can botch surgery.

These are straightforward enough as illustrative cases. Let me, though, for this discussion, put before us another sort of case—one involving a physician in the "penumbra" around a case involving a treatment situation especially complicated by urgency, family pressures, and still other factors, including political and quasi-moral elements that enter into decision making in tense situations. The case sketched in what follows is drawn from Abraham Verghese's book, *My Own Country*:

> Bobby Keller called me in the office as I was about to leave for home. He sounded shrill and alarmed.
>
> "Doc? Ed is *very* sick! He is *very, very* short of breath and running a fever. A hundred and three. Dr. Verghese, he's turning blue on me."
>
> "Bobby, call the emergency ambulance service—tell them to bring you to the Johnson City Medical Center." . . .
>
> I was at the Miracle Center well ahead of the ambulance. Soon it came roaring in, all its lights flashing. When the back door opened, I peeked in: Ed's eyes were rolled back in his head, and he was covered with a fine sheen of sweat. . . .
>
> Bobby . . . was on the verge of fainting.
>
> "Don't put him on no machines, whatever you do," Bobby begged me. "Please, no machines."
>
> "Why?"
>
> "Because that's what he told me. He doesn't want it."
>
> "When did he tell you? Just now?"
>
> "No. A long time ago."
>
> "Did he put it in writing? Does he have a living will?"
>
> "No. . . ."
>
> In the emergency room, I stabilized Ed as best I could. . . . Time was running out.
>
> Ed was moaning and muttering incomprehensibly. . . . I had only a few minutes before I had to either breathe for him, or let him go. I needed more guidance from Bobby as to Ed's wishes. . . .
>
> I hurried outside.

Bobby and three other men and one woman were near the ambulance entrance, smoking. . . . Bobby Keller, still trembling, introduced me to Ed's brothers, all younger than Ed. . . .

I addressed the brothers: "Ed is very sick. A few months ago we found out he has AIDS. . . . Now he has a bad pneumonia from the AIDS. I need to put him on a breathing machine in the next few minutes or he will die. . . . But Bobby tells me that Ed has expressed a desire *not* to be put on the machine." . . .

The family was clear-eyed, trying to stay calm. . . . I felt they were fond of their oldest brother, though perhaps disapproving of his relationship with Bobby.

"We need to discuss this," the older brother said.

"We have no time, I need to go right back in," I said.

[The family caucused and came back.]

"We want for you to do everything you can. Put him on the breathing machine, if you have to."

At this a little wail came out of Bobby Keller. . . .

The oldest brother spoke again. His tone was matter-of-fact and determined:

"*We* are his family. *We* are legally responsible for him. We want you to do *everything* for him."

We are his family. I watched Bobby's face crumble as he suddenly became a mere observer with no legal right to determine the fate of the man he had loved since he was seven years old. He was finally . . . an outsider.

I took him aside and said, "Bobby, I have to go on. There is no way for me not to at this point. . . ."

I rushed back in. Ed looked worse. As I went through the ritual of gowning and masking . . . it struck me that the entire situation had been in my power to dictate. All I had to do was to come out and say that the pneumonia did not look good, that it looked like the end. *I* mentioned the respirator, *I* offered it as an option. I could have just kept quiet. I had, when it came down to the final moment, given Ed's brothers the power of family. Not Bobby.

But there was no time to look back now. . . .

[A few hours later] a furious Code blue was in progress [but to no avail].

Bobby Keller and the Maupin family were in the quiet room. It was very difficult for me to go in there and tell them Ed had died. Bobby cried. . . . Ed's brothers covered their eyes or turned their heads away from me. The eldest came over and shook my hand and thanked me. Bobby came out with, "Praise the Lord, his suffering is over," and walked alone toward the door. . . .

I thought of funerals I had been to in Johnson City where the grieving widow was escorted to the memorial service by friends and family. Tears and hugs, happy memories, casseroles and condolences. Who would comfort Bobby Keller, I wondered.[8]

This case illustrates, I take it, how judgment can be affected in the urgency of circumstances. Notice again Verghese's remark, "All I had to do was to come out and say that the pneumonia did not look good, that it looked like the end. *I* mentioned the respirator, *I* offered it as an option. I could have just kept quiet. I had, when it came down to the final moment, given Ed's brothers the power of family. Not Bobby. But there was no time to look back now."

But there may, of course, be time later to look back. And that is where the danger usually is. One begins to rethink and "second-think" one's judgment; one begins to doubt one's judgment; one begins to want to go back and do things a different way. And I take it to be ordinary human experience in cases of this kind—not unique to physicians and their work—that one can begin to question one's judgment and in doing so come to jeopardize what comes next in one's work or even one's life. One may come to be "stuck" with a problematic event in one's own history— an event that remains embedded in one's past whether or not anyone else ever gives it attention. One seems stuck with the pain of guilt or shame and begins to doubt one's competence, and thus diminished agency makes engaging or negotiating the next cases difficult or impossible.

Here again the earlier point about individual differences in people becomes important. You may find that your friend is stuck with a problematic event in his or her past and be relieved that you are not similarly stuck. You may find, in line with the fashionable "modularity thesis" in contemporary philosophy of mind,[9] that your friend is vulnerable to being bothered by his or her past in ways that you are not. For if the self is "modular," that is, it is no unity or univocal competence but is instead a set or cluster of elements (dispositions, competencies, abilities, susceptibilities), the precise ingredients of which may very well be different from person to person; and if this is so, then we are not all the same in our vulnerabilities. Genetics may be involved. Heavy social conditioning may be involved. In the end you may or may not understand your friend very well in this respect. Sometimes we are baffled by people who apparently have problems in living their lives that we do not have. In some cases we manage to be understanding to some extent; too often, in my view, we end up impatient with and irritated by people who have difficulties we do not have.

Another even darker point: One cannot always tell how far one is oneself able to do x, or withstand pressure y, or rise to challenge z. I may be shy and think (with my friends, if I have any) that I ought to get past that; but I may in fact be constitutionally shy, in which case the degree to which I am "stuck" with shyness is for all practical purposes outside the power of my will; and I, as well as my friends, may do me damage by urging me to "get past" my shyness. Similarly, I may be vulnerable to loss of self-confidence and think that I ought to get past that, but I may in fact be constitutionally vulnerable in this respect, in which case getting past the vulnerability, and all that goes with it, is outside the power of my will.

In this view we are not all in command of our agency in the way our ordinary thinking about persons as rational beings may suggest we ought to be, and this plays havoc with how much we hold others and ourselves accountable for what happens—in, for example, urgent difficult circumstances—and, accordingly, with how much we suffer, tolerate, or are embarrassed by the problem of the restoration of agency, involving, as it does, the elements of peace of mind and self-confidence that I began with.

STRATEGIES FOR RECOVERY

Suppose, then, we recognize the restoration-of-agency problem for the complicated thing it can be. What follows? Are there strategies for recovery for someone whose agency is diminished by the remaindered sense of fault—mistake fault or moral fault—in what happened at an earlier point in life?[10] What can be said about the restoration of effective agency in a person who "does wrong" to another person, genuinely repents, and seeks ways to make amends (if any exist)? What can be said about the restoration of effective agency in a skilled physician who finds his or her professional life spattered not by the pain of awareness of deliberate wrongdoing but simply by negative emotional pain attending problematic judgments made in tense cluttered circumstances? What is the role of forgiveness, by others and by oneself, in the restoration of agency? Even if forgiveness cannot (logically) guarantee "recovery," can we have reasonable expectations that it can contribute toward the regaining of effective agency on the part of the person to whom it is offered?

I should say at once that I do not have slick new answers to such questions, and I do not trust the pop psychological answers I am aware of. In what follows I will discuss an interesting response to a problem like the restoration problem I have outlined above, namely, a response developed by Claudia Card to issues of recovery of agency in cases of child abuse and political oppression.[11] But before turning to Professor Card's views, let me make certain observations.

First, I need to observe how lame (in my opinion) the ordinary responses to this problem seem to be. You may urge your friend or yourself when pained by an awareness of mistake or wrongdoing to "disclose and apologize" and then "forget it and go on." But we all know that at any rate the latter part of this advice is not followable by just anyone—

and one sometimes suspects that those who can follow it, that is, those who can easily jettison problematic chunks of the past, are not fully serious people. You may urge your friend or yourself to excuse or somehow reinterpret the past so that a judgment made back then can be something other than wrong. But, again, the revisionist strategy is not promising, at least not among those who are seriously caught up in moral pain over what happened and are thus stuck with the decent person's typical respect for truth. In some cases the negative interpretation (that, e.g., the judgment made back then was wrong) may simply be true, and then excusing, rationalizing, and revising are forms of fraud.

A second observation concerns the important "variable" of self-knowledge relative to the reality of the restoration problem—or at any rate relative to how seriously the problem may be taken in real life. Despite the popular view that one knows oneself better than anyone else does, I think self-knowledge is not always in place and is, in fact, very hard to come by. I may be shy but not know that I am constitutionally shy; I may have a drinking problem but not know that I am what AA calls a "real alcoholic" (and thus stuck with a constitutional vulnerability). I may think of myself as self-confident but not realize that I am arrogant. I may be unsure of how smart or talented I am but simply not know how to give myself the morale-boosting pep talk that others can administer to themselves. It may be that such failures or distortions in self-knowledge are among the obstacles in the way of strategies for recovery being simple or very general in application.[12]

A third observation is that in theoretical settings it is tempting to approach the restoration issue in a way that counsels generosity. After all, the thought comes to mind that in the cases in question here—again, cases not of moral monsters performing evil acts but of ordinary decent people who have made mistakes or "done wrong" (and are sorry)—morality surely seeks the restoration of agency in such people. That is, morality does not ask or permit diminished agency to *stay* diminished forever or even for extended but limited periods of time.[13] There is more to this point than merely "wishing a person well." It may be that in cases in which forgiveness makes sense there is moral permission, and perhaps in some cases even an obligation, for it to be offered. For what is at stake when one speaks of the restoration of agency is in effect the restoration of moral personality—that "end in itself" that Kantian ethics finds to be the most precious of moral goods. And if *that* is what is at stake in cases of the sort we consider here, then indeed it might seem natural for theorists to suppose that generosity may play a role, or even lead the way, in our thinking about recovery.[14]

But I think the generosity imperative should be treated with caution, for even when we take the restoration problem seriously, cases come to mind in which generosity would not, in the real world, be advised or even safe. In some cases a person's makeup involves the dominance of depression, addiction, disorder, or simply low self-esteem, and our hearts go out to such a person and we want to encourage recovery. In other cases, a person's makeup involves the dominance of anger, viciousness, or very powerful ego and aggression, and self-protection requires in our lives with such a person (even when one is oneself such a person, and self-forgiveness is a possibility) something other than the actions that usually go with generosity. Even if we are different from one another, it does not follow that we or others are helpless, unthreatening, or eager to change.

The final observation on this list is the gloomy one that the life of anyone (not just physicians or other "professionals") who tries to live in the world rather than on its margins is a no-win life in this matter of challenges to effective agency. One *will* find oneself in urgent, complicated, dilemma-like circumstances in which one will be stampeded yet required to "decide." It does not follow from that, though, that what one decides does not matter or that what one decides, even at the highest level of responsibility and conscientiousness, will be morally okay when one reviews the situation in the quiet of the night. Perhaps some lives are more vulnerable to challenges to agency than others. But, so I suspect, there is such vulnerability in human lives in general, and thus the role of forgiveness in the recovery of agency is hardly of interest to only a few.

THE INTEGRITY PROJECT

Some of the salient features of Claudia Card's view about recovery when agency is diminished by child abuse or political oppression follow.

First, it makes sense, in her view, to speak of a person *becoming* a responsible agent. Here she writes, with Dewey in mind, that we are not born responsible but "at most with potentialities for becoming so, realizable to a greater or lesser extent with luck and hard work" (24).[15] So Card's conception of responsible agency is a degree notion. I assume that the "becoming" in question, then, can go either way: one may be "more" or "less" a responsible agent today than at some earlier point in one's history.

Second, Card describes her account as elucidating "the agent's forward-looking perspective" (24). She is not concerned with the backward-looking perspective of the moral observer or judge and thus is not chiefly concerned with "attributions of responsibility for what has already been done or occurred" (25).[16] Her account does not purport to be a completely general characterization of individual responsibility or of the agent's perspective. It is targeted on resistance to oppression or overcoming abuse, and the "agents" she has in mind are those whose "background stories" include "bad moral luck" in the form of a "history of child abuse" or a "heritage of oppression" (24).[17]

Third, relationships are important to an exposition of Card's conception in two ways. On the negative side, "early unchosen relationships with significant others" (33) may be involved in the abuse suffered or the oppression endured and, hence, may be, as it were, negative moral-luck "givens" in the history of the individual agent. On the positive side, relationships with others can function to support the individual's efforts to develop the self-esteem required to resist oppression and overcome abuse.

Finally, within the framework thus provided, to become a responsible agent is (as I will put it) to undertake and follow through on an "integrity project." Card is careful to distinguish an integrity project from (what I will call) an "autonomy project." To develop autonomy is, for Card, by and large "to develop *boundaries* between ourselves and our environments" (24). It is a "separating" of sorts (cf. 47–48). The integrity project, however, is not a matter of separating but, rather, a matter of developing "reliability and bases for self-esteem," and for these "interpersonal relationships can be critical" (24). How is this to be understood? Integrity, for Card, involves "basic commitments and values" (30). She writes, "Integrity—literally, wholeness, completeness, undividedness—involves considerations of consistency, coherence, and commitment, while autonomy involves considerations of dependence and independence" (32). In line with Lynne McFall's discussion of integrity,[18] Card writes that integrity requires of the agent the development of "an identity to which basic moral values and commitments are central" (32). And luck, she points out, "enters at several points": "Since some of our most deeply ingrained values and traits begin in early unchosen relationships with significant others, we may have difficult work to find their roots, assess them realistically, and come up with a tolerably coherent set" (33).

This seems the heart of the integrity project to me. Becoming a responsible agent is finally finding one's roots, assessing them realistically, and coming up with a "tolerably coherent set" of values and commitments. Thus, in "taking responsibility for ourselves," we "participate in constructing our own identities, and thus in constructing some of the conditions of our own integrity" (32). Becoming a responsible agent, then, may indeed be hard work.[19] The cases of child abuse and oppression are apt for this point. Here one's "roots" may be fragmented, garbled, and painful to sort out, and assessing them "realistically" may be a major project in itself (and, in my opinion, not always a feasible one). Beyond this matter of understanding one's roots, "coming up with a tolerably coherent set of values and commitments" may be a further major project of formidable proportions.

Professor Card does not minimize the difficulty. She likens the integrity project for an individual to the efforts of the membership of a community to come together to resist oppression. Just as the membership of a community might be at odds within itself, so an individual victim of abuse may be internally at odds within him- or herself. Card's helpful discussion of "dysfunctional multiples" offers a striking characterization of how a person may be "fragmented" or "scattered" on the inside.

At a certain point Card's analysis of the situation for victims of abuse begins to take on an air of exhortation and appeal to action that is appropriate, I think, to the subject. If taking responsibility is made complicated by the luck-damage of oppression and abuse, we are assured that "the character and values of the oppressed change drastically in the process of liberation" (41). Victims are urged to gear up and act: "Resistance can come only from within" (41). The oppressed and the abused have "responsibilities of their own to peers and descendants" and must turn themselves into "survivors" rather than "victims" (41). To do this one must achieve the integration that allows one to "cease complicity in one's own oppression or in maintaining one's own distress" (46). That is, one must achieve what is called "internal bonding" within oneself—a "reconciling" of one's different values, perceptions, and commitments (46). In fact, to this end autonomy (in the meaning earlier specified) may play an instrumental role, for against a "hostile environment," separation may be necessary "for healing and growth" (48). If indeed the acquisition of integrity can in the multiples case have "a life or death importance," even in less extreme cases it is "important to morale and to the possibility of self-esteem and pride" (46).

There is, thus, rather a Nietzschean dimension to Card's discussion here.[20] To *undertake* the integrity project is to attempt to overcome one's circumstances by a transfiguration of oneself from "victim" to "survivor." And, counter to the view that one's capacity for morally responsible agency is *threatened* by the factors of negative luck (abuse, oppression), Card argues instead that that capacity offers, via the energizing notion of *taking responsibility*, the prospect of change in, and even command of, one's life. Appreciation of luck, then, does not leave one skeptical of the value of morality; it instead transforms any such skepticism into a regard for morality as a conceptual facilitation of positive change in the life of the agent. Morality, via the idea of taking responsibility, presents the means by which to *seize* one's life. One may indeed, on this view, *recover* from victimization.

COMMENT

My first thought about Professor Card's discussion is in effect a worry about how seriously her view takes the specter of *constitutive* luck suggested by the modularity thesis mentioned above, relative to her discussion's positive estimate of the strength of the capacity for morally responsible agency. The integrity project supposes a self affected by the results of a history of oppression or abuse but not necessarily *constituted* by those results. Thus, those negative results can, in principle, be overcome through the development of integrity. Card notes at the end that our luck may be "to have to, or not to have to, work hard or self-consciously" (48) to cultivate the internal bonds at the heart of the integrity she wants victims to develop.

But my attachment to the modularity thesis leads me to worry about constitutive luck at a deeper level. Can the self suffering a history of abuse or oppression not only be affected by the history's results but in fact be constituted by them? Can it be my constitutive-luck fate not "to have to" but, in fact, to be *unable* to "work hard or self-consciously" at the integrity project Card outlines as an avenue of recovery from victimization?

I find two passages in Card's discussion that seem to allow constitutive luck at the deeper level. Early in her discussion she mentions, without elaboration, "a basic lack of justice in our *ability* to be moral" (29, emphasis added). And later she writes, "To determine whether it makes sense to hold an agent responsible, we need to know whether that agent's luck made the development or maintenance of integrity impossible or impossibly difficult" (33).[21] These passages—especially the second—seem to acknowledge that luck can be at the deeper level, that is, it can be of the sort that structures rather than "influences" the will.

Whether constitutive luck can be at the deeper level is an important matter philosophically, I think, for what is at stake are two different conceptions of the individual agent and, beyond that, the character of our moral-psychological responses to others and ourselves. In one conception, will is prior to luck factors; the latter may be heavy in their influence, but in principle they may be overcome. It thus makes sense for the individual to undertake recovery from victimization in the manner suggested by Professor Card's integrity project. In the other conception, some luck factors may be prior to the will, in the sense that they structure it (they are built into it) rather than influence it. These factors are true "givens"— necessities of the will—for the agent.[22] And, depending what these factors are, it may or may not make sense for the individual agent to undertake the integrity project Card has in mind.

As I say above, Card's "multiples" model suggests a victim of abuse whose self is fragmented or scattered. Will might be intact (though diminished in strength) in this case, but the properties of the will are in disarray. The suggested program of recovery is an integrity project cultivating "internal bonding" and thus the development of a sort of moral core allowing at least "cooperation" among the values and commitments present in the self (cf. 47). In contrast, the other conception of the agent just characterized allows us to imagine a victim of abuse—or indeed a victim of problematic judgment (as in the Verghese case) or even a remorseful perpetrator of unintentional wrongdoing—who is, in fact, *stuck* with regret, fear, resentment, self-pity, or some combination of these—perhaps a whole cluster of negative emotions—the whole mass of feeling laced with depression. The result may be a steady-state brooding despair, or generalized apprehension, that is quite paralyzing to thought and action. I am aware that this mass of feeling—this form of emotional sensibility—may indeed be, as the mental health professionals say, "ego-syntonic" and thus be temperament defining "to" as well as "of" the individual.

I suggest, then, that one's will can come to be structured by such feeling and that, in effect, one can be powerless over it. In chapter 2, I report that in the great meaning-of-life essays collected in *The Will to Believe*, William James's view sometimes appears to be that many of us, beneath the layers of ideology, are of "optimistic natural temperament," and this view helps support James's appeals to the legitimacy of "passional nature" in serious life decisions when rationality is inconclusive. But even James seems to allow that a person's *natural temperament* might instead be "pessimistic" and thus carry with it the bleak moral psychology of the negative sort described above.[23] I believe, given my own experience plus contact with others,[24] that there certainly is something like "pessimistic natural temperament." And my further thoughts are simply that (a) such temperament may be "constitutional" and (b) such temperament, that is, temperament constituted pessimistic, can be the residue of abuse and oppression or even of the realizations of mistakes or recognitions of wrongdoing that are at issue in this discussion of forgiveness.

PROSPECTS FOR RECOVERY

Suppose, then, that one is stuck with "pessimistic" temperament in the way, or at the level, I have just mentioned. Is "recovery" possible? Is there some way of restoring effective agency, including the peace of mind and self-confidence that we may suppose morality wants for moral agents? Perhaps there is a *sort* of recovery possible. But it may not take the form of the integrity project that Professor Card recommends. There is such a thing, I think, as learning to live *with* one's constitutive luck. But this "learning-to-live-with" will not be a matter of integrating value and commitment fragments as it is in the case of the victims of abuse or oppression for whom Card's "multiples" model is apt. It will perhaps be more a matter of understanding one's fate in the lotteries of nature and social contingency (including one's own history with personal relationships), then accepting it for what it is, and then designing—or redesigning—a life for oneself that sends one in some other direction or at least does not ask one to do the impossible. In the cases I have in mind, the results of one's history of abuse or oppression, or one's awareness of one's mistakes or wrongdoing, are not, as it were, present to one's will as items to be challenged and overcome; rather, they are *in* one's will, and they structure one's moral-emotional psychology ab initio.

Are there people whose shyness is constitutional? In the view I am exploring, it is a possibility that the answer is yes. And it is cruel to insist with a constitutionally shy person that he or she "overcome" shyness. Are the people who are called "alcoholics" really only "problem drinkers," or perhaps what Fingarette calls "heavy drinkers,"[25] or are they indeed (what AA calls) "real alcoholics," that is, people who *cannot* drink safely no matter how hard they try to control themselves? In the view I am exploring, there are real alcoholics—and the worst thing one can do for them, or to them, is try to teach them to drink "safely" (whatever that could mean). In a similar way, and despite the strange sound of the question, I need to ask, are there victims of abuse whose constitutive luck is such that they *cannot* "do" the integrity project Professor Card outlines for them? I think the answer must again be yes in the view I am exploring. And, again, it would be a form of cruelty to such people to urge on them a recovery program that their nature precludes. In the model I have in mind, the self "stuck" with the mass of feeling including anger, fear, resentment, and so forth, that is, the person for whom such a state is both systemic and ego-syntonic, is not a person who *can* respond to the energizing, morale-lifting strategies of common sense, religion, or frontline psychology—strategies, I rush to say, that have indeed been helpful and even inspiring to those not constituted in the same way. And all this, it perhaps goes without saying, I would apply to cases in which people are aware of mistakes they have made, or wrongdoing they have unwittingly committed, and are in the aftermath of their awarenesses being diminished in the negative constitutional way I have called attention to. For these people forgiveness by others may be ineffective regarding the restoration of effective agency, and self-forgiveness may be a sort of practical impossibility.

I do not wish to be misunderstood, and I do not wish to exaggerate. I am not proposing that all shy people be treated as constitutionally shy, or that all drunks be considered real alcoholics, or that all existential

nihilists be seen as systemically depressed, or that all those who procras-
tinate, lack discipline, or exhibit paranoia be viewed as constitutionally
so. And I am not proposing that forgiveness is futile, or should not be offered, or that self-forgiveness should not be urged on those one cares
about. To the question, "How does one tell whether J is x or constitutionally x?" I have nothing to say (here).[26] And—still a further point—those
who are constitutionally a certain way may not in fact remain that way
forever. There are cases in which one's depression "lifts," for example, or
one's phobias weaken, or one's absorption in one's own past diminishes.
This "just happens," sometimes slowly, sometimes rather quickly. How
this works is not, I think, well understood. Indeed, it may be that the very
effort of "stepping back" from oneself enough to bring into view certain
constitutive-luck factors about oneself is some sort of step toward their
becoming "influences" rather than "structures" of one's will. But there is,
in my view, no guarantee that understanding oneself will provide power
over oneself in this moral-emotional arena.

CONCLUDING THOUGHT

My exploration of the problem of the restoration of effective agency yields
a result that is gloomy in part. If J has made a mistake that results in serious damage to S or has done something very damaging to S that is in fact
morally wrong, then awareness of the mistake or the wrongdoing may
affect J in a way that reduces or diminishes agency, that is, disrupts the
peace of mind and self-confidence that J must have to carry on his or her
personal life or life in the workplace. If we assume that morality wants
J's agency restored, and that the conditions that morality imposes on restoration (e.g., repentance, amends, etc.) have been satisfied, then we may
engage in forgiveness of J, and urge self-forgiveness on J, as part of the
encouragement of recovery of agency. The point that my discussion leaves
us with is that there is no reason in logic or practical fact to suppose that
other-forgiveness will contribute to recovery or that self-forgiveness will
be possible for J. If J were "master of his or her fate" in the manner that
suggests control of the will, perhaps the practices of other-forgiveness and
self-forgiveness could be more promising relative to the restoration of
agency. But, so it seems to me, the fact that negative emotional experience
in some cases comes to structure the will, and not merely stand as a property of it, suggests that all bets are off regarding the expectations we may
have, relative to the restoration of agency, of the practices of other-forgiveness and self-forgiveness. One's agency may be reduced or diminished by
abuse in childhood, or political oppression, or awareness of how one's
mistakes have affected others, or recognition of one's own wrongdoing,

or any number of other things. When forgiveness (by others or oneself) does contribute to the restoration of agency, it does so by lifting a burden, that is, by ameliorating—not abolishing or "revising"—the pain generated by one's awareness of one's mistakes or moral wrongdoing and reflected in loss of confidence and disruption of peace of mind. But for those sensitive to morality—those decent people who take seriously their stake in their own moral history—forgiveness may or may not have its ameliorating effect. One may or may not be able to recover from the reduced or diminished agency one is left with.

4

✛

Self-Respect

THE IMPORTANCE OF SELF-RESPECT

It may be that the dominant moral value of our time is the societal value of *justice*. If one asks why this is so, at least one answer, from the standpoint of an interest in individuals, personal lives, and motivation, is that the societal value of justice, when realized, contributes to the cultivation and nurturing of *self-respect* in individuals. According to the most important contemporary treatment of justice, namely, John Rawls's *A Theory of Justice*,[1] self-respect is served by a society that takes justice seriously, and, in Rawls's view, self-respect is the most important of the "primary goods," that is, those things that every rational being wants, no matter what else he or she wants.[2] This as it stands seems to make of justice something of instrumental value, something whose value is a function of its leading on to self-respect; and, indeed, it seems also to make of self-respect something of instrumental value, for it suggests that the value of self-respect is a function of its leading on to "what one wants."

But, of course, something being of instrumental value does not preclude it from also being of intrinsic value, that is, in some sense valuable "in itself" or "for what it is, apart from what it leads on to." One can approach self-respect from a number of angles, for example, from an interest in economics, psychology, sociology, philosophy, or even literary criticism. These approaches may play up the instrumental value of self-respect. My approach to self-respect is from philosophy and, especially, from moral psychology. I hope my discussion will illuminate to some extent what it is to see self-respect as an especially important value for individuals. Whether

51

it should be counted an intrinsic value is a question I will not pursue here; to do so would require investigation of various conceptions of intrinsic value in ethical theory, and that would take me away from my main concerns.[3] It will be enough to display some different conceptions of self-respect and to attempt to understand how such conceptions can be important to us—in fact, motivating—regarding how we act.

I will begin by, as it were, backing into an account of self-respect. That is, I will consider some ways in which self-respect, in a person who has it or possesses it, can be threatened or challenged. My thought is simply that an exploration of some ways in which a person might be denied self-respect (by others or by him- or herself) may yield insights into what self-respect is. Actually, this way of approaching an account of self-respect is suggested to me by some remarks of Kant in *Lectures on Ethics*:

> We must reverence humanity in our own person, because apart from this man becomes an object of contempt, worthless in the eyes of his fellows and worthless in himself. . . . Only if our worth as human beings is intact can we perform our other duties; for it is the foundation stone of all other duties. A man who has destroyed and cast away his personality, has no intrinsic worth, and can no longer perform any manner of duty.[4]

I assume that when Kant speaks of "humanity in our own person" and "our worth" as persons being "intact," he speaks of something that fits with our notion of self-respect. The passage quoted goes back and forth between "intrinsic" and "instrumental" thinking about self-respect, I suppose, but, still, I find its suggestion that self-respect can be "destroyed and cast away" to be interesting.

Before turning to specific sorts of threats and challenges to self-respect, let me first mark some features of our ordinary thinking about it—features that seem in line with the passage from Kant. These are merely features of our thinking about self-respect, and they do not constitute a theory or explanation of self-respect.

First, I think we consider self-respect to be something of intense individual interest and concern. We would probably be puzzled and even troubled by a person who claimed to have no interest at all in his or her own self-respect. I think further that we consider it to be valuable apart from what it may lead to materially, emotionally, or even spiritually. Having it seems to us, I think, a sort of *security* for our person, and this I take to be a state or condition of our person that is independent of, say, physical, economic, or emotional security. (Being self-respecting is not, as I will emphasize later, simply "feeling good about oneself.")

Second, I think it is also a feature of our ordinary thinking about self-respect that possession of it is problematic—perhaps even problematic enough to make us suspect that self-respect is relatively rare in persons. Perhaps what makes it problematic for us is that having it is not entirely of one's own doing. I cannot, as it were, make myself self-respecting all by myself. My being self-respecting appears to involve at least (a) what others think of me in particular (as an individual, that is), (b) what others think of people of my sort (type, group, class, etc.), and (c) the makeup of certain of my community's institutions and practices. Apropos of these points, Rawls suggests that self-respect is supported by our "finding our person and deeds appreciated and confirmed by others who are likewise esteemed and their association enjoyed,"[5] and, too, he suggests that "it is clear that, although [self-respect] is a psychological state, social institutions are a basic instigating cause."[6] In moments of gloom it may see that *my* self-respect may be in important ways out of my control. (And this, in turn, may arouse anger or resentment.)

Third, we appear to view self-respect as a fragile state or condition—one that is constantly under siege or at risk of being damaged or taken away. Certainly the public discussion is filled with complaints and appeals involving (alleged) attacks on self-respect. Thus, women find their self-respect undermined by men, employees find themselves used by the businesses or agencies they work for, members of minority groups find their dignity ignored or denied by establishment people and their practices. This fragility is a troubling feature of our ordinary thinking about self-respect. For if self-respect is very important (as I think is so), yet possession of it is problematic—dependent in certain ways on the views and attitudes of others and the structure of society—and as a result even fragile (constantly under siege), then our having this very important thing may seem elusive and somehow beyond our grasp.

With this much elaboration of main features of our thinking about self-respect, let me turn to "threats and challenges" to it.

EXTERNAL AND PERSONAL THREATS

Perhaps it is common opinion that individual self-respect can be threatened by external forces, for example, corrupt institutions, popular ideologies, and so forth. But we can also imagine cases in which persons live under, or in the grip of, the most oppressive external forces, but their self-respect remains intact. So how to understand the bearing or pressures of external forces on self-respect is a difficult matter. It does not follow from the existence of oppressive institutions and ideologies that self-respect in the people oppressed is lacking or damaged; but still, these external factors are considered threatening to self-respect. And if we find that self-respect is lacking or damaged in some people or certain groups of people, we may consider that the oppressive institutions or ideologies they live with or under contributed to this result.

It is not difficult to list some of the external factors that we construe as being at odds with individual self-respect. High on most lists would be *misstructured social institutions and policies*, governing, for example, how education is conducted, or how the legal system operates, or how employment opportunities are made available. The terms by which institutions and policies structure these activities may, for example, be discriminatory in morally objectionable ways, so that some people under such institutions or policies find themselves subordinated or excluded in certain contexts for reasons or factors that are irrelevant to the activities in question. When this unfairness is seen to be so, we think that the self-respect of those thus victimized has been jeopardized. Similarly, the influence of *distorted social ideologies* can be such that people affected by them find themselves confined in artificial ways or perhaps thought of as inferior or ridiculous. Such ideologies may exploit alleged differences in the natures of men and women or the so-called traditional roles of men and women in (say) advertising and popular culture. Most of us are vulnerable to the influence of omnipresent ideologies, I think, especially because such ideologies are often "givens" in our lives and thus provide background premises for our thinking and action that are not immediate candidates for review or criticism. It is sometimes difficult, in one's own case, to pick out how far one is under the influence of this or that perhaps pernicious social ideology, and it is often hard to see how to resist such influence when it is recognized for what it is. Finally (for this discussion), *distortions in thinking about personal relations* promoting objectionable sorts of subordination or other "status" differences in such different contexts as the world of work or popular interpretations of sexuality need to be included among the external threats to self-respect—though these sometimes seem to be more matters of social custom and inertia than matters of ideology.

If self-respect can be threatened by such external forces, we should notice as well that we can ourselves, that is, by ourselves, threaten and indeed ruin our own self-respect. We might call these forces "personal threats," and many examples come to mind. Thus, our own *cruelty* (e.g., when we inflict gratuitous pain on a child, or stick pins in a kitten, or manipulate vulnerable people), when we are conscious of it, is a threat to self-respect. Our own *moral weakness* (e.g., when we fail to respond to another's needs from moderate fear, risk, or inconvenience or similarly fail to resist an injustice we are aware of)—again, when we are conscious of it—is also a threat to self-respect. Recognition of our own *egoism*, whereby we systematically put our own interests before those of others, can be a further threat to our self-respect. Our own awareness of being implicated in *unfair play*, for example, when we take advantage of others—even when doing so does not really cause pain to anyone (perhaps we fail to do our share or part in a cooperative scheme when the burden of co-operation falls on us)—too, has its way of threatening self-respect. And finally (for this discussion), the sense we have of *wasting ourselves*, for example, corrupting ourselves or letting ourselves deteriorate (as when one knows one cannot handle drugs, food, alcohol, or even free time but refuses to resist temptation), can diminish self-respect. In all these cases—and there are doubtless more "phenomena" in this area—one personally challenges one's own self-respect and as a result risks in extreme instances throwing oneself into self-contempt.

The logic of the connection between, for example, cruelty and self-respect seems to me to be interesting philosophically. Consider the difference between the threat to self-respect from what I call "external" factors (e.g., misstructured institutions or distorted social ideologies) and the threat from cruelty. In the first case the threat is just that—a threat. The misstructured institution does not *entail* loss of self-respect among those victimized by it. In the latter case the situation is different. I think that the knowing performance of cruelty (avoidable cruelty) *entails* a loss of self-respect on the part of the performing agent. This may be because, to borrow words from the quotation from Kant above, under misstructured institutions our "worth as human beings" can remain "intact," that is, we can persist in thinking of ourselves as taking seriously the principles of justice; but when we knowingly commit cruel acts, such persistence is fraudulent. It may be that faults and distortions in the institutions and ideologies that surround us and provide us a context in which to act are not the only—or even the most important—sources of damage to self-respect. In this area we may be our own worst enemies.

SERVILITY

In the discussion above I list some ways in which a person's self-respect might be threatened, damaged, or (in some cases) straightforwardly ruined. Let me here comment briefly on another aspect of this complicated subject. In some cases (e.g., cruelty) the threat to self-respect is very much a function of self-perception. On a phenomenological level, the performance of an act of cruelty can carry with it a sense that one's self-respect is "slipping away" *as* one performs the act. In other cases (e.g., the distorted ideology case) one may be aware of one's own resistance to the loss of self-respect. But this surface phenomenology of loss of self-respect or struggle against loss of self-respect is not present in all cases. There are

some cases in which we (if not the agent in question) want to speak of
someone lacking self-respect, yet that person's own awareness of the condition we are ascribing to him or her is simply missing. In cases in which
one suffers gradual or abrupt loss of self-respect, one may throw oneself
into *self-contempt*. In another sort of case the absence of self-respect is involved, but "awareness" may or may not be involved. I refer to the case
of *servility*.

How is servility to be understood? Let me briefly consider the response
to this question given by Thomas E. Hill Jr.[7] According to Hill, servility
is a moral defect that involves "a failure to understand and acknowledge
one's own moral rights" (9). Thus, servility from the start is understood
philosophically as related to one's capacity to have or possess rights.
Morally, it is a rights-based notion:

> I assume, without argument here, that each person has moral rights. Some
> of these rights may be basic human rights; that is, rights for which a person
> needs only to be human to qualify. Other rights will be derivative and con-
> tingent upon his special commitments, institutional affiliations, etc. Most
> rights will be *prima facie* ones; some may be absolute. Most can be waived
> under appropriate conditions; perhaps some cannot. The servile person does
> not, strictly speaking, violate his own rights. At least in our paradigm cases
> he fails to acknowledge fully his own moral status because he does not fully
> understand what his rights are, how they can be waived, and when they can
> be forfeited. [9]

Hill offers three main examples of the servility he has in mind: the
"Uncle Tom" figure is one who "displays an attitude that denies his moral
equality with whites" (9); the "Self-Deprecator" is one who "acts as if he
has forfeited many important rights which in fact he has not" (9); and the
"Deferential Housewife" is one "who fails to appreciate . . . that her consent to serve [her husband] is a valid waiver of her rights only under certain conditions," so that "if her consent is coerced, say, by the lack of viable options for women in her society, then her consent is worth little" (10).
And, further, the Deferential Housewife's "consent to defer constantly to
her husband is not a legitimate setting aside of her rights if it results from
her mistaken belief that she has a moral duty to do so. . . . When she says
that she freely gives up such a right, she is confused" (10).

We should remember that the servility we are considering here is not a
state or condition that the person suffering it is conscious of, and it may
be the result of what Hill calls "moral ignorance" or "confusion," in which
case "it need not be something for which a person is to blame" (10). But
what of the case in which the ignorance or confusion is cleared away and
the person in question persists in behavior "displaying attitudes" (as Hill

says) that we associate with servility? Two possibilities come to mind for Hill. First, "if the motive is a morally commendable one, or a desire to avert dire consequences to oneself, or even an ambition to set an oppressor up for a later fall, then I would not count the role player as servile" (11). Second, "the story is quite different, however, if a person continues in his deferential role just from laziness, timidity, or a desire for some minor advantage. . . . In these cases, I suggest, we have a kind of servility independent of any ignorance or confusion about one's rights" (11). And "the objectionable feature" in these cases is "a willingness to disavow one's moral status, publicly and systematically, in the absence of any strong reason to do so" (11). Thus, relative to my earlier remarks, Hill seems here to be considering how one might damage one's own self-respect: If one knowingly persists in, say, the deferential housewife role in a way that involves a willing "disavowal of one's moral status in the absence of any strong reason to do so," then one personally damages one's self-respect. And, relative again to my earlier remarks, in this case one may not merely "damage" but in effect "cancel" one's self-respect, at least for a time.

But we may ask at this point (as Hill asks), Why, when all is said and done, is this self-infliction of damage to (or the cancellation of) self-respect wrong? Hill answers in a way that is reminiscent of the points in the passage from Kant quoted above. Hill writes,

At least one sort of respect for persons is respect for the rights which the moral law accords them. If one respects the moral law, then one must respect one's own moral rights; and this amounts to having a kind of self-respect incompatible with servility.

The servile person, as such, does not express disrespect for the system of moral rights in the obvious way by violating the rights of others. His lack of respect is more subtly manifested by his acting before others as if he did not know or care about his position of equality under that system. [13–14]

Finally, Hill adds the further (Kantian) point that self-respect is a precondition of the sort of respect for others called for by morality:

Insofar as the servile person is ignorant of his own rights, he is not in an adequate position to appreciate the rights of others. . . . On the other hand, if he plays the servile role knowingly, then, barring special explanation, he displays a lack of concern to see the principles of morality acknowledged and respected and thus the absence of one motive which can move a person to respect the rights of others. In either case, the servile person's lack of self-respect necessarily puts him in a less than ideal position to respect others. [18]

OTHER CASES

So far I have classified "threats" to self-respect as either "external' or "personal." I suggest that there may be an important logical difference between these threats: the former seem, so to speak, contingently threatening, while the latter seem pretty much to entail the loss of self-respect, at least temporarily. I also considered Hill's account of servility, noting that in his view servility is a moral defect involving "a failure to understand and acknowledge one's own moral rights" (9). Servility in this case may be excusable, that is, not be blameworthy, when one is in ignorance or confusion about one's rights; but in another form—the case in which one understands one's moral rights but persists in the disavowal of them for no good reason— we have morally objectionable servility. In cases of this latter kind I think the servility belongs among my "personal" threats to self-respect.

However, there are "other" cases, which are interesting (as challenges to self-respect) but which I cannot myself easily classify as "external" or "personal." I will mention three such cases.[8] Call the first one the case of *having been cheated.* In this situation one learns something about one's life— and all of a sudden one has the sense of having lost out on self-respect. This is not a case of being self-respecting and then having one's possession of self-respect threatened, or diminished, or taken away either by external forces or by one's own doing. Rather, one realizes that one has been *denied* something one should have—or perhaps that one forfeited something without realizing it. A characteristic example is that of the older woman who learns from her feminist daughter that her life is, or has been, one of subordination and void (more or less) of autonomy.[9] A second case involves the risk to self-respect in *dirty-hands situations.* This is the case (kept simple here)[10] in which one must do something one knows to be *wrong* in order to get something *right* done. Not any case of this sort would damage self-respect, I suppose, for in some cases the right thing is *so* important, and the wrong thing *so* unimportant, that self-respect suffers only a light blow if any blow at all. But in other cases the *kind* of thing the wrong thing is—for example, the betrayal of a friend (in order to get the truth known in a matter of violation of the public trust), acquiescence in racist policies (in order to stay in office to pursue morally viable community goals)—might yield a significant blow to self-respect, as well as disrupting peace of mind in the form of regret, remorse, or even resentment. The third sort of case involves *loss of personal values* that are important to one's identity. This is the situation in which one's self-respect involves "setting and sticking to some personal values," which "are typically seen as inescapably a part of oneself": "Whether one sees them as objective or not, one genuinely takes the attitude that one is, in one's own view, better or worse according to how one measures up to them."[11] For present purposes we may recognize that these "personal values" may or may not be moral values. In some cases the values may be aesthetic commitments or attachments to organizational or discipline-oriented forms of style. In other cases they may be straightforward "personal moral absolutes" (e.g., "I will not torture—no matter what"). But the point is, if one sacrifices them or somehow comes to see that one lacks such values in one's life, then one suffers in the region of self-respect. One fails to have, or to meet, one's own personal standards, and one's identity comes to be in question. One is not what one ought to be or what one is supposed to be.[12]

TOWARD A GENERAL ACCOUNT

Given these several different cases, what can be said in general about how self-respect is to be understood? That is, what, in general, must self-respect be, if it can be threatened, canceled, or damaged in these various "external," "personal," or "other" ways?

Let me venture the following points.

First, it seems clear enough that self-respect is not just a matter of feelings—though this is not to say that the "surface phenomenology" I have mentioned at certain points does not involve feelings. This much seems true: one can be self-respecting even if one is tired or feeling ill. Self-respect is not itself "feeling good about oneself" as a sheer matter of affective response.[13] (If it were, of course, one could induce it with a drug.)

Second, being self-respecting is not reducible to being admiring of one's talents, skills, or even character traits as these are manifested in one's actions and activities. To be admiring of oneself in these respects may, if carried too far, be arrogance or conceit, and to be underadmiring of one's actual talents or other properties may, if carried too far, be an unfortunate kind of humility or at least a sort of excessive and "unhealthy" modesty. This point calls up an Aristotelian picture of a "continuum" involving perhaps "arrogance" and "conceit" at one end and "excessive humility" or "unhealthy modesty" at the other. But whatever the "mean" on this continuum is (and whatever the best vocabulary to describe it), I think the self-respect we are concerned about is independent of this continuum altogether.

If we set aside approaches involving feelings or means between extremes (useful in some contexts, to be sure), my positive suggestion is that self-respect is a matter of, or function of, *how one understands the security and viability of one's place, position, or standing in a community of autonomous or independent individuals*. I will refer to this proposition as a characterization of the "general idea of self-respect." Here are some comments about certain terms in this characterization.

When I refer to our "place, position, or standing" in a community, I do not refer to what we are "by nature" or what we are as a result of what John Rawls called "nature's lottery,"[14] for example, mathematically insightful, female, black, or blessed (cursed?) with perfect pitch. I refer instead to what we have in the way of *rights and responsibilities* (and, indeed, opportunities and privileges), insofar as we are participants with others in the practices and institutions of a community.

And *community* here is a term that might be applied to small things or big things—to local associations; to political, intellectual, or task-oriented communities of various sizes; or to what is perhaps the most important community of all so far as self-respect is concerned, namely, the "moral community."[15] I am inclined to say something like this. I may be concerned about my self-respect in the context of my membership in a local association or a large political community. But ultimately the most important context in which I may be concerned about my self-respect is that of the moral community. Here what I am concerned about is my understanding of the security and viability of my place, position, or standing in the human moral community of autonomous individuals. In Kant's words again, to "cast away and destroy" *that,* or to have one's possession of it jeopardized by misstructured social institutions or corrupt ideologies (e.g., in the form of stereotypical thinking by others),[16] is either a *moral tragedy* (as in the case of "personal threats," i.e., self-inflicted damage) or a *moral crime* (as in the case of the success of "external" threats). This view, of course, places the "moral community" at rather an abstract level. It is not that local or even national community (nation-state) in which one actually lives but, instead, that community to whose structure one appeals to mark injustices and other deep faults in one's local or national community.[17]

Finally, I will add a note on "autonomy." If self-respect is essentially a matter of the security of one's position in the moral community, we should note that this position not only *entitles* one to things (such as being taken account of and fairness) and *protects* one against things (such as torture, degradation, and exploitation); it also gives one *responsibilities.* Of course, what these latter responsibilities are (fair play, courtesy to others, compassion toward others in need, and a certain alertness to injustice come to mind) is a difficult philosophical problem. Some theorists would argue that among these responsibilities is a responsibility for our own "plan of life" (as Rawls calls it). And the extent to which we are autonomous relative to our choices of content for that plan, and to our implementation of it, is an important variable in the makeup of our own self-respect in ordinary life.

PLANS OF LIFE

Autonomy, of course, is a complicated notion. It has to do (surely) with the security of our *rights* as members of the moral community. But in perhaps a more immediate way it has to do (surely) with our standing among others in local and national communities and, as just suggested above, with how our choices and circumstances in those communities allow us to pursue our "plans of life."[18] Let me comment briefly in what follows on "plans of life" and how one's relationship to one's plan of life may be an object of self-respect, alongside the object provided by one's membership in the moral community.[19]

To be relevantly autonomous, in this more immediate context involving plans of life, one's relationship to one's plan of life itself must meet certain conditions. One of these conditions (surely) is that one's plan of life must be of one's own choosing—though in context, that is, in the environments provided by actual local and national communities, the notion of choosing involved here is doubtless a degree notion of sorts. That is, one's choices might not be the more abstract "free choices" of members of the moral community, unencumbered as they are by differences among them that are, in Rawls's words, "arbitrary from the moral point of view."[20] They are, instead, the "relatively free choices" that become possible when particulars about one's makeup (physical and intellectual) and the history and social circumstances attending one's existence in the world are taken into account. Still, within such parameters—as compared with situations in which people are forced or coerced into courses of action—we recognize some choices as (relatively) free. To be "of one's choosing," one's plan of life must the object of at least relatively free choice.

A second condition of autonomy in this real-world setting is that one's relationship to one's plan of life, apart from its contents, must be "rational." But, of course, the rationality here is more procedural than substantive; it does not pick out specifics in the way of content for plans of life. To be rational in the manner required, one must stand to one's plan of life in a way that involves awareness of relevant facts and a consideration of consequences.[21]

Two further conditions on the relationship in question are "sense of worth" and (for want of better terminology) "ego strength." By the first of these I mean both that one views one's plan of life as challenging and interesting relative to one's own natural talents, or at least one's estimate of one's own natural talents,[22] and that one finds the plan of life appreciated by others one respects, that is, by those "associates" in our communities whom we respect and from whom we seek respect.[23] And by the second I mean that one is reasonably confident of one's ability to carry through one's plan of life.[24] This latter condition is a crucial aspect of self-respect and seems psychological—and, indeed, visceral and volitional—in character. There is a difference between "feeling confident" of one's abilities and "being (with reason) confident" of them. We have interesting self-referential vocabulary that fits here: when a person feels confident of his or her abilities but has little or no reason to feel so, we may view him or her as guilty of wishful thinking or self-delusion; he or she may in fact be dangerous if his or her activities have serious consequences for others. On the other side, when a person can with reason be confident of his or her abilities but nevertheless fails to feel confident, the result may be indecision, lack of self-confidence, and different forms of immobility or paralysis. To be "reasonably confident" in this matter of being able to carry through one's plan of life is not easy.

Finally, to this list of autonomy conditions for the relationship between a person and his or her plan of life, I would add one's perspective on the range of "available" plans of life in one's real-world context. One needs to think of one's choice of a plan of life as not artificially limited. By this I mean that self-respect requires that the plan of life one sponsors be viewed by one as having been chosen from a reasonably wide range of plans widely considered desirable. Of course, the availability of candidate plans of life is in part a function of social circumstances and social ideology. As regards circumstances, it may be that in some cases economic or natural conditions preclude the feasibility of certain plans because material prerequisites are missing or in low supply. As regards ideology, during certain historical periods (e.g., hierarchical feudal society) it was widely believed that one's station in life was "assigned," and one's lot was to make the best of it, whatever it was. In this ideological context a certain attitude of resignation might be the most practical response to the task of life. I think such a view of one's situation is dangerous to the possibility of self-respect—or at any rate the form of self-respect being explored here. Of course, there may be situations in life in which resignation is appropriate and even, given coercion or no alternatives, both practical and admirable.

Many further details of an account of "plan of life self-respect" might be worked out, but I will not attempt to do that here. The idea that a person has a plan of life need not be simple. A plan of life might in effect be a nested arrangement of plans, with some indeterminacy about later phases or stages; and of course any sensible account must leave room for changes in plans of life given catastrophic events or even simply significant changes in circumstances. And, too, given persons' vulnerability to stress and cruelty from others, their plans of life may, as it were, slip from view from time to time.[25]

FOUR CONCEPTIONS OF SELF-RESPECT

With the discussion above in mind, I am inclined at this point to distinguish four conceptions of self-respect. There is, first, *basic rights self-respect*. Here I have in mind (with the help of Thomas Hill's account) one's general understanding of one's standing in the moral community, an understanding that emphasizes commonality with other persons but not the special properties (talents, abilities, local community memberships, etc.) by which one may be distinguished from others. This conception is egalitarian in character and places one "on a par" *with* others—in fact, in my interpretation, with all of humankind. Second, there is *plan of life self-respect*. Here I have in mind (with the help of the Rawlsian account) how one stands relative to local, national, and other communities regarding one's pursuit of a "plan of life" that is interesting to one and challenging to one's abilities, whatever they may in fact be. This form of self-respect does not place one "on a par" *with* others so that particular facts about oneself and others are not relevant. In this case particulars are of major importance (as is self-knowledge), for a human life is something like a project lived on certain terms (one's plan of life), and how one stands to those terms, in the real world, can be an object of respect or of dismay.

There is no reason for the discussion to ignore or set aside two more popular forms of self-respect. One of these, drawn from an example given earlier, we can call *personal values self-respect*. Here I have in mind, again, those valuational orientations we choose for ourselves and come to consider parts of our identity. Such valuational orientations may or may not be moral in nature. The valuational orientations that are moral in nature might be the "virtues" celebrated in Aristotelian ethics, and while there can be differences among people in regard to emphases, there is probably a certain core set of virtues that the moral community wants in all its members. But there is little or no commonality expected here on the non-moral valuational front. Thus, one person is, and insists on being, highly disciplined, forward looking, and entrepreneurial; another is, and must be, the "free spirit"; still another is, and has to be, the calm in the center of the storm. These sorts of "orientations" color our lives, and we have our ways of building them into who we are, so that action "out of character" can be challenging to self-respect.

Finally, let me include in this listing of conceptions the form of self-respect that may be most often on our minds as we worry our ways through ordinary life, namely, *achievement self-respect*. This is a largely meritocratic conception of self-respect in which one's concern is one's standing relative to others regarding the accomplishment of certain tasks or the display of one's talents. Here one is wondering whether one is "winning the race" (whatever its content), and the notion of winning the race is usually measurable by reference to money, fame, title, position, admission, and so on. I have the sense that concern about achievement self-respect among real people is very high, and I have no interest in playing down its practical importance.

One may ask at this point whether certain of these conceptions of self-respect are more important than others. And one may also ask whether a society, through its institutions and practices, can affect some, any, or all of these forms of self-respect in people. I end this discussion with some notes responding to these questions.

I think a society can do a great deal, through its institutions and practices, to cultivate basic rights self-respect. After all, a society, through its institutions, can express a view of persons as moral equals, as possessors of (equal) rights, and as equally deserving of fair treatment. It can also structure itself so as to convey the notion that the rights people have are rights they have as people (as members of the moral community, I want to say) and not rights held by them "at the whim" of the institutions themselves. It can structure itself so that the rights in question are indeed thought of as "natural," "basic," or "human" rights and thus not to be set aside or canceled for considerations of, say, economic benefit for some.[26] The difference between a society that discriminates against certain people, and in favor of certain other people, insofar as these people belong to different groups defined in terms that are arbitrary and irrelevant to the aims of social cooperation, and a society that does not do this is a difference between a society that destroys and one that cultivates self-respect of this first type.

A society can also, I think, contribute to the flourishing of plan of life self-respect—though here the ways it can do so are more difficult to make out. Despite the difficulty, it seems evident that societies can differ in the ways in which they restrict or broaden the range of plans of life available to individuals. Dominant ideologies are important, relative to this form of self-respect, and can be fostered or broken down, strengthened or weakened, by social action through the structure of institutions and practices. By leaving corrupt ideologies in place, that is, by inaction, societies can limit the recognition of opportunities and in this and many other related ways weaken plan of life self-respect.

I have my doubts whether society can or should do much at all regarding nonmoral personal values self-respect—at least not if that society means to be genuinely "open." If an open society is one that does not choose "the good life" for its members, I think it certainly does not choose their nonmoral valuational orientations for them either. There are of course limits on both these sorts of openness. The open society does not allow someone's implementation of a version of the "good life" that harms others, and it resists "valuational orientations" that are incompatible with what is required of people in order to secure and preserve justice in the basic structure of society. So even the open society is not an "anything goes" affair for plans of life or types of persons. But this is not to say that society should, or can, influence people toward one or another sort of valuational orientation within the range of those orientations that respect justice.

The main point I want to make about achievement self-respect is that, despite its "popularity," that is, despite the fact that it is a concern for most people, it has a dark side. For many of us, achievement self-respect is a source of unhappiness. It breeds a sensibility caught up in comparisons and contrasts, in many of which, in the nature of the case, given individuals may not fare well. (There is "almost always" someone who has done better at task x, and the races one has actually *won* rarely seem worth it after the fact.) One need not be "against" achievement to make these points. But persons can be brought to seek to achieve for the wrong reasons and at the costs of distortion in their view of what human life is or can be. I share the discomfort of many writers with the "meritocratic" society, and I worry that the source of the discomfort is the sense that such a society favors the "model" of a competitive, (very) competent person that is beyond the reach of many of us. On the other side, I see that the development and cultivation of (anyhow some) human talents and abilities—developed and cultivated for their own sake—are hardly objectionable.[27] The good society should indeed encourage and provide for human self-realization—but not (solely) to get races won.

Is there a *ranking* possible here? Can the conceptions of self-respect be lined up in some fashion, with certain ones thought of as morally higher or more important than the others? My thought here is simple and perhaps rather classical relative to the liberal tradition. What I want for myself and my children is, so to speak, "full" basic rights self-respect and also plan of life self-respect in a society that recognizes the importance of the latter and hence contributes to its flourishing. Nonmoral personal values self-respect, as characterized above, is something that society can afford to let people experiment with. The nonmoral "valuational orientations" are probably things serious persons should be reserved about committing themselves to in any case. And achievement self-respect (of the comparison-and-contrast kind) should probably be kept to a minimum, insofar as it breeds arrogance or despair. Human self-realization is a good thing but not because, relative to others, one has "won."

5

✛

Others' Needs

APPEALS TO NEED

Why are others' needs sometimes moving to me? That is, why do they disturb me and in some cases motivate me to act in a way that I think counts as a positive response to them? In some cases others' needs seem like simple facts, even though the philosophical accounts I know of typically treat them as values of sorts. When I am moved by others' needs, then, what is doing the moving? Are some facts about persons somehow already valuational? That is, are there facts about persons that are themselves normative in a logically ab initio way? Or is it really the case (analytically) that facts are facts, and when we are moved we are so via the logically separable involvement of values?

Appeals to the needs of persons are a staple of moral and political discourse. Social programs as well as individuals' other-regarding activities are commonly urged on the ground that they will meet certain needs, and when existing programs or activities are criticized, a typical part of the criticism is that they meet no needs or drain away efforts that could be put to meeting those needs or to meeting other more important needs. Sometimes entire social systems—for example, capitalist democracies—are objected to as "irrational" on the ground that their structure is such that they do not, or cannot, meet basic human needs.[1] Other systems, such as the modification of capitalist democracy we have come to call the Welfare State, may be recommended insofar as they involve a "conscious decision to allocate more of the country's resources according to criteria of social need."[2]

As this last point may intimate, appeals to need are often made in such a way that it appears that the needs appealed to are somehow in competition for attention and response with factors of other sorts; and a part of the point of making the appeals seems to be that the needs in question are, as it were, losing out in the competition. I say "appears" and "seems to be" here because it is this general picture of needs as factors in a competition for attention and response with other factors that I wish to discuss. The picture comes easily to mind, I think, when we consider, in contexts of moral and political recommendation and criticism, whether, for example, responding to persons' needs shall have priority over rewarding persons in virtue of their contributions to the public (the company's, the community's, the movement's) good; or whether claims of need typically should be subordinate to considerations of fairness (as this "competing factor" may be involved, for example, in institutional grievance procedures meant to satisfy demands for due process); or whether claims of need should regularly override considerations of efficiency and convenience (as these may be involved, say, in the operations of industries whose main mode of production is the assembly line).

This general picture of needs as competitive factors makes it tempting to suppose that an important part of political argument must consist in the *independent* (i.e., logically preliminary) identification of persons' needs. For plainly we cannot decide or even usefully mediate a competition among competing factors unless we have some notion of what those factors are. And it is tempting to suppose further that these needs we must independently identify are themselves (as indicated above) of a factual or empirical character. For if we are to make intelligent judgments about factors in a competition for attention and response, and thus must first identify what those factors are, then surely they must, in principle, be ascertainable in some reasonably straightforward way.

In what follows I attempt to work out my thought that an adequate philosophical characterization of human needs will pay special attention to our experience of them as "normative facts," that is, as facts that are ab initio valuational. There is, I suggest, a *conception of persons* behind appeals to need when the needs appealed to are serious and basic. And this conception of persons—persons as clusters of normative facts—is important to our understanding of morality. I think this conception of persons, articulated in different vocabularies, might be an important part of both the Kantian understanding of morality, whereby "rational beings" form a "realm of ends," and the utilitarian understanding of morality, whereby "social beings" are thought of as objects of "natural sympathy."

AN ANALYTIC VIEW

In contrast to the vigorous use of the concept of need in moral and political recommendation and criticism, philosophical treatments of the concept are rare.[3] That the concept is in use is of course recognized, and that it is difficult to analyze is acknowledged. It is tempting to move beyond the analysis of the concept to the question of whether the satisfaction of human needs may in some general way claim social priority over the satisfaction of certain other conditions that may be thought of as involved in the makeup of the good state.[4] I am interested in this question, but I can see that there are important prior questions about how the concept of need is to be understood that must be dealt with before one can move in this direction fruitfully. In what follows I discuss one of these prior questions, namely, whether appeals to need can have, as I will say, independent justificatory force.[5] The interest of the question is that an answer to it will govern, in part, how the project of determining the priority of satisfaction of human needs is to be understood.

Consider a view according to which appeals to need do not, as such, have independent justificatory force. In detailed presentation,[6] this view rests on the conceptual point that needs imply purposes. That is, to say of x that it is needed by J is to say that x is needed by J *for* (to secure, to do, etc.) p, where p is some end, object, condition, or state of affairs (e.g., being in good health), and x is some prerequisite (e.g., having decent food) of the existence of p. In this view, when needs are appealed to in argument, we must shift attention from the claim about what is needed to the claim (which may not be explicit) about what it is needed for. And so far as justification is concerned, the question of whether or not x should be supplied or provided turns not on the fact that x is needed but on the desirability of the end p for which x is needed, together with facts related to the desirability of p. Thus,

> When I say that "need" is not by itself a justificatory principle, I mean that no statement to the effect that x is necessary in order to produce y provides a reason for doing x. Before it can provide such a reason y must be shown to be (or taken to be) a desirable end to pursue. This much is necessary in order to provide *pro tanto* a reason for doing x. A *conclusive* reason would require showing that the cost of x . . . does not make it less advantageous than some alternative course of action, and that any disadvantageous side effects of x are outweighed by its advantage in producing y.[7]

This view has the interesting consequence that the very project of arguing that the claims of need have social priority over other claims is either mistaken in conception or a perhaps misleadingly oblique way of arguing for certain priorities among ends. And if we ask why it is that appeals to need are often regarded as having independent justificatory force, an answer is provided by supplementing the line of thought with the idea that there are limits on the ends that go with the needs ascribed to persons. This idea has been worked out by means of the metaphor of a "core" use of the concept of need in connection with the end of physical health. Beyond the core use, the concept may be used in connection with ends that "spread out" from the core. Thus, persons need privacy for mental well-being; students need access to sources of ideas to become educated; and older persons need a certain guarantee of financial security to maintain their dignity in later years. The result is that

> the nearer to the core the use of "need" is, the less linguistic propriety demands that the ends be supplied in the sentence and, of course, the easier it is to suppose that a need can somehow be established independently of an end. However, this modification does not affect the thesis that *no special account has to be taken of "need," for it is still derivative and the only interesting questions arise in connection with the ends.*[8]

My response to this line of thought is to grant its point regarding the structure of appeals to need but to qualify that point in a way that modifies its conclusion regarding the independent justificatory force of such appeals. That is, "*J* is in need of *x*" should, I think, be construed as "*J* is in need of *x* for *p*"; but it does not follow, I suggest, that the justificatory force of "*J* is in need of *x* for *p*" is simply derivative from the desirability of *p*, plus considerations connected therewith. To think that its justificatory force is thus derivative is to overlook that part of its force that derives from the fact that *J* is related to *p* in such a way that he or she is in *need* of *x* to secure *p*. In short, the line of thought in question leads us to concentrate on persons' ends at the expense of how they are related to their ends.

To show that appeals to need can have justificatory force that is not entirely derivative from considerations that have to do with the desirability of ends, it is not necessary to show that needs can be established independently of ends. It is sufficient to show that the *way* of being related to an end that is involved in a person's being in need is, in its own right, a separable and perhaps on occasion an important feature of that person's situation. If this can be shown, then it may be plausible to suppose that a feature of that sort could fall under a principle—perhaps a principle of moral and political importance—that relates it to a course of action of a general kind.

We can begin to show this by noticing some different ways in which persons can be related to their ends, when the claims that express these relations are triadic in form. For example, *J* may stand in relation to *p* such that *J* needs *x* to secure *p*; alternatively, *J* may stand in relation to *p* such that being provided with *x* would be (merely) a *convenient* way for him or her (or us) to secure *p*; alternatively again, *J* may stand in relation to *p* such that being supplied with *x* would be the way he or she would *like* to secure *p*. We can imagine cases in which, say, *x, y*, and *z* are different conditions of *J*'s securing *p* but in regard to which we would say that *J* needs *x* while he or she might like to be provided with *y*, whereas being supplied with *z* might be convenient for him or her (or us) and so forth. Cases in which there are "difficult but worthwhile" in contrast to "easy" ways of securing a certain end are among those that come to mind. Perhaps a student needs the rigorously structured guidance of a special tutor (to learn *a*), while he or she might like to work in a less structured, more independent way (to learn *a*), whereas it might be convenient all around, or especially for us, to place him or her in an existing program of regular classes (to learn *a*).

The point is not restricted to cases in which difficult but worthwhile ways contrast with easy ways of gaining ends. When we speak of persons being in need of decent food, we do not, in most contexts, have to fill out what we say with explicit reference to the end of physical well-being. But whether or not we refer explicitly to that end, it seems clear that in speaking of a person's need for decent food there is something more involved than the desirability of physical well-being and considerations related to it, though indeed these are involved. Roughly, so far as the condition of well-being is concerned, a person having decent food is no mere matter of convenience, taste, or efficiency relative to being in that condition but, rather, a matter of overriding relevance to achieving it. We require, in fact, a concept by which to express the character of overriding relevance that may attach to certain prerequisites of such ends. There are of course many prerequisites of an end of the generality of "well-being," and some of these may be such that their satisfaction is or can be a matter of convenience, taste, and the like. But when our concern with certain of these prerequisites is such that we think of persons as being in need of that which satisfies them, we distinguish what is involved in the satisfaction of such prerequisites from what is involved in the satisfaction of others. And my view is that the sense we have of the one sort of satisfaction or provision being distinct from the others is not to be accounted for solely in terms of a greater degree of desirability of relevant ends, together with related considerations.

Let me attempt to contribute to an account of the distinction in question, so as to suggest how the initial view described above is misleading regarding the character of the justificatory force of appeals to need. We may begin by contrasting different kinds of claims concerning persons' relationships to their ends against the background of the above view,[9] according to which the conditions of "J needs x for p" being even prima facie justificatory are (a) that p is desirable and (b) that having x is a means to securing p; and the further conditions of it providing a *conclusive* reason are (c) that having x is not a more costly way of securing p than, say, y or z and (d) that the desirability of p more than compensates any undesirable side effects of securing p by means of having x.

Notice first that the satisfaction of conditions a–d is not a sufficient condition of an appeal to need. Consider a group of claims of these kinds:

1. "J needs x for p."
2. "It would be convenient for J to secure p by means of x."
3. "J would like to secure p through x."

We can imagine cases in which conditions a–d are satisfied but in which a claim of kind 2 but not of kinds 1 or 3 could be made without prejudice. That is, J, x, and p might be related so that a–d are satisfied but without entailing that J *needs* x to secure p. For example, we can imagine a case in which giving J a regular program of courses (x) is a means of J learning a (p), such that conditions a–d are satisfied, but in which we view giving J this as a matter of convenience from our standpoint rather than as a matter of providing J with what he or she needs (which, we suppose, is not the regular program of courses but the guidance of a special tutor).

Second, we may build on this point by considering a group of claims of the following kinds:

4. "J needs x for p."
5. "It would be convenient for J to secure p by means of y."
6. "J would like to secure p through z."

Suppose the conditions a–d are satisfied for each of x, y, and z. In this event there is, according to the view in question, nothing to choose as regards whether J should be supplied with x, y, or z. Any of these will do, for there is conclusive reason for supplying any of them. But clearly, when 4, 5, and 6 are all true, and conditions a–d are satisfied for x, y, and z respectively, then J should be supplied with x: for J needs x (e.g., the special tutor), whereas it would be (merely) convenient (for us) if J were to have y (the regular program), and z (perhaps a program of independent, unstructured study) is (merely) what J would like to have.

In general, when we can make either x, y, or z available to J, then, in circumstances in which 4, 5, and 6 are true and a–d are satisfied for x, y, and z, we believe we are justified in giving x to J, in contrast to giving him or her either y or z. And when we can make either x, y, or z, but not all, available to J, then, in those circumstances, we believe that providing J

with x has priority over providing him or her with y or with z. But in the view in question there is no rationale for either of these beliefs. This suggests that the justificatory force of "J needs x for p" is not entirely derivative from the satisfaction of such conditions as a–d.

Now, an objection to these points might be that they overlook part c of the conditions of a conclusive reason. For if providing J with x is a matter of our convenience *rather than* a matter of satisfying J's need, then it must be more costly than providing J with what he or she needs: the very fact that providing x serves (our) convenience rather than (J's) need insures that it is more costly, given the contrast between the ideas of serving convenience and serving needs and given that unfulfilled needs constitute, in part, what we regard as the costs of different courses of action relevant to J securing p. The effect of this objection is that there cannot be a case in which the satisfaction of a–d supports (conclusively), or is even compatible with, providing J with x as a matter of convenience rather than need. And, aside from the reference to the contrast between serving convenience and serving needs, this effect is achieved by logically connecting the idea of an action leaving needs unfulfilled to the idea of that action being costly.

This objection is interesting, but I do not think that it can be made in defense of the view that appeals to need have no independent justificatory force. In the first place, the objection assumes that such appeals have justificatory force, but it simply leaves open whether that "force" is or is not "independent," that is, whether or not it is derivative from satisfaction of conditions such as a–d. To argue that a course of action is costly in the sense that it leaves needs unfulfilled is to appeal to needs as factors that justify certain (other) courses of action—in the absence, at any rate, of overriding considerations; but it is not to argue that those factors are not independently justificatory. In the second place, even if it is true that a course of action that leaves needs unfulfilled is costly, it does not follow that this course of action is *more* costly than other available courses of action relevant to J securing p.

But perhaps the same objection could be developed by switching attention to part d of the conditions of a conclusive reason. For we may suppose that one of the side effects of the case in which J is provided with x (to secure p) as a matter of (our) convenience is that J's need is left unfulfilled. It might be argued that the desirability of p cannot compensate for this, for unfulfilled needs are among what we view as the prohibitive costs of different courses of action. But framing it in this way poses the same difficulties for the objection in question: the objection in this form still assumes that needs have justificatory force but does not itself show that this force is entirely derivative from conditions a–d; and even if unfulfilled needs are among the prohibitive costs of a course of action, it does not follow that the costs of that course of action are prohibitive relative to other courses of action relevant to J securing p.

What is at issue is whether it follows from structural thesis T—"J needs x" is to be construed as "J needs x for p"—that the justificatory force of appeals to need is derivative from the desirability of the ends involved (perhaps only implicitly) in those appeals, plus related considerations, that is, in our more specific terms, from the satisfaction of conditions a–d. I suggest above that one way of testing this is to imagine a case in which conditions a–d are satisfied but also, in respect of J securing p, there *is* some question of whether providing J with x is a matter of convenience or a matter of meeting J's need. It would be a stipulation with no argument to say at this point that there can be no such question *because* the satisfaction of conditions a–d entails that providing J with x is to serve his or her needs. It does not, on the face of it, seem logically impossible that J, x, and p could be so related that the conditions a–d are satisfied but that there are yet different (reasonable) opinions as to whether providing J with x to secure p is a matter of serving our convenience or a matter of meeting J's need.

Even if conditions a–d are not sufficient for appeals to need, it might be supposed that whatever further conditions must be added to devise a set of sufficient conditions, a–d will be part of that set. That is, it might be supposed that appeals to need, when they give conclusive reasons for courses of action, entail the satisfaction of conditions a–d.

But there is doubt whether even this can be supposed about all appeals to need. In some cases, when J needs x for p (in contrast to it being a matter of convenience for J to have x or a matter of J's liking to have x), we seem to deal with the question of the costs of providing J with x by, as far as possible, setting it aside. Persons' needs sometimes have an urgency about them that makes it irrelevant whether, in accordance with part c of the conditions of a conclusive reason, the provision of x is more costly, as a way of securing p, than, say, the provision of y or z.[10] One thinks of cases involving persons in devastated regions who have immediate and urgent needs for shelter, food, and medical care. Or of cases in which a person comes into peril through accident or attack, such that he or she is in immediate and urgent need of, say, relief from pain or, again, some sort of medical treatment. In a less extreme way, this need may be for relief from discomfort or even from mere embarrassment. The point is that when needs are immediate and urgent, the niceties of cost involved in making the appropriate response to them seem beside the point.

It may be worth suggesting, in connection with this point, a possible link between the concept of need and the concept of justice. More precisely, there may be a similarity between the way in which the concept of justice operates so as to exclude considerations of utility and the way in which the concept of need, in some cases, operates to set aside considerations of cost. Meeting needs appears to require, in some instances, that we spare no expense.

How far this can be generalized is, of course, unclear.[11] There are probably many cases in which the question of whether needs are to be met involves careful estimates of the costs involved in meeting them, and in which we do not deny that needs exist when we decide not to meet them. There may even be cases in which moral grounds can be offered for providing what serves convenience rather than need. Nevertheless, the existence of cases in which needs have the character of making questions of cost seem irrelevant puts the general claim that appeals to need entail just the set of conditions a–d—in particular, part c of that set—in jeopardy.

It is tempting to speculate on the explanation of those cases in which appeals to need set aside considerations of cost. Perhaps we have certain concepts, or certain uses of a concept, that we can enlist to defend ourselves, as it were, against manipulation and by means of which we can express a conception of ourselves as of greater value than objects. If this is so, then it is meaningful to suppose that some of these concepts may give us a way of expressing the fact that a part of our humanity, that is, our value, is wrapped up in our access to certain ends. And it may be that we are related to those ends in such a way that when access to them is blocked, questions of the costs of restoring access are simply not relevant. My thought is that the concept of need, in some form, may be among those concepts that can serve us in this general way. If so, then the view of needs I have been concerned with here, according to which "the only interesting questions arise in connection with ends,"[12] obscures important questions about how we are related to those ends.

I will not attempt to develop this bit of speculation here. My concern at the moment has been for the question of whether appeals to need can have independent justificatory force. It is true that an appeal to the fact that J is in need of x to secure p can draw justificatory force from the desirability of p and related considerations as these are specified in conditions a–d. I have argued that beyond this there is a further question relevant to the problem of justificatory force arising from the fact that J is related to p such that J is in *need* of x. I see no reason yet why this question could not be susceptible to general treatment in terms of principles that serve to connect the fact that persons have certain needs to certain courses of action. It does not seem impossible that certain principles of this kind could occupy a place in a moral or political doctrine and that in such a doctrine they might have the effect of establishing certain priorities for political practice. What the content of those principles would be and how they could be argued for are questions I have not tried to answer here. I have argued, however, that there is more to the justificatory force that appeals to need can have than derives from estimates of the value of ends.

AWARENESS OF OTHERS' NEEDS

The discussion above modifies somewhat what is perhaps the received analytic view of needs, though it does not actually challenge the main lines of that received account. But I say at the beginning that in some cases others' needs seem like simple facts that are already normative or valuational. The notion that these appeals to serious and basic needs—very often motivationally disturbing—can always (logically) be taken apart into "fact" and "value" seems strained. In what follows I want to explore the "phenomenology" of needs, that is, what it is to experience, or be aware of, others' needs, and attempt to identify the conception of persons behind it, as promised at the beginning of this discussion.

It is part of appreciating that J is in *need* that one understands not only that something may be done respecting J but also, in more or less detail, what may be done respecting J. This is so because a person is never simply in need; rather, when a person is in need, he or she is in need of or has need for something. J may be in need of medical treatment, or money to pay debts, or spiritual or sexual fulfillment; but J is never just in need. Persons' needs have contents, as it were, and the contents they have specify in some if not complete detail the nature of a positive response to them. It follows that when nothing by way of response is indicated by such facts about a person as one is aware of, then one is not aware of that person's needs. Typically a response to a person's need consists in supplying or making up something he or she lacks, something that will allow him or her to meet a standard of personal or social well-being. But there is no such action as satisfying a need merely, though there are many actions that are instances of satisfying particular needs. I shall speak, then, of needs being *informative* regarding what may be done.

Of course, persons sometimes have needs we do not understand very well; sometimes these are psychological; or perhaps cultural, medical, or economic; or of some other general kind. And when we do not understand others' needs very well, we do not know in sufficient detail what may be done respecting them. (Interestingly, the latter epistemological shortfall may not diminish the power of an appreciation of the other's needs to move us, that is, disturb us.) I may encounter someone whose need is such that, so far as I can tell, it would be appropriate to provide him or her with medical or psychoanalytic treatment; but I may not myself know how to go beyond this point with him or her. But cases of this familiar sort are compatible with what I have said: what one understands about persons in such cases is that they have needs that one can identify only as instances of a general type; in such cases one's conception of what may be done may be shallow and unhelpful. But it remains that the needs persons have are informative respecting what may be done, albeit not always sufficiently so, given differences in our knowledge and experience. And their being informative is part of what makes it possible for others' needs to be *moving* in the sense I have in mind.

To say that for a need to be moving involves it being informative respecting what may be done is not to say merely that this involves it being *persuasive* to someone in some circumstances to do a certain thing. If there are no circumstances in which we could envisage someone being convinced by f to do a thing of a certain type, it follows that f cannot be described as moving or motivating.[13] But f can be persuasive to someone to do a certain thing without itself being informative as to what may be done. It may be that persons can be trained in such a way as to be persuaded by f to do a certain thing. Perhaps they may even be trained to find it "natural" not only to respond in a special way to persons possessing certain characteristics but also to believe themselves justified in doing so, that is, to believe that they have reason to do so. But to suggest these psychological points about training is not to say that the facts that persons may be trained to be persuaded by are informative respecting what may be done. When f is moving (disturbing, motivating) in the sense I am elaborating, it must indeed be what can persuade someone in some circumstances to do a certain thing, and perhaps we must admit too that such a response to persuasion can be brought about by training. This is to say (perhaps trivially) that being a persuader is a necessary condition of f being moving. But it is not the same condition of it being moving as that it be informative as to what may be done.

When f is moving or motivating in the sense I am exploring, it has the further property (as acknowledged above) of being "overridable" in a familiar way. When f is this way, it is something that is subject to being set aside in light of one's understanding of the consequences of the action that it moves one to perform. This is to say that it may be ultimately rejected, defeated, or set aside and that the action it moves one toward may not be performed if the consequences of performing the action are in one way or other unacceptable or intolerable. Their being open to defeats of this sort is a perfectly general point about the factors that move us to action, even those of the sort we identify in the language of needs. It does not follow, of course, that we *will* set aside what moves us when we understand that the consequences are unacceptable or intolerable. In some cases what moves us is, so to speak, insistent.

Finally, the general fact that what moves us to action may be overridable makes it possible for another conditional property to come into the picture. This is the sense we have that in the absence of overriding considerations, f's moving or disturbing quality carries with it a characteristic pressure to act in the way indicated. This is a way of expressing the familiar notion that, for example, when S recognizes that J is in need of medical care, S experiences the pressure (in the absence of overriding considerations) to provide or make available such care or to take steps to see to it that such care is provided by those able to do so. There is something morally puzzling, and perhaps logically odd, in the imagined case in which one is aware of another's need for relief from intense pain, one is able (directly or indirectly) to provide relief in the circumstances, and one is unaware of any considerations that override the other's need, yet one feels no pressure to respond.

A CONCEPTION OF PERSONS

Many theorists have claimed that persons are "by nature" social beings. I suspect that many of these theorists would be comfortable with the view that persons are characterized by features, attributes, and properties (for short, "facts") that have a way of putting pressure on those who deal with them in ordinary life. And these facts that generate such pressure do so prior to, or independently of, conscious applications of rules or principles. In this view it is a logical point that one does not stop to imagine in what circumstances a person's need for relief from intense pain puts pressure on one to respond in the obvious way. Put another way, one "finds" persons characterized by a network of facts, some of which are accompanied by an urgency that requires action, more precisely, some form of *responding to* them.[14] It may be that because of some overriding consideration one will end up not responding to a person having a certain need on a particular occasion. But that the pressure may be set aside does not affect the point that a person of whom such a fact is true thereby presents one who is aware of it with the burden of response.

It is important to recognize that what is at stake here is a certain view of what it is to be a person. It seems that the pressure-generating facts about persons carry with them their own metaphysics of personhood. According to this view, persons are "bundles" of (among other things) pressure-generating facts; and to be a person is thus to be at once a source of direction and aims for others and calls for responses from them as well. This is indeed to say that persons are social beings, for in this view persons are tied to others of their kind in their capacity to elicit responses from others as well as in their capacity to respond to others. In sum, a person is a being to whom, per se, one may be pressured to respond, rather than a being to whom, per se, one may be indifferent; and this relationship among persons is "natural," or prior to the workings of social institutions, rather than "artificial," or posterior to social institutions.

This conception of persons as clusters of normatively loaded facts is not strange or unfamiliar. It has been, I think, a part of the fabric of informal liberal thought, and in particular it has been useful as a basis for social criticism and social commentary directed to the quality of life in societies that prize individual liberty. It may be some support for this conception of persons to note that the contrasting view of persons—as bundles of facts, none of which puts pressure on others to respond—does not allow us to make sense of an important tradition of social criticism and appeals for reform. The contrasting view disallows the point of classical liberal appeals to conscience and humanity. It makes both the historical appeals for toleration and noninterference and the appeals for members of society to function in at least a minimal way as their "brother's keeper" at best a vague kind of sentimentalism and at worst simply capricious. The contrasting view goes against a tradition of social concern that has had, in my opinion, a beneficial effect on the development of social and political institutions and practices.

Consider this question: Are there facts about persons that *must* be pressure generating in our ordinary lives with others? The contrasting view I mention rests ultimately on a view of facts that entails a negative answer to this question. This is the view of facts whereby there is no fact about a person that cannot be pressure generating and no fact about a person that must be pressure generating. And this is so, in this view, because facts are what may be *taken* (or not taken) to be pressure generating, and there is nothing "in the facts themselves" that, as it were, necessitates certain of them being taken to be pressure generating.

Against this contrasting view (according to which facts are "neutral" and not "value laden"), I am inclined to think that it is a necessary truth that some facts about persons are of the pressure-generating sort. I am inclined to think this because to think otherwise ultimately risks losing the conceptual underpinnings of ordinary social thought and criticism, in particular an important social notion of *responding to* a person, and, accordingly, the conception of person involved in the claim that persons are social beings. But, of course, the kind of "necessity" involved in such a claim and the nature of the conceptual losses we risk in not granting it require explanation.

I attempt to explain them by asking first what it is for one to *respond to* a person *in virtue of* some fact about him or her of which one is aware.

When I respond to a person I do not merely react to him or her. It is true that I may both respond to and react to a person in light of some fact about him or her of which I am aware. It is not the awareness itself that distinguishes them. But in the former case the fact about the person of which I am aware must give direction to what I do, while this need not be so in the latter case. A fact being informative respecting what may be done is not a condition of me (merely) reacting to a person in light of that fact. However, though responding to a person in light of a fact about him or her is something different from reacting to a person in light of a fact about him or her, it is not yet responding to a person "in virtue of" a fact about him or her. This further idea, that is, the social concept of responding to a person in virtue of some fact about him or her, rests on the possibility of a fact being not only informative respecting what may be done but also generative of pressure respecting what may be done. Put another way, when I respond to *J* in virtue of some fact about him or her of which I am aware, the fact of which I am aware must give direction to what I do and enable me to answer the question, "Why did you respond to *J* rather than do something else?"

The contrasting position is that a citation of a fact about *J*—even a citation of *J*'s need—would not itself stop the why question from occurring here. That is, if on some occasion there exists pressure to respond to *J*, who is in need of *x*, its "source" will be something other than *J*'s need. An answer to the why question will require (logically) reference beyond *J*'s need to this source (perhaps, e.g., a rule or principle sanctioning responding to *J* when he or she is in need generally or when he or she is in need of *x* but not *y*) to account for one being pressured to respond to *J* rather than do something else. In this contrasting view, it is never a full answer to the question, "Why did you respond to *J*?" to say, "Because *J* was in need of *x*."

It does not seem to me that the contrasting account is logically absurd. That is, it does not seem inconceivable that it could be true or that it could come to be true. If this is so, it is not possible to say that the claim that there are some facts about persons (e.g., their basic needs) that generate pressure for responses is logically necessary. But it does not follow from granting this that there is no sense in which this claim is a necessary truth.

What is it that is supposed to be at least logically possible in the contrasting account? It is not merely that there are occasions on which a person is under no pressure to respond to another when he or she is aware of the other's need. And it is not that there is no such thing as pressure to respond to a person. If this is so, it does not seem possible to say that persons being characterized by pressure-generating facts is a condition of understanding persons as moral agents. If the claim is necessary, it must be so in some other way.

I want to say that the claim that persons are characterized by pressure-generating facts is necessary in the sense that it states a condition of understanding our practical thought about persons as social beings, that is, as beings that live in society as we know it, containing, among much else, technology, institutions, and practices that develop and change—and alternately frustrate, satisfy, or fulfill human needs, rights, and interests.[15]

The contrasting view does not account for the dimension of our ordinary moral and social thought which consists of assessment of how adequately our technology, institutions, and practices serve us as vehicles of our "respondings to" each other "in virtue of" our needs, interests, and rights. It is only by granting that persons are "by nature" sources of pressure for others that one can make sense of our ways of evaluating and criticizing technology and institutions as social instruments we have devised to serve each other. According to the contrasting view, a person is no source of pressures for others to respond, for a person is not characterized by pressure-generating facts. In such a view of persons it is possible that persons could have needs, and recognize needs that others have, but never feel the pressure to respond to their needs. And this remains possible even if something counts for such persons as, say, sources of *obligations,* for there is no guarantee that the obligations put down by this source will include obligations to respond to others' needs. If such persons were by chance obliged to respond to the needs of, say, a hurt child, their being so arises not from the child's needs but from some other source. Similarly, if such persons were to engage in assessing the workings of social institutions, any obligations to persons that they acknowledged (it is logically possible that there could be none) as involved as standards in their evaluation of these institutions would arise not from the persons "served" by the institutions but from some other source.

Now, this is a conception of persons as lacking (logically) in what Mill calls the "powerful natural sentiment of sympathy" and according to which there are no facts about persons of the kind I believe critics have in mind when they speak of persons "qua persons" as having certain needs and interests and possessing certain rights. As such, it seems to me quite foreign to our ordinary moral and social thought. In short, I think we are too far committed to thinking of institutions and technology as vehicles of our respondings to each other in virtue of our needs, interests, and rights to believe that the contrasting account applies to persons as social beings. It may be that we do not need the conception of persons as characterized by pressure-generating facts to secure the idea of obligation, but it does not follow that without it we can secure an idea under which we can recognize ourselves as the social beings we are.

Mill writes in *Utilitarianism* that "few but those whose mind is a moral blank, could bear to lay out their course of life on the plan of paying no regard to others except so far as their own private interest compels."[16] Notice that in the contrasting account a person is, if not a being "whose mind is a moral blank," then at any rate a being whose mind is blank respecting what we ordinarily think it is for a person to be a social being, for the being Mill imagines must have some "plan" to have reason to pay regard to others *at all*. (And notice further that it is at least doubtful whether such a being could consistently adopt even the special plan that Mill mentions, for the notion of a "compelling private interest" seems to be sufficiently close to the notion of a pressure-generating fact about a person, in this case a fact that pushes a person to respond to him- or herself by paying regard to others, to be inconsistent, strictly, with the contrasting view.)

In sum, we design social and political institutions, or conceive of them as designable, for ourselves as social beings, and we criticize them when they do not serve us as such; and it is necessary, as a condition of understanding the designing, criticizing, and sometimes redesigning we undertake in this connection, to construe the "social being" at stake as a being characterized by pressure-generating facts. To think of persons as not so characterized would be to make equally opaque our appeals for reform in the name of persons' needs, rights, or interests and the important efforts at fulfilling and satisfying them made by persons through the social and political institutions they devise.

It must be added, of course, that not all facts about persons can be pressure generating in the manner I have been concerned with; for, if they were, it would be logically impossible to *respond to* a person in virtue of a fact about him or her at all. The notion of responding to a person would have no application in circumstances in which all facts about him or her were pressure generating. There is no such action as undifferentiated responding to a person, just as there is no such fact about a person as that he or she is merely in need. But if the concept of person were such that the infinite number of facts about a person were all of the pressure-generating sort, and if there is no such action as undifferentiated responding to a person, then one could not respond to a person at all, for though one may sometimes be pressured to respond to a person in several ways at once, one cannot be pressured to respond to a person in an infinite number of ways at once. And it does not help to think that one might respond serially to a person. For if a person were such that all facts about him or her were generative of pressure for others, then it would be impossible to begin to respond to him or her in a particular way. For it is a condition of responding to a person in virtue of a fact about him or her that one understand a certain fact about him or her as informative respecting what one's particular response is to be; but if an infinite number of facts about a person is informative in this way, one cannot begin to respond, for an infinite number of such facts is not informative as regards what in particular is to be done. There is logically no place to begin to respond to such a person.

The claims I have made are, I suppose, "formal" in character. They do not themselves tell us which facts about persons are pressure generating (and which are not); nor do they tell us how we come to apply a specific notion of a pressure-generating fact, for example, being in need of something, to a person. I have assumed that our notions of serious and important needs treat those needs as pressure-generating facts; it seems plain that our concepts of rights do as well; and there are surely other types of concepts (e.g., concepts of interests) that also operate in this way. I have not provided a list of these types of concepts, nor have I attempted to draw distinctions within any one type, for example, distinctions among kinds or classes of needs. My aim has been to argue the prior point that there must be facts about persons that operate in our ordinary moral and social thought as generative of pressure. In the moral-emotional nature we have as human beings,[17] our ordinary moral and social thinking finds that our human colleagues are marked by facts that call for responses.

NORMATIVE IMPLICATIONS

If human needs are the pushy normative facts I have made them out to be, then we may ask if there are consequences of such a view for how individuals—individuals in a world filled with such facts—are supposed to conduct their lives. Let me explore this question in the sections that follow.

I begin with some simple, and I hope uncontroversial, remarks about the character of the human condition in our time.[18] If we stand back from our own lives in our local and national communities and make the effort to understand the situation for humankind at a more general level, then we confront certain crude facts about the human condition that immediately offend our sense of how life in the modern world ought to be. These troubling facts have at their base unmet human needs.

I will point to just three of these troubling facts. First, there are millions upon millions of people in today's world who suffer destitution in some or many forms. *Destitution,* for my purposes here, need be no technical term. It simply refers to extreme deprivation relative to basic human needs. I have in mind people whose lives are stifled through malnutrition, homelessness, or total lack of education. Destitution may be the result of natural or social factors, including political oppression or war. But I do not wish to address the problem of causation here. It is enough to note that more than a full billion in a total population of roughly six billion human beings in the world community face life-threatening destitution in some or many forms at this moment. Second, the levels of life affecting people's opportunities for self-realization are grossly disparate in today's world. The world community contains millions of people in destitution, millions in affluence, and millions at the many points between. No human life is free of struggle. But, whatever its woes, the life of the reasonably well-off "competent individual" in a free, affluent society, with its material base, its opportunities for self-realization, and perhaps its measure of luxury, is hardly a struggle with extreme deprivation relative to basic needs. The third troubling fact is that efforts to ameliorate the destitution and gross disparity in levels of life in the world community through charitable institutions and nation-state programs of "foreign aid" are meager and inadequate. Even in the best of years, such aid, as a percentage of the wealth of the contributing nations, is miniscule; and too often the aid that is given misses its target or is lost to corruption or political interests. The problem of survival faced by millions of destitute people in the world, when it is not linked to national self-interest, is consigned to the secondary moral category of national or individual charity, or it is simply neglected.

One might respond to this recitation of familiar facts in a defiant way or perhaps with indignation. One might ask, So what? I think, however, that one cannot sustain the belligerence or indignation for very long. There may in fact be different moral emotions, attitudes, and underlying beliefs, rationalizations, and defensive maneuvers at work in us as we attempt to confront and take in such painful moral data. The facts in question are offensive to one's moral sense of what ought to be, whether or not one grants, as some argue, that we are all implicated in them.[19] Ignorance of these facts would be a blessing of sorts. Such facts are cruel, and there is no sophistication about them.

At a minimum one may experience sorrow in reaction to the facts of extreme deprivation. These facts are, after all, matters of suffering, unmet basic need, and stifled lives, and (I assume) they call up joy in no one. But sorrow is probably not the only element in our moral-psychological response to the bleak underside of the human condition in our time. The facts in question—the destitution, the gross disparity in levels of life, the meager response—may occasion guilt in many of us, even as we rush to say that we personally are not responsible for them. The facts in question make one sharply self-conscious about one's level of life. When I contemplate them, I become suspicious of the legitimacy of my efforts to pursue *my* interests and of my efforts to develop *my* talents. One is reminded of Rousseau's impatient pronouncement, "It is plainly contrary to the law of nature, however defined, that children should command old men, fools

wise men, and that the privileged few should gorge themselves with su-
perfluities, while the starving multitude are in want of the bare necessities of life."[20]

Perhaps once one is aware of the troubling facts of the human condition in today's world, one then faces what might be called "the problem
of living with oneself." If one reviews one's life and finds in it, relative to
the flaws in the human condition, little or no attention given to the plight
of others or, perhaps worse, a certain indifference to the human pain involved, then one might very well suffer the feeling of *having cheated.* One
feels that one has somehow gotten away with something that one is not
entitled to. Perhaps one very quickly moves from this feeling to feelings
of anger or indignation at finding oneself "stuck" in a human condition
that is as cosmically unfair as ours is. But it is not part of my aim here to
fuss about the correct label for one's feelings when one's review of one's
life reveals indifference to others. It is enough that one's feelings are
troubled and disturbing ones. The recognition of one's indifference to others may even be as painful (albeit in a self-indulgent sort of way) as one's
awareness of the original destitution, gross disparity in levels of life, and
meager efforts to help which mark the human condition in our time.

SHARED-FATE INDIVIDUALISM

If the human condition is marked by the troubling facts I point to, and
our moral-psychological response is along the lines I just indicated, then,
surely, we have interest in how we are to respond to the situation. We
need, in effect, a conception of individual responsibility that provides
guidance for thought and conduct relative to the pressure-generating facts
of unmet basic need all around us. I call the conception of individual responsibility that I think the situation calls for "shared-fate individualism."
This conception, I believe, is not a strange "new ethics" but is instead a
familiar part of the form of moral life we already share. This form of moral
life we share, with its general interpretation of (all) persons as equal members of the moral community, is what makes our attention to the destitution and gross inequality in the human condition quickly become unbear-
able. For these facts of the human condition—again, largely facts of unmet
need—when we stand back and view them from the standpoint of our
ordinary morality, are not only painful to contemplate; they are also contingent in logical character—which is to say that the human condition as
we know it *can* be different. Indeed, it might even be, I believe, through
human effort, "changed for the better"—which is to say that it might be
brought more nearly in line with our conception of what the situation in

the moral community ought to be. When we recognize the cruelties of the human condition for the contingent facts they are, and also take the prospect of amelioration seriously, then shared-fate individualism is seen to be a moral orientation to the human condition that in its own way affirms the importance of the life of the individual. For it says, in effect, that each and every individual life is important: so important, in fact, that in the circumstances of today's world "putting oneself first," as a matter of moral policy for individuals, would be to deny the importance of many—perhaps a great many—individual lives.

The central idea in shared-fate individualism is that morality requires of competent individuals in circumstances such as those that characterize today's world that they place the value of *service to others* over the value of *self-realization* in deliberations on relevant serious life decisions. An example of a "serious life decision" is career choice. As a first reaction, of course, some will find this idea to be objectionably overwhelming in its implications. My proposal will seem "morally strenuous" in a way that is simply extreme. Because the cruelties in the human condition as we know it cannot in fact be ameliorated easily or soon, shared-fate individualism seems to project a picture in which we are called on to make a *great* sacrifice. The notion that the burden of making that great sacrifice falls on *us* may seem entirely arbitrary—the "luck of the draw" in some silly cosmic lottery. One may indeed be inclined to dismiss shared-fate individualism as impossibly extreme, despite the fact that the human condition as we know it *is* both cruel and ameliorable.

But even if one finds oneself impatient with the central idea in shared-fate individualism, it does not follow, so far as I can see, that one may after all legitimately "put oneself first" in the relevant serious life decisions. If the human condition is thought of as something that *must* be constituted by destitution and gross disparity in levels of life, then perhaps "putting oneself first" might make sense as a policy reflecting resignation. The intelligibility of this me-first policy would in that case rest on the notion that "there is nothing we can do" about the troubling facts. But *our* human condition (so I assume) is not somehow necessarily constituted by destitution. Given our human condition, that is, the one that is flawed but ameliorable through human effort, I do not see that the idea of putting oneself first can gain a foothold in a conception of individual responsibility that draws directly on the form of moral life we share.

Another form of impatience with the central idea in shared-fate individualism might lead one to sponsor what could be called "liberal individualism." This is the recommendation that in serious life decisions one may indeed "put oneself first" so long as one then implements one's decisions in such a way that one's courses of action are at least of some service to others. This recommendation might be thought of as following on a reaction to shared-fate individualism not as "impossibly extreme" but, rather, as "unreasonably extreme." It finds shared-fate individualism to be not batty but merely "excessive" in its call for sacrifice. It attempts to accommodate the human condition as shared-fate individualism views it but also to make room, so to speak, for the moral legitimacy of the self-realizationist aspirations of competent individuals who happen to be in fortunate circumstances.

My worry about liberal individualism is that it represents not so much "what morality requires," given the human condition in today's world, as a *compromise* with "what morality requires." The best practical antidote for the thought that the ordering of values involved in shared-fate individualism (namely, service before self-realization) yields demands that are excessive continues to be further attention to the cruel contingent facts of the human condition. It is not puzzling to suppose that the form of moral life we have may, in difficult circumstances, make demands on persons that would be excessive in circumstances that are not difficult. Indeed, what *would* be puzzling is our having a form of moral life that does *not* shift and adjust its requirements (and permissions) according to differences in the circumstances of those who share it. Once one genuinely attends to the cruel facts about the human condition in our time, the liberal-individualist response cannot but seem (I believe) to be a moral shortfall. I do not myself see the implausibility in the general idea that there may be certain situations in which *heavy sacrifice* on the part of relevantly able individuals is not *heroic* but simply *required*. It is this general idea that shared-fate individualism finds applicable to the human condition in our time. It may be unfortunate that the circumstances in the human community today are such that this general idea is applicable. But it is no aid to clarity about individual responsibility to ignore those circumstances, or be indifferent to them, or pretend that they are other than what they are. Shared-fate individualism avoids all these obstacles to clarity.

ART AND PUBLIC ART

Suppose that shared-fate individualism, or some conception relevantly like it in its capacity to see the troubling facts about the human condition in our time for what they are, is correct as a conception of responsibility for individuals. What, if anything, follows for those who undertake "ground projects,"[21] whose point may be aesthetic fulfillment, progress in esoteric scholarship in a discipline, or exploration of the hidden promises of a new technology? If we accept shared-fate individualism, what, in general, of projects that are of absorbing intrinsic interest but do not make an immediate or even apparent response to the facts of unmet need discussed above? I will approach this issue by discussing briefly art and artists—with, as it were, special reference to recent discussion of what is called "public art."

Views that attempt to ascribe a univocal self-regarding point or purpose to art and to artists are of course familiar. In a review of an exhibit of the work of de Kooning in New York in 1984, Dale Harris writes in the London *Guardian* that the "abstraction" involved in abstract expressionism "was a declaration of independence, an assertion of the artist's freedom from social responsibility, an expression of his need to follow an inner calling, no matter how private and esoteric."[22] The public art I have in mind pushes away from the professional egoism involved in this sort of "inner calling" conception of art. In a 1983 piece about "public art" in *The New Yorker*, Calvin Tomkins writes,

> One thing Armajani, Irwin, Fleischner, Burton, and their colleagues seem to agree on is that working in the public sector means getting rid of several common myths about being an artist. To a large extent, it means getting rid of the artist's ego. . . . Self-expression, which Irwin defines as the lowest form of artistic incentive, clearly has no place here.[23]

Not only does the public art I am interested in push away from the inner calling conception; it also carries with it a willingness not to be entrapped in self-reflexive effort within the "discipline" of art to "define its own essence"—as, indeed, was said to be the aim of modernist art by such critics as Clement Greenberg and Michael Fried. There is, in the art I have in mind, a willingness on the part of the artist to set aside, or at least temper, the motive of getting on with the internal development of art itself in favor of reaching out to the public—perhaps even in favor of making a social, political, or moral point or, indeed (shades of Tolstoy), in favor of making a point about the religious sensibility of the day.[24] Mary Miss has written that in public art "engagement of the public is part of the work's motivation."[25] I am struck, in this connection, by the words of artist Athena Tacha in a statement from a 1980 interview:

> I feel that, given the present state of the world, it would be morally untenable to pursue an art career unless one makes art available to everybody (not only the financially or educationally privileged). One way of achieving this aim is to bring art into the urban environment and to endow it with a social function. . . . Another way is to make art approachable by avoiding deliberate offensiveness and by allowing the work to be attractive. I am not interested in shocking the middle class . . . and I am not afraid of beauty.

Rendering art functional or beautiful does not need to entail an artistic compromise—it merely makes art less of an act of self-indulgence . . . I believe
this is a crucial difference in attitude between artists who matured in the
early sixties, such as the minimal and earth sculptors, and my generation.
Only this new attitude can engender truly public art.[26]

I will, then, for the purposes of this discussion, characterize what interests me in this way. It is art that is not dominated by the demands of
an "inner calling," that is, egoism and self-expression; it is also not dominated by the demands of an internalist disciplinary project of working out
the essence of art. Even if it is not entirely free of these demands, it nevertheless proposes—deliberately—to "engage people" and even in some
cases to make a social, moral, or political point. What this "social point"
is, of course, is hardly uniform in the artworks themselves or in the writings and utterances of those involved in or concerned about art.

Therein, in a sense, lies the problem I want to address here. What is the
appropriate social, political, or moral point for art in our day? There are
less-than-serious treatments of this question, of course. Not long ago I was
walking the halls of my college in the area of the art studios, and I over-
heard one new and youngish faculty studio artist discussing the nature
of art in his time with a colleague. He said—seriously, I believe, though I
was only eavesdropping—that the point of art is to *shock*: "You have to
shock 'em out of their minds [he said *skulls,* actually], that's when you
know that what you've got is really art." I do not know what I think of
such a view. I *hope* the moral point of art does not reduce to shocking
people for the sake of shocking them. If it does, then strange things, such
as terrorism without purpose and Disneyland horror halls, become possible artworks. There are serious answers to the question, of course, and
these are usually more interesting, if in some cases more difficult to make
out. Tomkins reports Robert Irwin as saying that the artist's job "is to
maintain the human scale, to assert individual values in the midst of high-
tech decision-making."[27] Patricia C. Phillips's (vaguely environmentalist)
idea is that "public art is in the unique position to reconstitute the idea
of the common."[28] More concretely, some artworks may directly address
particular social issues, for example, the issues of battered women or the
homeless. Other artworks may seek to remind us of past horrors. (I have
in mind here Athena Tacha's series of "Massacre Memorials," including
a "Jewish Holocaust" memorial, an "India/Pakistan" memorial, and an
"Hiroshima/Nagasaki" memorial.[29]) It may be the point of still other artworks to educate in a certain way or to affirm cultural identity. (Here I
think of Judith Baca's muralist art in Los Angeles—art that has been characterized by one writer as "socially concerned, artistically captivating, and
collectively produced."[30]) In the notes that follow, I will make my own

suggestion about an appropriate moral point for art and thus offer an interpretation about what it is, or might be, for art to "engage the people." My suggestion flows from my thoughts above about what is required of responsible individuals in our time, as I will explain next.

SELF-REALIZATION

It might seem tempting to say that the obvious answer to the normative question about what follows for art and artists from my earlier discussion regarding shared-fate individualism is a short and brutal one. It says that artists—or anyhow the "competent individuals" among them—should give up or set aside their work as artists and become participants in a worldwide crash effort to move food to the starving, to shelter the homeless, and to educate those without the rudiments of language, concepts, and numbers. Frankly, I worry that there might be more to this short and brutal answer than I wish to admit. Still, even if the short and brutal answer has its point, I think it is not a complete answer.

There are, in fact, many ways to "serve" others. I seriously doubt that the artist must give up art in order to serve any more than the elementary school teacher must leave teaching to serve or the lawyer must abandon his or her skills to serve. Nor do I assume that if the artist is to serve, he or she must produce only works whose sole function is to moralize at us in a single way—by, for example, representing or portraying for us, narrowly and repeatedly, the dreary facts of destitution and gross inequality. My view cannot object to works that function in that way, of course. But I think, again, that any such response to the general question before us is too limited.

What is the *point* of "service to others," according to the conception of individual responsibility I have called "shared-fate individualism"? In the vocabulary I have found it helpful to use, the point of service is *to position others to self-realize*. Let me, in what follows, explore this notion a little.[31] The aim of the exploration is to remind us of some of what it is to be positioned to self-realize. (I say "remind us" of this because the idea, or the phenomenon itself, is hardly new.) Beyond that, the aim is to work out how, if at all, art does, or could, bear on positioning people to self-realize.

It is a familiar view—a view with powerful moral credentials—that persons (who are positioned to do so) owe it to themselves to cultivate their native endowments as these exist in the form of talents, skills, capacities, and abilities. Even Marx, who found much wrong with capitalist society, held that one of the cruelest features of such a society is that it channels its members into fixed, repetitive modes of activity and in that way blocks the realization of the many talents and capacities that are to be found in any individual human being. Marx's familiar appeal was as follows: let my society encourage me to "do one thing today and another tomorrow, to hunt in the morning, fish in the afternoon, rear cattle in the evening, criticize after dinner, just as I have a mind, without ever becoming hunter, fisherman, shepherd or critic."[32]

Despite the familiarity of the idea of self-realization, and its generally acknowledged moral standing, it seems plain that how far one succeeds at the task of developing one's potential will depend on many contingent factors (some of them more or less beyond one's control), such as what one's native endowments are in fact, what one has available to one in the way of resources for their development (e.g., energy, health, imagination, time, teachers), and what one's opportunities are for actually carrying out the different (and often difficult) tasks involved in self-realizing. One person's self-realizationist results may not be as technically proficient or artistically significant as another person's, for there may be, after all, limited natural gifts or resource and opportunity failures; but these results may still *be*, from the moral perspective, self-realizationist results and thus "count" as the fruits of the self-realizationist project available, perhaps relatively uniquely, to a certain human being and thus prized by our moral form of life.

Now, when we think of "native endowments" or "potential" as something to be "realized" or "developed," we obviously do not have in mind just the individual human being's genetic heritage or physiological equipment. What *I* consider to be my native endowments *now* are features of mine that have already been infused (to some extent) with training, education, opportunities seized (others lost), interests pursued (others forgotten), and so forth. Each of us may indeed have what Kant calls "fortunate natural gifts" (some talents and skills, say),[33] but each of these is itself rather a mix of "basic" capacities (e.g., intelligence, physical dexterity, mathematical insight) and what has been done *to* and *for* these capacities by oneself, by others (e.g., parents and teachers), and by certain institutions and practices (such as schools, of course, but also the economic system, class structure, art world, and "streets" of the society one lives in). In a word, the realization of our fortunate natural gifts is relative to the *ways of life* available to us. And such ways of life are structured by material circumstances, modern agriculture, recent technological innovation, ideologies about the state of natural resources, easy or difficult communications systems, efficient or inefficient bureaucracies, modes of transportation, the practices and institutions of our art world, and much else.

MEDIA

My earlier remarks about shared-fate individualism, with its emphasis on service to others as a task for competent individuals in today's world, thus presuppose emphasis on the moral priority of positioning people to self-realize. Those remarks, together with the notes just made about the nature of self-realization, lead me now to consider how art might "serve." What can be done through art to "position" people to self-realize?

When we speak of something being done "through art" to contribute toward people being positioned to self-realize, it is convenient to recall that artists work through media. We are all familiar with media. They are everywhere—in art, of course, but also in communication, politics, science, and even the humanities. Music is a medium—one that is mainly auditory—and it can be broken down into many submedia. Poetry and fiction are media (for present purposes)—the pieces in them "work" via being read (and poetry in some cases via being heard). If we think of primarily "visual" media, many forms come to mind: for example, painting, photography, film, theater. For my purposes here the term *medium* refers to many different things, and there can certainly be new media and variations on old media. But apart from whatever list of media we might generate, and whatever plurality of media we might be prepared to recognize, what *are* media in general?

Stanley Cavell responds to this question in ways I find helpful. In a book about the movies, Cavell writes,

> A medium is something through which or by means of which something specific gets done or said in particular ways. It provides, one might say, particular ways to get through to someone, to make sense; in art, they are forms, like forms of speech. To discover ways of making sense is always a matter of the relation of an artist to his art, each discovering the other.[34]

So, media are "ways of making sense." And, for Cavell, a medium imposes a certain "ontology" or structure on what gets produced by it or through it. What is produced *in* a certain medium is (in part) a product *of* the ontology, that is, the structural elements, of that medium. Media organize and structure data to some extent and thereby make certain opportunities for experience available; and thus, so I think, media can be means by which artists can contribute to the self-realizationist projects of other people.

Sometimes our view of what medium a work is in figures importantly in how we understand it. When Schoenberg offered his earliest twelve-tone works, they were considered controversial, and part of the controversy concerned whether such pieces were or were not works of *music*.

For some listeners, they seemed formless, chaotic, and weirdly dissonant, and this was in part because they could not be found "within" the category of music as these auditors understood it.[35] Now things are rather different, and for many serious people the medium of music easily countenances such works. Some argue that in the course of this coming to be so—that is, in the course of it coming to be that twelve-tone pieces are works of music—something about the essentials of the medium of music itself was learned. Similarly, some critics (e.g., Greenberg, Fried) find that certain modernist works—visual works that feature flatness of surface and lack representational items entirely—are best understood as efforts to reveal what is essential to the very idea of a painting itself. In fact, some understand modernism to *be*—at the most general level—that impulse to find the essence of art itself. (Accordingly, some understand "postmodernism" to *be*—at the most general level—the impulse to deny that "art itself" has any "essence" at all.) Here, with the modernist claim in mind, I am reminded of words from Paul Klee: "If my works sometimes give a primitive expression, then this primitiveness is the result of my practice of reducing things to a few essentials. It is economy alone, thus the ultimate professional knowledge. In other words the opposite of true primitiveness."[36]

RADICAL CONCEPTUALIZATION

I am moved by the capacity of artists to contribute to others through their media—sometimes media newly invented: a certain type of opportunity for experience that seems to me to be of crucial importance for what I have been calling self-realization. What I have in mind as the contribution of artists is (obviously) not on the material level of contributions of food or shelter. But it does not follow from that fact that what I have in mind is not necessary for self-realization. It may be that through the media in which they work artists can convey their vision, their feelings, their individuality, their social messages, or, as was so important for the modernist critics, their conceptions of what constituted what Greenberg calls the "irreducible working essence of art itself."[37] I have no wish to dispute these glosses on the point of art or to diminish their importance to, say, aesthetics or to theories about the internalist or externalist aims of art. I mean only to note that there is something more basic to be identified in what can be done through art—something that surfaces, I think, when one thinks hard about how one might, through art, speak to the matter of positioning people to self-realize.

To put words on the point, I venture the thought that what artists can offer to others through their media is *radical conceptualization*—in some cases *reconceptualization*—of the *elements of experience.* I mean by *radical* here not "dangerous" but, rather, "fundamental." I do not know how to argue for my point, other than to illustrate it. I will work through one illustration in some detail and then attempt to draw out the general message I have in mind.

The example I have in mind is drawn from the well-known work of the American music theorist and composer, John Cage. I refer to the subject in Cage's work that has been said to be its "most consistent feature,"[38] namely, his treatment of *silence.* Of course, this treatment of silence is really, or really involves, a *conception of sound*—a conception that is indeed "radical," I should think, relative to our ordinary, lay theoretical interpretation of the idea of sound.

What is our ordinary, lay theoretical conception of sound? Cage calls it an "ignorant" conception and then renders it in terms of a *contrast* plus a *recommendation* about what counts as a proper presentation of sound. The ignorant conception claims first that "sound has, as its clearly defined opposite, silence," and this contrast forms the basis for the recommendation that "since duration is the only characteristic of sound that is measurable in terms of silence, therefore any valid structure involving sounds and silences should be based, not as occidentally traditional, on frequency, but rightly on duration."[39] How is this conception "ignorant"? Well, it is shown to be so in empirical fashion, that is, by auditory observation, which means, in this case, by close listening in relevantly "pure" circumstances. Cage writes,

> When . . . one enters an anechoic chamber, as silent as technologically possible in 1951, to discover that one hears two sounds of one's own unintentional making (nerve's systematic operation, blood's circulation), the situation one is clearly in is not objective (sound-silence), but rather subjective (sounds only), those intended and those others (so-called silence) not intended.[40]

This is to say that the ordinary conception's contrast of "sound" and "silence" as "clearly defined opposites" is importantly bogus. The "real" situation (phenomenologically) is that *silence is a form of sound.* Sound and silence differ, of course. But they differ not as ultimate categories but, more simply and less ultimately, as merely the *intended* and the *not intended* differ.

So the new conception of sound redoes the lay theoretical conception in a novel way. Cage's treatment of sound is radical in the sense that it moves *into* the idea of sound an element that the ordinary conception leaves *outside* it altogether—outside it as, indeed, something "polar opposite" to sound per se, namely, silence. In the new conception, silence itself (conceptually) assumes a position (and hence legitimacy) inside the idea of sound. Silence takes a rightful place as a form of sound alongside other forms of sound. In Cage's own striking vocabulary, "sitting still anywhere . . . listening" is "the stereophonic, multiple-loud-speaker manner of operation in the everyday production of sounds and noises."[41]

I want to say that Cage's treatment of sound exemplifies a radical conceptualization of the elements of experience and that the contribution art makes to persons when it conveys this sort of conceptualization is a contribution to their powers of self-realization. There are two moves in Cage's treatment that reflect conceptual ingenuity and also suggest implications for art and for ordinary experience. They are (a) the incorporation of an element into a concept that (traditionally) we figured sat outside it (so that now silence *is* a form of sound) and (b) the transformation of our experience of silence from a passive sort of inactivity or "marking time" to an active sort of "doing" or "producing" (so that now sitting still anywhere listening is *producing* sounds and noises).

Let me ask now, what is the interest—for "art and ordinary experience"—of Cage's conceptual ingenuity, and why should we be concerned to understand it? And, indeed, what is *radical* about it? Theorists in many fields, after all, move conceptual bits and pieces in and out of notions all the time, and some even try out alterations in the logical character of certain of our experiences occasionally; but in some cases such efforts end up at best as games or at worst as misleading or obfuscating. But of course in the case of John Cage's work, the basic concept at stake is *sound,* and to be ingenious with *it* is, or might be, to challenge expectations and, finally, to alter thinking in areas (e.g., music) in which the concept is central.

Here are some notes about the power of Cage's ingenuity. The interesting point is that Cage's treatment of sound carries with it what might be called a "morality" of sound—an *ethics* of sorts—to fit the new, "unignorant" conception he sponsors. My thought is that this accompanying ethics is *part of* the radical conceptualization of the elements of experience in question, and my further thought is that the fact that the conceptualization extends into this ethical terrain is important to an understanding of how art can contribute to people being positioned to self-realize.

The first point in (what I call) Cage's ethics of sound is that the distinction between sound and silence in the new conception—now a distinction between sounds that are intended and sounds that are not intended—allows us to conceive of the possibility of not discriminating between the intended and the not intended. We may notice that the first effect of the nondiscrimination is to increase what *counts* as sound. One commentator writes that for Cage silence becomes "the door through which might enter the sounds of the environment."[42] The next effect is to get us to take seriously the project of treating sounds in ways that are independent of what anyone intends with or of them. So the second point in the ethics is that, if we take up this project (we do not *have* to, I assume), we must take seriously sounds per se, that is, sounds *void* of intentions, imposed structures, prior interpretations, expectations grounded in familiar cultural or aesthetic routines—in short, sounds *void of thought*. Cage's own words are helpful here:

> Sound does not view itself as thought, as ought, as needing another sound for its elucidation, as etc.; it has no time for any consideration—it is occupied with the performance of its characteristics: before it has died away it must have made perfectly exact its frequency, its loudness, its length, its overtone structure, the precise morphology of these and of itself.
>
> Urgent, unique, uninformed about history and theory, beyond the imagination, central to a sphere without surface, its becoming is unimpeded, energetically broadcast.[43]

The thesis here, put short and negatively, is that sounds are not thoughts. But how is the thesis to be understood on the positive side? This much seems clear: the new music, for Cage, begins by ridding sounds of (our) purposes and other structures of thought. The teaching is that we are to attend to sounds per se as "things" whose value is "intrinsic" and not instrumental relative to *our* aims and goals. The point—about sounds—is reminiscent of Kant's humanity imperative about persons, namely, that they are to be treated as "ends in themselves" and never as means only. An apt metaphor might be that, for Cage, sounds have *rights*—not welfare rights, of course, but the so-called negative rights of individual liberty, the rights that impose duties on the rest of us not to interfere. In this account, Cage's ethics of sound is even libertarian: "Patterns, repetitions, and variations will arise and disappear" but *not* via structures *we* impose.[44] And such patterns, repetitions, and variations as finally emerge (via a compositional "invisible hand," as it were) we must not judge later "in terms of success and failure." A truly "experimental" music, Cage says, is "an act the outcome of which is unknown."[45] If one asks, "Then what is the purpose of this 'experimental' music?" Cage answers, "No purposes. Sounds."[46]

The last point I will mention in connection with Cage's views concerns change, or openness to change, and affirms the propriety of, as it were, "continual revolution." The worst thing we can do, in respect of sounds, and perhaps of life generally, is develop *habits*. We must take steps to avoid becoming what Cage calls "musicians in ruts."[47] And we take these steps not just "to recall or extend known musical possibilities" but, rather, to introduce ourselves "to the unknown with such sharp clarity that anyone has the opportunity of having his habits blown away like dust."[48] But the openness to change I wish to emphasize here is perhaps only misleadingly characterized by use of the word *revolution*. After all, Cage's radical conception of sound is not itself belligerent, and it involves no repudiation of anything. It means to stretch the mind and to make us alive to what we have been accustomed to ignoring. That, in a nutshell, it seems to me, is how it contributes to our being positioned to self-realize. From one angle, Cage's treatment of sound is, in fact, a gentle doctrine. For to move silence into the world of sound is, among other things, to make us alive in a new way to what is around us, to our environment in the most general sense, and without prior commitments to "ideology." The revolution is not in a protest based on a substantive "vision" of what ought to be, or what everyone ought to believe, but, rather, in the humble but striking thought that even in sitting still anywhere listening, one is making sound and possibly music. Such a thought brings to mind Thoreau, and Cage's notes about Thoreau reflect his own view of what genuine openness of mind is. Cage writes, "No greater American has lived than Thoreau. Emerson called him a speaker and actor of the truth. Other great men have vision. Thoreau had none. Each day his eyes and ears were open and empty to see and hear the world he lived in. Music, he said, is continuous; only listening is intermittent."[49]

REVIEW

Let me now review what I have said in the latter normative part of this lengthy discussion of others' needs, offer my conclusions, and suggest some implications of my discussion.

I begin the normative discussion with some notes about the human condition in our time. It is marked by (among other things) destitution on a massive scale, gross inequality in levels of life available to different human beings, that is, fellow members of the moral community, and very limited efforts to ameliorate these troubling facts. These facts—largely facts of unmet basic need—become sharply problematic for responsible individuals, I suspect, when viewed from the perspective of the relative, and rather general, affluence to be found in certain parts of the world community.

So far as moral theory is concerned, I respond to this desperate situation in today's world by suggesting that (what I call) "shared-fate individualism" is a conception of individual responsibility relevant to it. Indeed, I suggest that shared-fate individualism, demanding that competent individuals put "service" before "self-realization" in serious life decisions, is required in the circumstances of today's world by the form of moral life we already share.

I then ask what (if anything) this has to do with art and artists. I do not suggest that artists are to drop their work and join hunger relief organizations—though I suppose that my view would not allow me to *object* were an artist to follow that course. I also do not suggest that artists are to produce only moralizing works that only portray the dreary facts about the human condition, somehow meaning to shame members of the public into increasing their charitable donations—though, again, I suppose my view would not *object* were some artists to follow that course. What I do suggest is that artists consider, or perhaps simply remember, that morality requires that members of the human community be positioned to self-realize, and that artists consider further what it is for human beings to contribute to other human beings being positioned to self-realize. In this connection I indicate that I am moved by the capacity of artists through their media to contribute to others certain types of opportunity for experience that are indeed important for human self-realization.

My view is that through their various media artists can give others opportunities to conceptualize or reconceptualize their experience, and sometimes these conceptualizations or reconceptualizations may be quite radical, that is, fundamental, in character. This seems to me of great importance. For I believe that self-realization is not possible for people who have no experience of alternative conceptualizations of salient facts in their experience. There are many ways, in my view, of being destitute. When destitution is discussed our minds go, naturally enough, to shortages or shortfalls in food, material goods, shelter, and perhaps education. My view insists that these matters be attended to. But it does not follow from that necessary emphasis that a certain minimal level of material goods, food, shelter, and education is sufficient to self-realization. People must be able to *move in their minds* if they are to be able to nurture and cultivate their fortunate natural gifts, whatever they are. My thought is that, in principle, art can make a contribution to the satisfaction of the conditions of self-realization in a person, just as much as proper diet or decent living space can.

As an example of a "radical conceptualization" conveyable through art, I nominate John Cage's treatment of sound. Here is a new manner of thinking directed to something very close to us, namely, our experience of sound. Cage's art and theorizing make us rethink our experience at a deep level. In words I quote from Cage's writings, his art and theorizing introduce us "to the unknown with such sharp clarity" that a person who takes in Cage's point "has the opportunity of having his habits blown away like dust." In a less colorful phrase, his art and theorizing stretch our minds. By doing this, or helping us do this, this work contributes toward our being positioned to self-realize.

I am aware that my line of thought raises many questions. Perhaps the most important of these is a question I am not myself qualified to answer. What "radical conceptualizations" can this or that form of art, medium, or genre effectively convey? I have my own ideas on this subject, of course. The points from Robert Irwin and Patricia Phillips that I mention earlier— the "assertion of individual values in the midst of high-tech decision-making" and the "reconstitution of the idea of the commons," respectively—seem to me loaded with radical conceptualization possibilities. The very different work of public artists Athena Tacha and Judith Bacca seems to me similarly loaded with such possibilities. In a general way, given my own estimates about the serious problems before humankind at this point, environmentalist reconceptualizations also seem to me paramount in moral importance, along with the basic conceptual connections that need to be drawn to give human beings the sensibility that goes with shared-fate individualism. But there are many other possibilities. If Tacha's "Massacre Memorial" of the Jewish Holocaust can serve to fix for us a sense of our enormous capacity for evil, and Baca's "Great Wall" muralist project can alter our sense of what constitutes our collective identity, then in a still different way perhaps an artwork might be able to bring home to people the point that numbers are beautiful and attractive, rather than frightening and intimidating, and thereby motivate quantitative literacy. Perhaps still other artworks can do something with the dismal fact that large cities in the United States have very high annual homicide rates or the tragic fact that one in four young black males is in prison or on probation. These may be facts that are "local" rather than "global" relative to the wider perspective on humankind encouraged by shared-fate individualism, but the *failure of community* that is at their heart is a theme that has received treatment by artists in the past and needs now, in my opinion, fresh attention.

CENSORSHIP

Before closing I will mention a modest implication of my line of thought for a subject of intense contemporary concern, namely, censorship. Given the moral point I have assigned to art, that is, the task of making possible radical conceptualizations or reconceptualizations of the elements of experience as a contribution to the positioning of people for self-realization, it seems plain enough that the freedom of the artist must be stable and wide ranging. "Invention" at the deep level I have in mind cannot flourish in contexts in which the moralisms of some are enforced at the law or expressed in restrictions on artists or others embedded in policies on, say, funding or other art-related ventures. At the same time, I must say that I am not an "anything goes, no qualifications" theorist in this matter. In the fall of 1990, an art student entered a work in a show at the Cleveland State University Art Gallery. His work involved the photograph of a teenager named Diah Harris, and the artwork connected this photograph with sketches of this young person portraying her in sexually explicit scenes. The young woman thus shown and interpreted in the work was viciously killed—not far, in fact, from the art gallery itself—a short time before the artist and the gallery placed this work on exhibit. Shw was a very real person; her death by murder included the dismemberment of her body. Her family, still grieving, was itself living in the same area, taking such steps as it could to go on with life. When the work was exhibited, outrage was expressed in Cleveland. I understand that the art student proceeded to withdraw his work from the exhibit. A Cleveland newspaper suggests that perhaps he feared "physical retribution for his controversial art show entry."[50] The paper also notes that the "intent of the art show" was "a celebration of First Amendment rights for freedom of expression."[51] My point is really very simple. There is no real reason, so far as I can see, for the freedom so necessary to "invention" at the deep level that I have in mind to be exercised in a way that violates the sensibilities of a family and others grieving the loss of a young person by a most dreadful form of murder. There is, as moral and political philosophers have often noted, a distinction between, on the one side, *having* a certain freedom, and thus a certain *entitlement* to action in a certain range, and, on the other side, the *wise use* of that *precious* entitlement. I indicated earlier that I hope that shocking people for the sake of shocking them is not the point of art. Art *can* "shock," of course. Sometimes "shock" can have positive value, I suppose—but not in any and every case. In some instances it is silly, nonsensical, or just cruel—and it fails to reach any worthwhile goal. In the view I have suggested, art can and should have a point—a moral point, in fact—and in virtue of that point my view strongly endorses the freedom of the artist; but it does not find its moral point importantly advanced by artistic statements that in given circumstances constitute gratuitous cruelty to innocent people already in pain. Artists who seek to contribute to the self-realization of people, and thus require the entitlement of freedom, can do better than that.

The limits to the radical conceptualization I have discussed are merely the limits of our imagination and ability to draw connections and also, given what I have just said about the abuse of freedom, the limits afforded by our own sense of decency and respect for the emotional pain people may suffer as they take the low blows that life sends them. Of course, my emphasis here has been almost entirely on our imagination and ability to draw connections. For Thoreau, being quiet in a woods could be a positive act, for it could be a "being at one" with nature. For Cage, sitting quietly listening could be a positive act, for it could be a producing of sound and possibly of music. As Cage reorients our experience of sound, so another artist, or artist-*cum*-theorist, might conceptualize, or re-conceptualize, our experience of place, location, situation, and environment in alternative ways or even our experience of our relationships with one another in alternative ways. Perhaps, in a manner that seems to me structurally reminiscent of Cage's work, my just being in my community could, through art, also be a positive act, an act that connects me with my environment and its people in a manner that affects my sensibilities as a person for the better. Of course, how one "implements" one's adventures in conceptualizing or reconceptualizing alternatives to our current forms of experience, that is, how one gets from "idea" to "artwork," I gratefully leave to others and, in particular, to artists. For that aspect of the matter is very much beyond my competence. Artists are needed for that.

6

✢

Future People and Novel Ideas

A MOTIVATION PROBLEM

Suppose we are independent policy makers for a free society.[1] Our job is to formulate policies and put them before the larger community for approval. While we as individuals are members of the society we make policy for—we live in it and know it well—our appointments as independent policy makers give us enough security so that we may be disinterested and impartial in our work. We are free to consider what morality requires in the matters raised by the various policy questions we take up, and we in fact attempt to devise satisfactory policy solutions for our society's problems which are in line with what morality requires—so far, of course, as we can make out what morality requires in particular cases. But, given the context in which we work, we are also mindful of the fact that ours is a free society, and in such a society it is best for the implementation of public policy to flow from general *support* for it on the part of the people and not just from, say, legal coercion. Questions about the *availability* and *reliability* of such support recur in our work on policy questions.[2] Finally, our recommendations to the larger community are respected: they will be considered seriously. In the past our recommendations have often been accepted.

Our task at this point is to prepare morally principled policies concerning our society's legacy to "the world of the future."[3] These policies deal with many things but (for convenience here) principally with the distribution and conservation of natural resources and the control and impact of our physical plant on the environment. Suppose it becomes clear that

103

the policies we find emerging from our work—the policies we develop under the guidance of our conception of what morality requires of us in this matter of our legacy to the world of the future—will not be *easy* to implement. We see that they call for *serious* sacrifice on the part of ordinary people.

Now, because we are policy makers for a free society, and hence we seek to recommend policies whose implementation can command general support, the fact that the morally principled policies we have developed make heavy demands for sacrifice by ordinary people is something we cannot pass over lightly. We recognize that the people of our society—our fellow citizens—have deep interests in the ways of life they labor (hard and honestly, in most cases) to build and maintain. These ways of life reflect our fellow citizens' different interpretations of the value of self-realization, and in some cases their ways of life reflect aspirations they have for those close to them, such as their children or even friends and associates. Such interests, values, and aspirations seem legitimate to us (though we may quarrel with their interpretations or contents in some cases). Indeed, as members of society we too have such interests, values, and aspirations. We may pause over the fact that the unbridled pursuit of self-realization can become corrupted into self-absorption.[4] But that is an extreme, and the possibility of its occurrence does not impugn our thought that there are things that the individual member of a free society owes to him- or herself. A person who takes seriously his or her personal development and the wellbeing of those close to him or her is not thereby morally unserious. We realize that a sacrifice can be perceived as being too great relative to one's legitimate interests in one's own realization, one's aspirations for others, and the ways of life related to these interests and aspirations. We recognize that to many of our fellow citizens these considerations may seem to be *defenses* against the demands for sacrifice involved in the policies we are entertaining.

Nevertheless, after further work, let us suppose that we see that the policies that demand this sacrifice are indeed *required* by morality and that these familiar defenses we have considered are *overridden*.[5] In that case, we (independent policy makers for a free society) face the following question: What (apart from legal or other forms of coercion) is available and reliable in the way of support for the morally principled policies we now see we must recommend to the larger community? Alternatively put, what in people can we draw on to *motivate* them to follow the policies that morality requires regarding our legacy for the world of the future? I refer to this as the *motivation problem* for public policy regarding the future or, for short, the future generations motivation problem.

NOTES

Here are some introductory notes about how this motivation problem is to be understood. In the first place, the problem at issue is not that of justifying morality to a thoroughgoing egoist, or what Hume calls a "sensible knave."[6] The problem concerns the motivation of quite ordinary decent people, and they are not, in general (so I shall assume), egoists or knaves. Some may be, but not all or most.

Second, while it may be reasonably easy to generalize negatively that ordinary decent people are neither egoists nor knaves, it may be much more difficult to generalize positively about the motivation of such people. What in fact moves people becomes at some point an empirical question, and this already suggests that there are limits to what philosophical work on this subject can achieve. A philosophical discussion of motivation available to support public policies guided by what morality requires for the world of the future will not, for example, yield statistical generalizations about the likelihood of the population of this or that nation-state to be moved by a given motivational factor, such as a "sense of tradition" or the "love of mankind." But there are nevertheless certain aspects of this future generations motivational problem which seem open to philosophical treatment. In what follows I restrict my attention to some of these.

Third, I assume that the availability and reliability of relevant motivation is a condition of the acceptability of proposals for social policy in a free society. Supporting motivational factors are of course only some among the many types of considerations bearing on the acceptability of policies.[7] But they may be of special importance in the context of the development of policies concerning our legacy for the future. I assume that policies are unacceptable when it is known that rational persons of integrity cannot follow them or can follow them only with extraordinary difficulty such that they make demands nearly "exceeding the capacity of human nature."[8] Besides, as a purely practical matter, if we understand that our ways of life—our individual activities and collective projects, together with our means of conducting and implementing them—jeopardize or seriously risk damaging the interests and prospects of future people, and if we understand further that in these circumstances morality requires substantial—even radical—changes in our ways of life, then it would surely *help* in the choice of social policies developed with the requirements of morality in mind to determine what motivation in support of such policies is available and reliable among the people expected to follow them.

Finally, let me mention that the motivation problem I wish to explore is not unique to the policy context in which we deal with what morality requires for the world of the future. It may be that the problem typically arises when public policy calls for sacrifice, and the sacrifice is thought of as for the sake of people who are distant enough from us to be faceless and impersonal. Of course, the condition and plight (e.g., the destitution) of *current* people who are distant from us can often be revealed to us through the gathering of particular facts. Individual current people, at any rate, can (in principle) become known to each other.[9] But the same opportunity to know future people in similar detail is not available to us. This, I think, affects our motivation to do (if not our understanding of) what morality requires for the world of the future. But it does not restrict the motivation problem to the context in which we are concerned with acceptable policy for the future.

"CONCERN FOR GENERATIONS TO COME"

Some theorists claim that people as we know them are not, and even cannot be expected to be, motivated by "a concern for generations to come" to act on what morality requires for the world of the future. Robert L. Heilbroner, for example, offers the following overview of our situation:

> A crucial problem for the world of the future will be a concern for generations to come. . . . [H]umanity may react to the approach of environmental danger by indulging in a vast fling while it is still possible. . . . On what private, "rational" consideration, after all, should we make sacrifices now to ease the lot of generations whom we will never live to see?
> There is only one possible answer to this question. It lies in our capacity to form a collective bond of identity with those future generations. . . . *Indeed, it is the absence of just such a bond with the future that casts doubt on the ability of nation-states or socio-economic orders to take now the measures needed to mitigate the problems of the future.*[10]

Heilbroner here raises the motivation problem I have in mind. It may be useful to be aware of his own estimate of its seriousness:

> There seems no hope for rapid changes in the human character traits that would have to be modified to bring about a peaceful, organized reorientation of life styles. . . . [T]herefore the outlook is for what we may call "convulsive change"—change forced upon us by external events rather than by conscious choice, by catastrophe rather than by calculation. . . . [N]ature will provide the checks, if foresight and "morality" do not. Thus in all likelihood we must brace ourselves for the consequences of which we have spoken— the risk of "wars of redistribution" or of "preemptive seizure," the rise of social tensions in the industrialized nations over the division of an ever more

slow-growing or even diminishing product, and the prospect of a far more coercive exercise of national power as the means by which we will attempt to bring these disruptive processes under control. From that period of harsh adjustment, I can see no realistic escape. Rationalize as we will, stretch the figures as favorably as honesty will permit, we cannot reconcile the requirements for a lengthy continuation of the present rate of industrialization of the globe with the capacity of existing resources or the fragile biosphere to permit or to tolerate the effects of that industrialization. Nor is it easy to foresee a willing acquiescence of humankind, individually or through its existing social organizations, in the alterations of lifeways that foresight would dictate. If then, by the question "Is there hope for man?" we ask whether it is possible to meet the challenges of the future without the payment of a fearful price, the answer must be: No, there is no such hope.[11]

This is (to put it modestly) a troubling view. It rests directly on a pessimistic claim about the motivation of ordinary people: namely, that they do not, and perhaps (given their social conditioning) cannot, feel responsible for future people deeply enough to move them to "acquiesce" in policies demanding substantial "alterations" in their "lifeways."[12] If my assumption is fair—that the availability and reliability of relevant motivation is a condition of the acceptability of public policies in a free society—then this pessimistic motivational claim presents a matter of great importance to the design and adequacy of any policies for natural resources and our physical plant which we propose seriously for adoption in a heavily industrialized "affluent" society such as our own.

Let me ask what this *concern for generations to come*—which is said to be absent or weak—consists in and amounts to. In what follows I explore a small number of ways in which such a motivational factor may be interpreted.

STIPULATIONS

Let us call people who live fifty generations after us "future people." Let us call ourselves "current people." In order to begin my exploration of the motivation problem, I must make four initial points. They are stipulations, and I will not attempt to argue for them.

The first point is that morality requires something of us regarding our legacy to the world of the future. Morality, as it were, speaks on this subject. What morality requires of us regarding future people is a full philosophical problem in its own right, and I do not take up that problem here. I only suggest some maxims that might stand as the "requirements of morality" regarding the world of the future.

We may begin by agreeing with Joel Feinberg's remark that "surely we owe it to future generations to pass on a world that is not a used up garbage heap."[13] Beyond this, let us suppose first that morality requires (among other things) an equal opportunity maxim, according to which what we owe to future people is a world at least no worse off than the one we received. As Brian Barry puts it, "the overall range of opportunities open to successor generations should not be narrowed." Second, it may require (among other things) what we might call a custody maxim, according to which current people are to regard themselves as "custodians rather than owners of the planet, and ought to pass it on in at least no worse shape than they found it in." This is to say, I take it, that morality may require a change in our attitudes (and relevant practices) toward the things of the earth. We may have to give up the view of the world as a cluster of resources which we can come to possess or own and adopt a view of the world as a cluster of resources of which we are temporary custodians or stewards.[14]

I will not attempt to argue either for these maxims or against other candidates that may come to mind. Let us simply regard the maxims I have mentioned as plausible candidates to figure in an account of what morality requires of us in behalf of the world of the future.

The second point is that what morality requires of us is indeed what we (current people) would count as *sacrifice*. What exactly the sacrifice consists of I must leave indeterminate. Experts appear to make different estimates of what our natural resources situation is and of what shape our physical plant is in. The fact that current humankind is organized into nation-states is not helpful in this matter of information and estimates. Our approaches to the facts get cluttered, so to speak, with politics.

But however far away we are from accurate information about our physical plant and resources, I share with many people a growing uneasiness about our situation. As laypersons relative to the technical matters sometimes involved, we have the impression that our resources are drying up or being squandered and that our physical plant is in disrepair or of the wrong kind to serve human needs in growing populations. All this portends sacrifice. The future has the bleak look of a burden about it. The vocabulary of the policies we are asked to consider is that of "pulling back," "seeking alternatives," "using less," "curbing," "lowering," and "restricting." Those who see something objectionable in ways of life supported by affluence and considerable energy consumption may welcome the prospect. But many of us do not.

The third point is a reminder of a distinction that allows the motivation problem to arise: it is one thing to understand what morality requires and another thing to be moved to do what morality requires. If understanding what morality requires operated in us in such a way that, in Kant's words, the actions that we recognize to be "objectively necessary" were also "subjectively necessary," then the motivation problem I have in mind would not arise. But—so I assume here, following Kant—this is not so.[15] As I discuss in chapter 1, there is no *tight* connection between understanding what morality requires and being moved to do what morality requires. It does not follow, of course, that understanding what morality requires has no motivating power. But it does follow that an account that shows what morality requires in some category of cases does not *thereby* make clear (at least not directly) the motivation of people to do or act on what morality requires in that category of cases.[16]

ABOUT FUTURE PEOPLE

Future people (those who live many generations after us) are faceless and impersonal to current people. The details that make people at least interesting to each other personally are missing. We do not know what their lifestyles are, what they stand for, whether they think much of us, or whether they are concerned about people who live many generations after them. Face-to-face encounters are out of the question.

We are not totally ignorant of what future people are like, of course. If (ex hypothesi) our descendants are still *people,* then we have now a body of "salient facts" about them.[17] They will almost certainly have wants, needs, hopes, and fears; they will almost certainly love and hate and perhaps even experience resentment and feel guilt. We may say, in overview fashion, that future people will have interests. And current people can do things now, so it seems, that affect those interests. We can do things now that hurt future people. We can damage the environment, for example, or use up finite resources (without researching and providing for alternatives) and thereby affect how many future people there are or make the circumstances in which future people live very difficult to bear.

These facts—that future people will be *people* and will have *interests* that current people can affect—may make it *intelligible* to say that people of both sorts (future and current) have rights and, in an abstract sense, belong to one moral community. And if this can be said, perhaps it in turn helps show that indeed morality requires something of current people relative to future people. But, of course, even if such claims are intelligible, it does not follow that we should adopt them or base social policies on them.[18] Indeed, the whole idea that we and future people are members of a common moral community may seem strange. There is no mutual cooperation in such a community, and there are no exchanges "in kind";

as a consequence this community is not characterized by mutual benefit or joint participation in common activities in *any* familiar ways.[19] The one "exchange" I can think of is that for the sacrifices we make in order to deliver an inhabitable globe to future people, they are grateful. They at least do not think little of us. But this "exchange" is hardly "in kind," and, in fact, it never reaches us.

In what follows I explore what these few notes about future people suggest concerning the motivation of current people to make the sacrifices required by morality on behalf of future people.

MOTIVATION AND PARTICULARITY

It would be unrealistic for policy makers to rely on *love* or *concern* to motivate current people to do what morality requires for the world of the future.[20] This is suggested by the faceless and impersonal character of future people. Future people cannot arouse love or concern in current people—at least not in the way other (typically nearby) current people can. Whatever may be the full explanation of this fact, it involves, I think, the nonparticularity—the facelessness and impersonality—of future people. As I remark above, the details that make people at least interesting to each other are missing in the case of future people, and *the capacity to interest* is a precondition of, or perhaps a constituent part of, the capacity to arouse in us such "motivational factors" as love or concern. Somehow being moved by love or concern for a person or group of people involves having more of him, her, or them before one than one has in the case of future people.

But perhaps this might be replied to: we note earlier that future people will have interests—call them "salient fact interests"—that we can know about now and which we can affect now. Is that particularity not enough to make it possible that love, concern, or other strong feeling might be aroused? Perhaps we can love or have concern for future people insofar as they may be construed as interests we can affect now.[21]

But I do not think this response is helpful. I do not think one can love or have concern for interests per se, and so it does not help make motivation in the form of love or concern flourish or even exist to semireduce future people to their interests. What is at stake here *is* motivation, in particular, motivation to do what morality requires. The fact that future people have interests that we can affect now may indeed be relevant to the philosophical problem of determining whether or not we have responsibilities to future people and beyond that to the philosophical problem of determining what, morally, is adequate provision for future people. But, again, what thus helps us see or understand what morality requires is not thereby what motivates us to do what morality requires. And in any case the nonparticularity problem remains. The interests of future people, construed as derived from their wants, needs, hopes, and fears, are radically indeterminate. Insofar as this is so (and risking the air of paradox), the interests of future people do not have the capacity to interest us. Therefore, so I suggest, a condition of them having the capacity to arouse love, concern, or other strong feelings in us is not satisfied.

I say above that it would be unrealistic for policy makers to rely on love or concern to motivate current people to do what morality requires for the world of the future. Perhaps the term *unrealistic* is after all too weak. The discussion I have offered suggests that policy makers *cannot* rely on motivation in the form of love or concern because motivation in this form is not available in the context of policy for the future. More exactly, what is not available is love or concern, each of which has as a condition of its possibility (a) the capacity of its object to interest us, which involves (b) what I have called "particularity." If a person were to profess or claim to be moved by love or concern for future people, or even for future people qua interests, I would have to say that something other than the love or concern I have indicated is being referred to or perhaps that the characteristic feelings associated with the love or concern I have indicated were aroused by something else, that is, something other than future people, future people qua interests, or the idea of either of these. (Perhaps they were aroused by a drug.)

In general, insofar as motivation to do what morality requires is tied down to particularity about persons, such motivation is not available to support widespread acquiescence in public policies meant to implement what morality requires for the world of the future.

COMMUNITY BONDING AND RECIPROCATION

A second form of motivation that is sometimes available to prompt us to do what morality requires may be labeled (for purposes of this discussion) as *community bonding*. Even if this term is not ordinary, what I have in mind is familiar enough. We are commonly and often moved to act in ways that may be in line with principles (and hence, on occasion, with moral principles) by a regard for other persons which derives from their membership with us in a common community, association, enterprise, or project of some sort.[22] At a minimum, motivation of this sort involves a *sense of belonging to some joint enterprise with others*. The motivational factor constituted by this sense of belonging may carry with it the feeling

tones of solidarity, comradeship, loyalty, mutual confidence and trust, or
at least a sense of being on the same side. And the sense of belonging with
others to a joint enterprise has a certain directionality to it. It is not indis-
criminate in its objects. It selects *those* "others" who belong with one to
that common enterprise. It picks out others who stand with one as co-
members of some identifiable body, association, or community. In the
event that one fails the association, violates the community, or lets down
the side, one may incur feelings of guilt or be dismayed or experience
regret.[23]

My thought is that just as there is a condition for the occurrence of
motivation in the form of love or concern, namely, what I call "particularity," so there is a condition (probably many conditions) for the occurrence of motivation in the form of community bonding. I title this condition *reciprocation*. By *reciprocation* I have in mind the exchange of ideas and
conceptions of purposes that must be available to persons before they can
be considered to stand as joint participants in a common project. We
should distinguish this condition of reciprocation from that of prospective mutual benefit. Joint participation in common enterprises often has
mutual benefit as its aim. But reciprocation is at a deeper level than the
cooperation appropriate to mutual-benefit associations. There are communities, associations, enterprises, and projects that we participate in or endure (perhaps reluctantly) but which we do not view as directed toward
mutual benefit. But still, participation in or endurance of these different
associations and enterprises may arouse motivation in the form of community bonding,[24] yet these various modes of joint participation cannot
occur in the absence of the reciprocation I have in mind. People may find
themselves in routines and regimens in which their behavior is controlled
for them (e.g., as unwitting victims of medical experimentation), and these
routines and regimens may occur in the absence of reciprocation (and give
rise to still different kinds of "motivational factors," such as resentment).
But such modes of control or manipulation of behavior are not communities, enterprises, associations, or projects. The latter rest on a ground of
exchange of ideas and interpretations of ends among participants in
them—an exchange that is sometimes one-sided, no doubt, but nevertheless (to whatever minimal degree) present.

If we ask at this point whether motivation in the form of community
bonding is available and reliable to support policies designed to implement what morality requires of us on behalf of the world of the future, I
think the answer must be no. We (current people) and they (future people)
are not positioned in such a way as to be able to reciprocate with each
other concerning the constituent ideas and controlling aims of any associations or enterprises that we jointly participate in or endure.[25] In the

absence of the possibility of such reciprocation, I do not see how motivation in the form of community bonding can arise. The feeling tones of solidarity or loyalty, or even the sense of being on the same side, are foreign to our relationship (whatever it is) to future people. Accordingly, the experiences of guilt, dismay, or regret, as they are known to us from our acquaintance with what it is to damage or destroy the associations we have with persons with whom we exchange ideas and interpretations of ends—these experiences cannot arise from our relationship (whatever it is) to future people. If a person should claim to feel guilt as a result of faults in his or her conduct toward future people, I would have to say that the experience of guilt referred to is of a different kind from that which may be explained by reference to motivation in the form of community bonding.

In general, insofar as motivation to do what morality requires is tied down to reciprocation with other persons concerning the ideas and aims of shared enterprises, as is so in the case of community bonding, then it is not available to support policies implementing what morality requires for the world of the future.

EXTENDED SHARED-FATE MOTIVATION

Finally, let me take up—or, more exactly, speculate about—a form of motivation that seems very different from love or concern and community bonding. In those cases the motivation was construed as grounded either in the particularity of other persons or in reciprocation with them concerning the ideas and aims of joint enterprises. The motivation I wish to touch on now is more abstract in character. I will call it *extended* or *unbounded shared-fate motivation*. I have in mind the sense of common humanity we have (if we have it, and to whatever extent we have it), which involves at some level the notion that in a very general way human beings as such "belong together," or are "in life together," *irrespective* of differences in time and location among them.

Let me offer a series of thoughts, in no special order, about motivation of this kind.

First we need some account or picture of what extended shared-fate motivation consists of or at least what it is like. The following passage from Rawls's *A Theory of Justice* is suggestive, I think, regarding the possibility of the form of motivation I have in mind:

> Individuals in their role as citizens with a full understanding of the content of the principles of justice may be moved to act upon them largely because

of their bonds to particular persons and an attachment to their own society. Once a morality of principles is accepted, however, moral attitudes are no longer connected solely with the well-being and approval of particular individuals and groups, but are shaped by a conception of right chosen irrespective of these contingencies. Our moral sentiments display an independence from the accidental circumstances of the world.[26]

What attracts my attention in this passage is just its suggestion that motivation may be grounded in an idea in a way that is independent of what I have called particularity about persons or reciprocation between persons. Given my general approach in this chapter, let us ask what such an idea would have to be *of* in order to serve as a ground for motivation supporting public policies operating on behalf of the world of the future.

So far as I can see, the most straightforward candidate for an idea that could serve this function—analogously to the role of particularity in the case of love or concern and the role of reciprocation in the case of community bonding—is the idea of a community of persons who may be at any temporal or social location and who nevertheless construe themselves as "being in life together" or "sharing fate" according to the contents of an appropriate conception of what morality requires of the members of such a community.[27] And we must note at once that the idea of community thus brought before the mind (an idea very like, I believe, the Kantian conception of persons as members of "the realm of ends") is unusual in important ways. First, it is an idea of a community in which not all or even very many of the members can reciprocate with each other, that is, engage in an exchange with each other over the ideas and purposes of their community. No real *joint* decision making, no matter to what extent representation is employed, can take place in it.[28] Second, it is an idea of a community in which not all or even very many of the members have—in principle—particularity for each other. Most of its members are, and must remain, faceless and impersonal to each other. Third, it is an idea of a community in which the membership is *unbounded* in *all* the ordinary ways. Thus it has no national or even geographical limits, and its membership extends into the future indefinitely if not infinitely.

Once the idea that might ground extended shared-fate motivation is sketched in this way, we may ask, Can an idea of this sort in fact be *motivating* among persons as we know them? That is, can we not only conceive of a community of this sort, and of ourselves as members of it, but also imagine ourselves developing *a sense of belonging to it,* such that this *sense* might be available and reliable in support of policies meant to implement what morality requires for the world of the future? It is one thing, we may suppose, for us to be able to form the conception of humankind as an unbounded (yet) shared-fate community and quite another thing for such a conception to arouse in us, say, *affection for* the community.

I will close with just three notes about the prospect of the idea of an unbounded community of mostly nonreciprocating persons who are nonparticular for each other being motivating among people as we know them. First, it is worth mentioning that reference to the idea in question is an occasional part of ordinary moral discourse—though this occasional use of the idea may not indicate serious appeal to the content I have suggested the idea might have. I have in mind, in the context of discussions of policy for the future, appeals to common humanity in the form of appeals to the fact that *persons*, after all, may be hurt by what we do now. As Feinberg remarks, "The vagueness of the human future does not weaken its claim on us in light of the nearly certain knowledge that it will, after all, be human."[29]

The second note is that if we follow Rawls's lead, we may then think of the development of certain forms of motivation as describable by very general psychological laws linking their emergence to institutional structures and practices.[30] Thus, *given* a society or social setting of a certain sort, together with persons' natural sentiments, we may *expect* certain forms of motivation to be aroused in the human beings who live in that society or social setting. In this fashion, what Rawls calls "the sense of justice" is a form of motivation that is the *product* of life in what he thinks of as a "well-ordered society," that is, a society that is, and that is known to be, governed by the conception of justice as fairness. To think in this way about the development of motivation leads us in the present case to ask whether our society is such that we may reasonably expect the people who have their lives in *it* to develop extended shared-fate motivation.[31]

Finally, when we raise this latter question, my own estimate is that our society is not one that lends itself to the cultivation of extended shared-fate motivation. To show why this is so would be a large project, and I will not attempt it here. It would involve discussion of the structures, institutions, practices, and moral ideology characteristic of our society;[32] argument about how far this social entity as a whole meets the criteria of "well-orderedness"; and then treatment of the still further questions of what sorts of social structures would lend themselves to the development in persons of a sense of belonging to an unbounded community of human beings which could be efficacious enough to be relevant to the motivational problem of making available reliable support for public policies implementing what morality requires for the world of the future. Without meaning to beg important questions, I suspect that this large project would find that certain elements in the makeup of our society— for example, the lack of good Samaritan rules in our legal system, the self-interested psychology of competitive appropriation fostered by our economic life, the emphasis on self-realization in our educational system, and the prizing of immediate sensibility so powerfully supported by everyday commerce and culture—all operate *against* the development in us of what I have called extended shared-fate motivation.

In general, I think extended shared-fate motivation is intelligible—we can imagine its presence in persons—and I think it "fits" our thoughts concerning what motivation would have to be like to be serviceable in the context of policies implementing what morality requires for the world of the future. But there is nevertheless serious empirical doubt, I think, about its availability and reliability as support for public policies in a society such as ours. Given the influence on us of certain dominating institutional elements in the makeup of society, plus our current received moral ideology, it may be that motivation of the unbounded shared-fate sort is somehow beyond us, or too difficult for very many of us to develop, at this time. The discussion above of love or concern (grounded in particularity about persons) and of community bonding (grounded in reciprocation) brings to our attention features of our nature that are familiar to us. But extended shared-fate motivation is, while not unknown to us, nevertheless not similarly familiar to us.

SUMMARY

The discussion of this chapter is offered as an exploration of what I called the "motivation problem" in the context of the task of formulating morally principled social policies on behalf of the world of the future. I touch on motivation of three different kinds. I suggest that motivation in the familiar form of *love* or *concern*, grounded in what I called "particularity" about persons, is not available to support policies for the world of the future. I also suggest that motivation in the familiar form of *community bonding*, grounded in what I call "reciprocation" between persons, is similarly unavailable. Finally, I offer a brief account of *extended shared-fate motivation* and speculate that, while this may be intelligible to us as a possible form of motivation among human beings, it may not be widely available or reliable.

At the beginning of this chapter I call attention to Robert L. Heilbroner's view that "a crucial problem for the world of the future will be a concern for generations to come." And I indicate that Heilbroner is very pessimistic about the availability of this concern as motivation that could support policies on behalf of the world of the future among current people. My discussion may deepen somewhat how this notion of "concern for generations to come" is to be understood, and, so far as it goes, the discussion supports Heilbroner's pessimism. If we imagine ourselves in the place of independent policy makers for a free society (as sketched at the beginning of the discussion), we may well be dismayed by the apparent fact that certain familiar sorts of motivation are not available to support policies demanding serious sacrifice for the sake of future generations, and we may well be discouraged by the further apparent fact that the cultivation of a form of motivation directly supportive of such policies might require something close to an overhaul of main elements in the makeup of our society which influence the moral psychology of citizens.[33] Whether these difficulties would or should be enough to make us recommend policies other than those required by morality (e.g., less demanding policies) or, indeed, no policies for the world of the future at all, I am uncertain. It might occur to us that we should stay with our recommendation of the policies required by morality, even at the cost of reliance on coercion of some sorts for implementation. But in that case it appears that we face the problem of determining what kinds and levels of coercion would be tolerable—a problem whose difficulty is emphasized by the fact that ours is a free society.

TOWARD OTHER SORTS OF MOTIVATION

The "future generations problem" resembles those challenges to individual responsibility involving our awareness of human problems or suffering beyond our family connections, personal friendships, and cooperative social or political associations. In these cases that are outside our relationships and associations, we may feel burdened or irritated by the notion that we should help people who are in fact strangers to us. Sometimes we may offer our help, but we do not always do so, for we may not know how to help, or we may be pressed by competing demands, or we may simply not care enough to respond.

In the future generations case, of course, the responsibility of helping may seem weak not just because it is directed to strangers but also because it involves helping others who cannot be personally known to us in any of the usual ways in which people identify one another. When people are not just members of the next generation but members of distant future generations, then the particulars of their identity, so many of which are socially and economically conditioned, are blocked from view in ways we cannot really overcome, even through technology or strenuous exercises of imagination.

One might acknowledge this epistemological blockage but find it not to be a difficulty for an intellectual part of the future generations problem. For one might argue that although we may not know future people

in ordinary ways, we can recognize that they are, or will be, *human*; and
one might then suggest that this is basis enough for us to formulate appropriate principles of justice to guide our lives so that the lives of future
people may be adequately protected and prepared for.

This may be right as far as it goes. I assume above that the facelessness
and impersonality of future people need not prevent our developing a
conception of justice appropriate to their well-being. But I suggest that this
epistemological blockage raises *another* problem that needs our attention.
For it is not enough for us to formulate a conception of justice that takes
future generations into account; we must also understand better than we
do what motivational factors are available now to support action that is
in line with the principles and policies of justice toward future generations.

This is to say that there are at least two important questions within the
future generations problem. One of these is a question of *normative content,* that is, of principles and policies, and is thus a question of *what morality requires* (if anything) of responsible individuals relative to the
identityless strangers at stake. The other is a question of *motivation,* that
is, a question of what will, could, or should *move* responsible individuals
to do what morality requires. The latter question, which I focus on here,
may seem to be a question of psychology rather than a problem for philosophy. I believe, however, that theorists from many disciplines and back-
grounds can contribute to the motivation problem and that the problem
itself is not the possession of any one discipline or field of expertise. I also
believe that the motivation problem is a *very* important part of the general problem of future generations: if we do not face it, I think future
people will be endangered as much as they will be if we fail to respond
to the normative question of principles and policies.

Let us assume again—what is surely plausible—that what morality requires of current members of humankind relative to distant future people
is demanding. We may suppose, for example, that morality requires serious changes in current ways of life involving heavy use of natural resources. We need not suppose that such use is always indulgent "consumerism"; in some cases it is in the service of health or the provision of
welfare and is called for by justice itself. We may say that, relative to future generations, morality requires serious changes in our ways of life but
without moralizing that our current "ways of life" are in some general way
corrupt.

What, then, is to move us to undertake the serious changes in our ways
of life that we suppose morality requires of us? If, intellectually, we understand something of what justice prescribes in this matter, what forms
of motivation are available and reliable to bring it about that we as individuals *do* what we understand justice to prescribe?

We may recognize again that factors of different kinds move people to act—and, too, in some cases their actions may very well be in line with justice. Self-interest might be high on a list of such factors for many people; but fear, hate, ambition, and pity can also function in some cases to move people to do what happens to be right. Interestingly, the trouble with all these familiar forms of motivation, for our purposes, is that they are not *reliably* connected to one doing the *right* thing. If, for example, we let the notion of self-interest have its ordinary meaning and do not stretch that meaning to accommodate our theoretical ambitions of the moment, then clearly *what* is "in my interest" is not necessarily *what* "morality requires" in any given case. The connection between the other motivations I have mentioned and what morality requires in particular cases is similarly contingent. Let us not artificially solve the motivation problem by inventing interpretations of such motives that make them conceptually yield conduct that their ordinary interpretations carefully refuse to guarantee. Self-interest and pity, say, may indeed be available in many individual human beings, but such forms of motivation are not necessarily connected to what morality requires.

Similar points must be made even about forms of motivation that we might *want* to be available and reliable in support of justice toward future generations. I claim above that serious sacrifice called for by morally principled public policy cannot really be motivated by appeals to "love" or "concern" for members of distant future generations—at any rate, not the love or concern that rests for its intelligibility upon awareness of the details or "particularity" of its objects. Nor can it be motivated by appeals to the sort of "bonding" with others that rests on the possibility of reciprocity with them, for, after all, we have no reciprocity in any plain sense with members of distant future generations. Certain secular as well as religious traditions refer to a very general form of "love of humankind" that does not require current or future strangers to be close to us either temporally, geographically, or socially. But even if this form of motivation—which I call "extended shared-fate motivation"—is intelligible, there is nevertheless, I believe, serious empirical doubt about its availability and reliability as support for public policies taking seriously the fate of future people—perhaps especially in those societies whose popular culture emphasizes me-first consumerism, with secondary motivational recognition reserved for loyalty to one's family, friends, and, perhaps, nation-state.

Reflection on all this leads to pessimism in one's estimates of our chances of offering a decent legacy to future generations. Are there other sorts of motivation we should explore? In what follows I discuss a form of motivation that is both familiar yet different in kind from certain of the factors mentioned above. It is different from what seems involved in "love" or "concern" and "community bonding," though indeed it is suggested by the structural feature of what I call extended shared-fate motivation, whereby that form of motivation rests ultimately on a very general *conception* of community. I have in mind what has traditionally been called *the power of ideas* and what I will here call *the motivational power of novel ideas*. By *novel ideas* I mean broad conceptualizations of the world we experience that are, relative to our current conceptualizations, unusual, intellectually odd or challenging, and sometimes different in what they suggest for attitudes and action. By the *motivational power* of these ideas I refer to the power these new ideas can come to have to guide our thoughts and thus our actions. It is the power these ideas have when they "take" in us, that is, become "operative" in our ways of thinking about the world, and, in effect, constitute a part of "common knowledge" for us.

ON NOVEL IDEAS

It seems to me uncontroversial that novel ideas can come to have motivational power. Here are two examples of what I mean.

The first example is an egalitarian moral idea, namely, the idea that persons—all of them—have certain rights (e.g., "natural rights" or "basic rights") and are in that way morally on a par with one another. This idea is both widespread and familiar; it expresses an ideal that is profound for many people; it moves some people to conduct their lives in certain ways—in some cases in ways involving protest and radical political action. At one time this idea was novel, but over time it caught on and became motivating. Now it is to many of us not novel at all; we are used to it, and it is so entrenched in us that its way of structuring our thoughts about how persons are to be understood seems to us a matter of common knowledge. It is even operative among people whose governments do not take it seriously or even acknowledge it; and it survives even when there is controversy over what the basic rights are.

The second example is an interpretive idea about the conditions of life for many people. It holds that poverty is not necessarily a natural state that some members of society must be in but is instead a function of conventions, such as economic systems influencing political and legal systems. This idea that poverty is a conventional rather than natural state was a novel idea at one time; but over time it "took," that is, it caught on and became motivating, and now, again, it is to many of us not novel at all, even though we differ in our views of how we should respond to the poverty around us. If the sky is cloudy today, that is (in most cases) a natural fact, and while one may not like the fact, one is not morally offended by it. But if one becomes aware of extensive poverty in one's

local or national community, or even in the world community, one's reactions are different: if one attends to the situation and learns about its
details, one very likely will be offended by it. There is something wrong
with extensive, deep, life-stifling poverty. It ought not to exist.

Of course, even if poverty ought not to exist, and one believes that this
is so in a way that involves the idea that poverty is artificial rather than
natural, it does not follow that one will *do* anything about the poverty that
exists, for example, work to ameliorate or eradicate it. But the problem I
have in mind is not the one prompted by this fact that people sometimes
do not do what they believe they ought to do. (Sometimes people have
reasons they find compelling for not doing what they believe they ought
to do.) The motivation problem I have in mind is located at an earlier
point. It does not have to do with moving from understanding the right
to doing the right. It has to do with how candidate novel ideas come to
have standing in one's understanding of the right *so that* the familiar problem of choosing whether or not to do what one recognizes to be right *can
then arise* in a way that involves reference to those ideas.

How is it, then, that a new idea might not only intrigue us but also come
to *count* with us such that we think differently about certain elements in
our experience and perhaps, as a result, actually alter our conduct or ways
of life respecting those elements? If certain ideas (such as that all persons
have basic rights or that poverty is artificial) are "regulative" for us, and
thus operate as standing presumptions for our conduct, so that our *not*
acting in line with their normative content requires an explanation, how
do candidate novel ideas come to be regulative for us? I should say that
my interest in this question (in this discussion) is not in the part of it that
has to do with the analysis or assessment of ideas, that is, with the "contents" of a conception or with the arguments, evidence, or justifications
available to it. It is no part of my view that the questions of analysis and
assessment are not important or not answerable. But I suggest that the
"motivation problem" I have in mind remains, in particular cases, even
when the analytic and assessment questions are satisfactorily responded
to. Even when a broad conceptualization is clear, and the arguments for
it strong, it does not *follow* that it will "take" in one. And, too—perhaps
unfortunately—when a conceptualization is not clear, or the arguments
for it not strong, it sometimes "takes" in one nevertheless. My attention
here goes not to what makes a novel idea a good or bad idea; it goes instead to what is involved in an idea becoming a functioning part of one's
practical outlook in some domain of experience.[34]

Of course, the ideas I have mentioned—about persons and poverty—
are hardly novel for most of us. Let me next explore the future generations motivation problem by discussing a less familiar idea. It is an idea

important in environmental ethics. But while this idea may be familiar to theorists in environmental ethics, my impression is that it is not (yet) an idea that is operative among people generally.

AN ENVIRONMENTALIST IDEA

The idea in question belongs to the branch of environmentalism that goes beyond appeals to prudence in our use of the environment and its resources for human purposes. This branch of environmentalism holds that the environmental crisis we face in fact calls into question our sense of our own standing in the larger whole of nature itself.[35] In this view, while we may indeed develop and pursue public and personal strategies for cutting back our consumerist ways of life and increase our efforts in technological research and the development of alternative sources of energy, we must first rethink our place among the natural creatures, objects, and systems that make up our environment. Indeed, we must move away from our received anthropocentric sense of ourselves as the sole moral agents in the natural world to the cultivation of an "ecological conscience" that treats human beings as members *with* other members (i.e., other natural creatures, objects, and systems) of a larger whole, namely, the biotic community itself. A general prudence regarding the environment may permit us to continue to think of ourselves in the familiar terms of the anthropocentric ethical traditions we have inherited. But that response, so it is argued by the environmentalism I have in mind, is shallow and not morally adequate to the serious crisis we face. The development of a genuinely "ecological conscience" is, according to this environmentalism, the required next step in the ethical evolution of humankind.

This notion of "ecological conscience" involves relatively novel ideas, I think, but it is worth noting that ecological conscience itself is not totally unfamiliar to us. (It is not found only in the moral and cultural sensibility of "native peoples.") Thoreau's *Walden* is a classic of the Western literature we think of as American,[36] and Thoreau's combination book and journal elucidates the notion of ecological conscience in moving detail. Thoreau's love for Walden is not just "appreciation of nature" in the way in which from time to time most of us are moved by natural phenomena. This love for Walden has wrapped up in it Thoreau's responses to certain philosophical problems about how one is to live and what kind of person one is to be. To some extent Thoreau's responses are negative: they push us away from concern for the externals that tend to overwhelm our lives, such as property, material goods, power, and reputation. On the positive side, Thoreau drives us in on ourselves. The "individuality" that Thoreau is famous for encouraging turns out not to be a matter of the idiosyncrasies or features of temperament and possessions by which one differentiates oneself from others. It is, rather, the essential core of "significant and vital experiences" we all share.[37] Thoreau's "experiment in simple living" is "to live deliberately... to drive life into a corner, and reduce it to its lowest terms."[38] Among these significant and vital experiences, for Thoreau, is a sense of membership in the natural world involving a recognition of values in nature, that is, values *in* (not "projected into") the various items and systems that make up the natural order. Thoreau's critique of our life "in society," that is, life not "in the woods," is that we have raised ourselves above nature, subordinated it to our purposes, and made it instrumental to our material interests. Thoreau objects to the reduction of nature to "our property," and he admonishes us "to enjoy the land, but own it not."[39] His thought is that, in the larger view, we belong *with* the other creatures and elements he finds in his life at Walden under "the greater Benefactor and intelligence."[40] Our smaller view, whereby we give ourselves special standing in the order of things, he regards as the corruption of vanity.[41]

This idea of a form of membership in nature that involves the recognition of value *in* the environment and the items and systems that make it up is, to the environmentalism I am sketching, of central importance to the achievement of depth in our thinking about environmental crisis. Already in the foreword to *A Sand County Almanac*, Aldo Leopold writes, "We abuse land because we regard it as a commodity belonging to us."[42] When instead we regard ourselves as parts of the natural order, other parts of which have value, then "we see land as a community to which we belong," and "we may begin to use it with love and respect."[43] In *Philosophy Gone Wild* and *Environmental Ethics* by Holmes Rolston III,[44] the idea of value *in* nature is again a main object of attention, though now the philosophically problematic aspects of the idea are faced directly. Rolston indicates that to attempt to develop this idea is to "swim against the stream of a long-standing paradigm that conceives of value as [merely] a product of human interest satisfaction."[45] It is nevertheless his view (echoing Thoreau and Leopold) that nature is not to be reduced to "instrumental value" but, rather, is to be considered a reservoir of "intrinsic value" and that recognition of this fact is central to an adequate response to the environmental crisis.

NOTES ON THE POWER OF NOVEL IDEAS

What can we glean from this small discussion of novel ideas—two examples of ideas once novel but no longer so, one example of an idea now (relatively) novel but, as it were, a serious contender for a place in thought and action? What is it for novel ideas to "take" in us in such a way that thought and action are influenced? Could the idea of "ecological conscience"—an idea that radically reconceives our place in nature—come to have motivational power in us?

I offer some notes that respond to these questions—though my notes do not reach to the techniques and strategies involved, say, in politics or in coercive manipulations of persons, no matter how noble or benevolent their ends. My notes concern what it is for novel ideas to "take" at (I think) a more basic level. In any case, I would regret discovering that a positive result for future generations rests only on manipulation or external coercion of persons.

Notice first that for novel ideas to be motivating they apparently must be *interesting*—intellectually interesting—in some way or other. They must, so to speak, catch the attention of the mind. When classical theorists claim that persons have certain basic rights (whether government agrees or not), or Marx (for example) urges us to see that poverty is not natural but a function of conventions, or the environmentalist finds intrinsic value in the natural order—in all these cases there is some conceptual maneuvering occurring.[46] Reconceptualizations of familiar items (persons, poverty, the environment)[47] are proposed, and those of us concerned to understand the world and not just walk around in it become intellectually fascinated.

But that, of course, is not enough for "motivational power." An idea can be interesting in its manner of contrasting with current or received ideas but fail to be motivational. What else is involved?

I notice further, in the examples I have worked with, that in each case, beyond the reconceptualizing of familiar items, there is a *normative proposal,* that is, a proposal bearing on our attitudes and through them our actions. This seems to me germane to the issue of how an idea can have motivational power. For the point of a normative proposal is to urge us to adopt a new way of *valuing* what the novel idea is of or about. Thus, the reconceptualization carries with it, typically, implications concerning the importance of its subject and how it is to be treated. From this angle, then, the egalitarian basic rights theorist is saying that persons—all of them—are worthy of respect, whether they are tall or short, smart or dumb, religious or not, and they ought to be treated accordingly. Marx is saying that poverty is objectionable as well as eliminable, and we ought to think about and act toward it accordingly. Certainly the environmentalists are saying that the natural world and its constituent parts have intrinsic value and, thus, worth independent of human-projected value, and we ought to think about and act toward them accordingly.[48]

I think the normative element in the novel idea is important: the candidate novel idea offers not only a different reading of some item in or

part of experience but one that is charged with the energy of recommendation, demand, or objection. This aspect of the situation raises interesting and difficult questions about states of mind in both the "source" and
the "recipient" of the candidate idea insofar as it is possible for one to
receive a novel idea *as* recommendation or demand (or threat or opportunity) when no such thing is intended. But I will not pursue these com-
plexities here. The more intriguing point, for this discussion, is that even
when a novel idea is intellectually interesting and contains a normative
proposal (correctly received, say), this may not be sufficient for the idea
to "take" in one. Notoriously, normative proposals generally, even in the
form of justified ethical demands—for example, principled calls for respect
for items of this or that kind—do not necessarily move us into thought
and action in line with their contents. I ask again, what else is involved
when a novel idea comes to have power in us? In what follows I offer
some speculative notes regarding this question. I do not have a full answer to it, though I believe that the question itself has a place in the development of a comprehensive understanding of how ideas relate to action.[49]

The first note is reminiscent of one of Rousseau's themes in *A Discourse
on the Origin of Inequality* (1755).[50] It is that over and beyond the intellectual interest elements and the normative element in a novel idea, it *helps*
that novel idea be or become motivating if the idea "strikes a primitive
chord" in us. There are, of course, different kinds of "primitive chord striking." In one sort of case, we may imagine that the idea penetrates through
the conceptual layers we have taken on through education and under the
pressures of various social and cultural forces and reaches to some original experience we have had. Perhaps most of us have had our share of
experiences in which we have "felt" ourselves to be part of nature. The
environmentalist novel idea may function, in part, to recall one's experiences of this kind (if any), and insofar as the idea functions in this way, it
might somehow gain what I have been calling motivational power. It
might draw such power from the power of the original experience in
one—supposing, of course, that the original experience itself had salience
in a relevant positive or negative fashion.

In another sort of case, the primitive chord striking may be rather different. Here we imagine the situation in which one's life is filled with failure and frustration, and one's experience is confusing and filled with
moral-emotional dissonance. It seems to one, in such a case, that within
one's life routine ways of thinking are ineffective, and one's agency is
diminished. In these circumstances novel ideas can (in some cases) provide a combination of illumination and guidance that serves to facilitate
the recovery of agency, and when this is so it *helps* the novel ideas "take"
in one even though the "taking" is not guaranteed. I think that, in fact,

such recovery linked to novel ideas occurs—though it remains mysterious to me how the "gap" between the availability of the novel idea and it "taking" so that recovery is facilitated is to be described. Internally, the novel idea seems to sort experiences for one in helpful ways—"taking" might be reflected in one's sense of finally having "insights" into one's experiences—and the recovery of agency comes to seem possible to one. One is able to "move on" in one's life. There may be an "externalist" version of this sort of case, too. For it *helps* a novel idea become motivating if it speaks to or addresses (through its normative element) external facts or situations that are both troubling (e.g., they offend moral sensibility) and objects of repeated attention. For example, if it is a novel idea that our responsibility to aid others in distress extends far beyond those close to us (family members, friends) to suffering members of humankind in general, then it helps this novel idea gain in motivational power when one gives repeated attention to the troubling facts of destitution and inequality in levels of life available to members of humankind in today's flawed world community.[51] It appears that as we become more intimate with certain troubling facts, a novel idea that addresses them, even if initially strange, comes to seem serious, familiar, relevant, and finally (sometimes) even right. Again, in circumstances of these kinds, a novel idea may sort the troubling experiences and in doing so afford guidance for action.

A second note is this: Suppose a given novel idea urges one to respect items in a range different from the range whose items one is used to giving respect. Then (I think) one is more nearly ready to take this proposal seriously if one has already learned to give respect to certain other items that are also outside the range of those items to which one is used to according respect. For example, I suspect it becomes easier to be moved to respect items in the environment, and ecosystems of various dimensions, if one has already begun to offer respect to, say, animals as well as human beings. Perhaps, indeed, if one is used to offering respect to persons, and then the relevant idea "takes" in one such that one also offers respect to animals, one might then find motivating the idea that still other items in the environment (e.g., wilderness tracts or, more generally, ecosystems of various dimensions) are worthy of respect.

The third note looks at the other end of the motivational process. I think that if a novel idea in fact comes to have power for one, then one cannot, as it were, "go back." If the idea that poverty is a function of conventions "takes" in me, then the earlier notion, that poverty is a natural state for some people, is lost to me. Similarly, if the environmentalist's idea of ecological conscience "takes" in me, I think the older idea, whereby the natural order and its items are merely resources or instruments for me, is lost to me. Of course, one might intellectually study or review older ideas, and

as a result of such study or review one might move to a revised or deep-
ened version of an older idea. But motivationally a novel idea that "takes"
seems to cancel the *power* of the original older idea. Later one might move
from a novel idea to still another novel idea in some domain of experience; but, in general, when a novel idea becomes motivating, it diminishes
and perhaps terminates the power of the particular idea it replaces or
supplants.

I should mention that I do not hold that novel ideas always motivate
(when they do) because they make one "feel good" or otherwise "serve
one's interest." I am reminded here of Aldo Leopold's sad remark, "One
of the penalties of an ecological education is that one lives alone in a world
of wounds."[52] Indeed, to take seriously the environmentalist's idea of ecological conscience in today's world would be to bring into view many
"wounds" to our planet; but this (ordinarily) would not lead to one "feeling good," and whether or not it serves one's interests would depend on
the circumstances and the nature of those interests. When a novel idea
"takes," this is not always because of the standard motivational factors
recognized by consumerist ideologies and interests-oriented politics.

The fourth note makes apparent that my observations here are indeed
speculative. Suppose that the environmentalist's idea that nature has intrinsic value has power for one. Perhaps this is so because it combines
intellectual interest and a normative proposal and somehow reaches into
one, through the conceptual layering, to make contact with original experiences one has had. Suppose further that the appeal of this idea, when
first encountered, was immediate and easy for one. (Perhaps it was put
forward by very able teachers.) In contrast, in other cases this general
subject brings to mind, an idea coming to have motivational power is
much more labor intensive and struggle filled. (The "taking" comes
harder, so to speak.) Consider, for example, the case of the novel ideas
offered to the (alleged) hopeless drunk "bottoming out" after, say, a thirty-
year drinking history. There are cases in which through the good work of
Alcoholics Anonymous (AA), self-destructing human beings have been
coaxed back to sobriety and then have successfully moved on to vigorous lives involving families and careers. Now, "ideas" are not the only
things involved in the typical AA recovery story, of course. The recover-
ing alcoholic in AA is surrounded and supported by people and invited
to move slowly and patiently through daily study and discussion of the
AA twelve-step recovery program (the "novel idea," for the purposes of
this note). This is not the place to explain this program or discuss this fascinating sort of case in detail.[53] What is important for this part of my discussion is that the ideas that AA offers its new members are often *not*
motivating *at first*; they *become* so as time passes and as the new member,

typically suffering the residual effects of his or her past and greatly fearful of (and at once attracted by) the prospect of returning to drink, takes
slow steps among the members and with the program of AA. In some
cases, over time, the novel ideas, perhaps even hated in the beginning,
somehow come to have power. The dynamics of this process need to be
better understood. They involve pain and suffering in a way that is not
so apparent in the imagined case in which the environmentalist's idea
"takes." But I cannot explore the process here; I only acknowledge its existence and in that way record it among these notes.

REMARKS

I end with some perhaps obvious caveats. The first of these is a recognition of the difficulty of theorizing about what I have described as an idea
coming to have "motivational power." It seems to be a fact—one taken
into account in the discussion above—that an idea that "takes" in one
person may not "take" in another, despite, say, the achievement of a similar level in the idea's clarity and justification for both persons. One might
worry, then, that the "taking" of an idea in a person is "subjective" in a
sense that prevents it from being an object of a theory or philosophical
account; perhaps there is no list of "conditions" that a theory or account
might provide such that when those conditions are satisfied, then the candidate idea "takes." In this view the ideas that are operational in us do
not come to be so (merely) by meeting conditions of clarity or justification, or satisfying other rational or cognitive tests, and it is inferred that
"coming to be operational" is outside the ken of theory.

My thought here is that it does not follow from this worry about subjectivity that nothing illuminating can be said about what it is for an idea
to "take" when it does. Doubtless many different things are involved in
an idea "taking" or "not taking" in a person—things as disparate as social pressures, misunderstandings of facts, vulnerability to self-deception
or gullibility, needs for stability, self-confidence, even chemical imbalances
in the brain. Still, the facts that there is such complexity and that an idea
that "takes" in one person may not "take" in another do not themselves
render the "taking" of an idea opaque to theory or philosophical description. Besides, apart from how far a theory might be helpful in understanding these facts (and illuminating the complexity), the initial point that the
"taking" of ideas is logically beyond satisfaction of conditions of clarity
and justification itself has a place in a philosophical account of how ideas
relate to thought and action. There is no reason yet to infer that this "taking" cannot be an object of theory.

The second caveat is that I hold no special brief for "novel ideas" in general. I recognize that not all novel ideas are morally admirable, even as I also recognize (especially in retrospect) that some novel ideas are meritorious and should come to have motivational power. Clearly, the sheer fact that an idea involves a reconceptualization of experience plus a normative proposal does not mean that that idea *should* "take." We must be on guard with novel ideas, as with ideas generally. Still, apart from how we attempt to clarify and thus understand the ideas we find interesting and then assess them in terms of cogency, internal consistency, evidence, and justification, there is, I think, a question about what it is for them to come to have motivational power that should be given attention. Nothing I have said suggests that a novel idea coming to be motivating is either easy or simple; nothing I have said means to minimize uncritically the power (or merit) of older ideas we possess and live by; nothing I have said limits what may count as "motivational factors" affecting thought and action. In some cases it is a good thing for a novel idea to come to have motivational power; in other cases it is not a good thing; in cases of either kind what it is for a novel idea to come to have motivational power is a philosophical puzzle.

7

✢

Indifference and Reconciliation

In the studies above I have been interested not so much in the principles of morality as in the motivation we have for paying attention to them. But I have found it to be important that my subject is not motivation simpliciter, that is, motivation somehow in itself (and hence out of context), but, rather, motivation issues generated by taking seriously the demands of the moral life in certain areas.

Morality is an artifact[1]—that is, it is a framework of rules, principles, and policies carrying with it some distinctive demands, permissions, invitations, and challenges to agency, including challenges to the motivational side of our nature as human beings. My view is that we ordinarily think of the morally good person not as someone who merely obeys the moral rules but as someone who takes such rules seriously and who, as a consequence, has a certain moral psychology. This is not to say that all morally good persons (decent people) have the same feelings about life and its constituent activities, tasks, and dilemmas, any more than it is to say that they all have the same moral opinions on all moral issues. But it is to say that morally good persons, when, for example, they understand that they have done something wrong, suffer moral pain in some form (guilt, shame, regret, remorse, etc.), depending on circumstances and differences in types of wrongdoing. It is also to say that they prize (rather than merely know about) the self-respect that is theirs when their basic rights as full members of the moral community are respected and when they enjoy a reasonable autonomy in their relationship with their own plans of life. It is also to say that they have the compassion to appreciate what it is for others to have serious needs and thus are moved to respond,

131

and, too, that they see the point of arguments appealing for sacrifice relative to the rights and needs of people who will live many years in the future yet whom they cannot know personally.[2] It is also to say that they have a sense of themselves as agents with histories, and when those histories are marked by moral flaws, this troubles them and draws down their energy and their capacities for self-realization and compassion.

In this account, decent people are not just "persons of principle"; they have, as a part of their moral goodness, moral-emotional lives. My aim in this book has been to explore some of what is involved, for morally good people, in having moral-emotional lives.[3] In this final discussion I wish to explore a rather negative aspect of what it is for decent people to have moral-emotional lives. I want to discuss what might be called "ordinary indifference" to morality. I should emphasize the word *ordinary* here. I will approach this topic by touching on certain accounts of moral indifference, but although the agents characterized by these accounts are interesting and important, I want in the end to characterize the moral indifference of ordinary decent people—an indifference of a sort that is much more familiar and everyday-like than these accounts suggest. I think real-life morally good persons *are* vulnerable to flat, episodic bouts of indifference to morality—indeed, I think this sort of experience is also a part of human nature. The indifference in question, though familiar and known to all, raises what I call a "reconciliation problem." If taking morality seriously is a constituent part of the makeup of morally good persons— enough so as to provide them with moral-emotional life—then how are they to think about and live with their own vulnerability to episodic indifference to morality?

ALIENATION

I think a first attempt at understanding what is involved in "indifference to morality" might target the idea of *alienation* for study. Intuitively, to be alienated is to be separated from something in a way that is considered normatively to be negative or unfortunate. And while *alienation* is a messy term, it may be that a study of a detailed interpretation of the idea of alienation could throw light on moral indifference. Perhaps moral indifference is a sort of alienation. Perhaps alienation produces or cultivates moral indifference.

The idea of alienation has been invoked in moralized political criticism of society to call attention to a *separation* between *individual* and *society* that the critic finds objectionable. But the notions of "separation," "society," and even "individual" are, by themselves, unclear. In an interpretation informed by Kantian moral theory, the claimed separation of individual and society concerns society's manner of treatment of its members. The moral point is that society—chiefly though perhaps not solely through the workings of its economic institutions and practices—alienates its members in the sense that it treats them in instrumental terms, that is, it "reduces" persons to "means only" or "means mainly" and thus accords them less than the respect owed to equal autonomous agents who are, morally, on a par with each other. I suspect that an interpretation making this point may fit the critique of capitalist society from the idea of alienation given by Marx in the famous essay fragment "Alienated Labor."[4] Such an interpretation, suitably qualified, could also be incorporated in a form of philosophical liberalism (e.g., that of John Rawls)[5] that supports the welfare state and countenances capitalism or socialism in the economic life of society. The interpretation I have in mind connects, too, with the account given earlier (in chapter 4) of "basic rights self-respect." In the remarks that follow I focus on Marx's critique.

If one approaches Marx's early theory of alienation in a way that reflects Kant's moral philosophy, then it is plausible, in my view, to see its general theme to be that the fault in capitalist society—even capitalist society that is "liberal" in its political life—is its incompatibility with the moral nature of human beings. I take it that if the case exhibiting such a fault were to be made out, then we might have a critique powerful enough to justify a radical restructuring of capitalist society even when it is liberal in its political life.[6] But my more modest purpose here is to explore whether the alienation from society that Marx has in mind might, from the angle of our interest in moral psychology, be or contribute to a form of indifference to morality in the people who suffer it. How, then, is capitalism supposed to be incompatible with human nature?

Let me schematize the account given in Marx's essay "Alienated Labor" in the following way:

1. Capitalism involves the institution of private property.
2. The institution of private property operates in such a way as to *alienate* persons.
3. When persons are alienated they are alienated from something: more fully, they are in *relation to x* such that *x* is both *independent of* (Marx says "external to") them and *usable*, that is, usable by *A* for purpose(s) *e*.
4. The variable *x* here, according to Marx,[7] covers (at least) "products," "labor," "species-being," and "other persons." That is, the institution of private property operates so as to alienate persons from the products of their labor, from their labor itself, from their "species-being," and from other persons.

5. Persons being in the condition of alienation is *objectionable,* for then
   (a) The products of the labor of persons may be used by other agents
       (or agencies) in such a way as to bring the latter "profit" with-
       out appropriate return to the former.
   (b) The labor of persons may be "exploited," that is, used by other
       agents (or agencies) for the purposes (e.g., material gain, repu-
       tation, power) of the latter without appropriate return to the
       former.
   (c) Persons' "species-being" (their "essence," I think Marx means),
       namely, their laboring function or capacity to produce, is made
       independent of them and construed as usable—which is to say
       usable by *A* for *e,* where *A* may be those persons or other agents
       · or agencies and where *e* may be the purpose(s) of those persons,
       of others, or of neither.
   (d) Similarly, other persons may be viewed as both independent of
       oneself and usable.

Notice that a and b under point 5 do not by themselves support the
characteristic radical social prescription that accompanies the Marxist critique. For what they specify to be objectionable *could* be dealt with by the
establishment and enforcement of fair rules concerning what is to count
as "appropriate" return within the framework of a liberal capitalist society. They do not by themselves require, say, the abolition of private property—though this is not to say that they lend no support at all to the case
for that radical prescription.

Let us focus, then, on c and d under point 5. The following thoughts
come to mind. First, despite (or perhaps because of) the technical term
species-being, these points bring to mind the Kantian imperative that persons are to be treated as "ends."[8] That is, as I attempt to understand the
point of Marx's claims in this area of his treatment of the idea of alienation, I find that I understand them best, or most easily, when I read them
with the language of Kant's humanity imperative in mind. Second, there
may nevertheless be a difference between Marx and Kant concerning how
this imperative is to be understood. The difference might be expressed in
the following way: for Kant the ideal is treatment of persons as ends and
never as means *only;* for Marx the ideal may be treatment of persons as
ends and *never* as means. Third, it may even be that, in principle, the
Kantian expression of the ideal is compatible with capitalism. The critique
we are considering (i.e., a critique strong enough to support the radical
prescription of the abolition of private property) must argue, among other
things, that the ideal expressed sans the final *only* is not compatible with
capitalism, even, in particular, a just liberal capitalism incorporating guarantees of rights and certain welfare transfer practices.[9]

Consider 5(c) in more detail. It may be that this part of Marx's critique is simply obscure as it stands, insofar as the notion of "species-being" (or the alternative notion of "essence") is obscure. But perhaps we do not need a philosophically full account of "species-being" or "essence" (or a justification of the identification of the two) for present purposes. Perhaps the point is clear enough if we say the following: According to 5(c) the fault in capitalism is that it makes of one's productive capacities (which may involve common or rare talents, abilities, or powers) something for one or others to view instrumentally, that is, as "tools" to be used for such purposes as one, or others, may have (or be forced to have), given social necessity, social position, and so on. In general, in this view capitalism imposes on persons a pervasive ideology according to which productive activity (i.e., what flows from productive capacities) is not valued for its own sake, or for the sake of "self-realization," but for the results it may bring.[10]

I do not mean to suggest by these few remarks that the Marxist form of the criticism from alienation is successful or unsuccessful against liberal capitalism. It may be that a controversial "utopian" element is present in what I include in 5(c) and 5(d), for while the account is meant to be a criticism of liberal capitalism, its presupposition appears to be that the ideal society is one in which persons are treated as ends and *never* as means, that is, the ideal is construed as a situation in which social intercourse ("life with others") never involves persons "using" one another for purposes that are not necessarily those of the latter. This ideal, while conceptually coherent, may seem so out of reach as to be a practical impossibility. The *form* of a liberal response to the Marxist critique might then begin to emerge in the dialectic. The response would consist of arguing, first, that no society in which persons are never treated as means is a real possibility and, second, that liberal capitalism can, in principle, be structured so that persons are treated as ends and never as means *only*. The latter can be done by political acts that, through guarantees of certain rights, liberties, and opportunities, specify what it is for persons to be "ends"; in general, the idea is that we can bring political and other institutions to bear on the capitalism of our economic life in such a way as to make liberal capitalist society as a whole morally tolerable when judged by a reasonable interpretation of the Kantian humanity imperative.

Now, when the Marxist criticism from alienation is interpreted in a Kantian way, it assumes a certain *conception of the person* that construes the dignity of individuals (their moral status as "ends") as a function of their equal rational nature. In this account, the "self" is essentially a capacity for choice, and what morality protects (e.g., when it is claimed that liberal capitalism is incompatible with the moral nature of human beings) is this *capacity for choice* and not any particular *choices*. Further, this account of the self places the self prior to one's choices, and thus what may flow from them, such as community relationships, projects, or features of character, are, logically, contingent and "outside" the self per se.[11] Above all, we need to observe that none of the contents of such choices (e.g., community ties, linkages to others, projects, features of character)—*constitutes* the self "proper." The great Kantian theory of the autonomous self as the central ingredient in moral agency, when applied in interpretation of the Marxist critique of liberal capitalism from alienation, makes the central point of the critique be that capitalism fails to respect the autonomy—the prized capacity for choice—of the moral agent and instead coerces the individual in the exercise of that capacity. Capitalism "reduces" human beings essentially or mainly to "means" in *that* way. In the account thus generated, the Marxist critique from alienation assumes that there is an important distinction between the self qua capacity for choice and the contents of the choices (community ties, projects, etc.) *of* that self.

Does, then, the Marxist critique of capitalist society from the idea of alienation provide an account of the ordinary episodic "indifference to morality" that even morally good people experience from time to time? I would have to say that the alienation Marx characterizes seems to me very important. It is hardly an attractive feature of capitalist society that it should entail alienation.[12] Still, the alienation Marx has in mind is not, I think, equivalent to the moral indifference experienced from time to time by decent people. One can imagine the case (as Marx did) in which people are suffering alienation but are not indifferent to morality at all—in fact, they may very well be appealing to morality for the judgment that the alienation they are stuck with in their economic and political lives is objectionable. Of course, this is to imagine a situation in which the people in question, while they suffer alienation, have such a strong sense of themselves as moral agents, that is, as members of the moral community (a community transcending their capitalist society), that they rise to protest the situation in their capitalist society. The other possibility is that they do not have this strong sense of themselves as members of the moral community. They may recognize the terms of their existence in capitalist society for what they are—they are systemically "used" by their society—but they may be, in effect, psychologically numbed by their situation. Their moral psychology may come, or seem, to be that of resignation more than anything else. But even this is no necessary consequence. Capitalist society radiates a conception of persons as competitive users of one another, and some persons who are caught up in this psychology are probably calculative, and some among them are probably prone to anger and resentment. A psychology of this sort, like the one involving resignation, is not likely to cultivate and nourish the sorts of attitudes that go with "taking morality seriously." In a capitalist society, appeals to morality might be reserved for public ceremonies and other special occasions, safely located outside the hurly-burly of everyday life. There is a *sort* of "indifference to morality" here of course, but it does not seem to be the kind of troubling episodic moral indifference that morally good people are vulnerable to. The alienation that Marx has in mind is grounded in something "external," namely, a form of organization of economic life that is objectionable; but the moral indifference that I have in mind is "internal"—its ground is moral nature itself, apart from whatever may be our external social, economic, and political circumstances.

MENTAL ILLNESS

Let me next touch briefly on another factor often associated with moral indifference. I refer to "mental illness." The intuitive idea here is that those who suffer mental illness often exhibit disinterest in morality and a skewed understanding of the demands that go with it. This association is not "tight," of course, for it is not unusual for those suffering one or another form of mental illness to be very sensitive indeed to moral value, the imperatives of morality, and their own rights.

I cannot here offer a full discussion of mental illness. Fortunately, for our purposes we have a good book on our topic by a writer competent in both psychology and law. I refer to *The Rules of Insanity: Moral Responsibility and the Mentally Ill Offender* by Carl Elliott.[13] I will proceed by following Elliott's discussion in some detail and then commenting on his results with our questions about moral indifference in mind.

The subject of Elliott's discussion is how wrongdoers who are mentally ill "fit" in the moral community. Elliott speaks of our "scheme of moral responsibility" (104) and our "universe of morally responsible agents" (118) and then wonders when and how far those who suffer mental disorders of one sort or other are to be held to account for any wrongdoing they perform or commit. Elliott means to focus on moral responsibility rather than legal responsibility, though there are words about the latter in most chapters. In respect of background ethical theory, the account leans on the views about voluntary action and responsibility in Aristotle's *Nicomachean Ethics* rather than, say, the moral theories of Kant or the utilitarians.

Elliott's subject seems to me timely, for our public discussion now often draws attention to cases in which attempts are made to excuse, set aside, or diminish wrongdoing by reference to an increasingly varied number of psychological conditions people may suffer. To take these cases seriously is to experience having one's moral intuitions jerked around—and sometimes baffled.[14] When we learn that *J* has murdered many people in the local fast food restaurant, we are outraged and filled with moral anger. When we *then* learn that *J*'s life history is filled with abuse and deprivation, leaving him (say the experts) with "disorders" of kind *K, M,* and *O,* our hearts go out to him, and our anger is frustrated if not dissolved. But *then* what? When we look at the agent's life history, we cannot just "go back" to outrage and anger; when we look at the action, we cannot just "forgive," "forget," or "do nothing." We end up stuck in a negative moral-emotional experience that is internally "conflicted," to say the least.

Elliott's discussion is helpful about this situation (and others). It proposes to explain the seriousness of the mental disorders that are invoked in such cases, that is, how powerful these disorders can (legitimately) be in providing "moral exoneration" from responsibility. I believe that a philosophical treatment of this matter has at least three things to do. On a first level, it should provide an account that sorts and explains the disorders. On a second level, it needs a further account that indicates when disorders of different kinds do or do not defeat our ascriptions of responsibility. On a third level, it should identify and assess the general principles operating behind the scenes to explain why the accounts on the other levels are what they are. Elliott's discussion seems to me very instructive on the first level, at least plausible if not uncontroversial on the second level, but not fully filled out on the third level.

In response to the first-level issue, Elliott provides a "moral taxonomy" (his phrase). With Aristotle in mind, the idea is that the "normal" case is one in which a person is held (morally) responsible for his or her intentional actions, such that responsibility is a function of the *connection* between the person and his or her action. The disorders that provide responsibility exemptions, then, break the connection or render it "absent" (123–24), and they do this through (again, following Aristotle) finding the agent trapped in *compulsion* or caught up in *ignorance.* In the former case we have "volitional disorders," including, for example, kleptomania, necrophilia, exhibitionism, and pyromania. In the latter case we have "cognitive disorders" involving a person's beliefs, including schizophrenia, bipolar affective disorder, psychotic depression, or extreme delusion. Interestingly, Elliott's taxonomy goes on to include cases in which a person suffers radical psychological change so that we may have to say that he or she is "not the same person." And it goes even beyond that to cases in which extreme disorders (e.g., the incapacitation and incompetence in severe chronic schizophrenia) place sufferers outside our moral community. In all these cases Elliott's account tends to exempt sufferers from responsibility.

The situation is different, however, with *personality disorders*. For Elliott, the move toward exemption from responsibility is here largely halted. Personality disorders are

> relatively longstanding, maladaptive character traits that may affect a person's life dramatically, often making her miserable, perhaps more often making other people miserable. People with personality disorders are troubling because very often they come from backgrounds that argue for sympathy and understanding; on the other hand, they often behave very badly, and do it intentionally. [3]

The last point is important, for in Elliott's account the personality disorders "should *not* be an excuse" because "a personality disorder does not break the connection between agent and action: the person with a personality disorder ordinarily *intended* to act as he did" (124). Elliott makes an exception to his denial of exemption here for the psychopath: "The psychopath is exceptional because he does not appear to understand fully the moral aspects of his actions," and "without understanding the moral aspects of one's actions, one cannot be held fully responsible for them" (124).

While I find Elliott's discussion very helpful, I nevertheless have certain difficulties with the view. First, any view that allows exemptions for disorders of some kind or other raises an epistemological issue for participants in ordinary moral life. Elliott says very little about "how we tell" whether the persons we deal with are genuinely sufferers of this or that disorder in the taxonomy. Late in the book, when he discusses what it is for persons to "fall above and below the threshold of responsible agency," Elliott compares judgments of responsible agency with judgments "made routinely by clinicians who must decide whether patients are mentally capable of making decisions about their medical care" (122). But the comparison is left without specifics. Responsible agency is said to involve, for example, "the ability to communicate, to deliberate, to manipulate information, to have some degree of knowledge about one's actions" (122), and so forth. There is nothing obviously false here, nor is there anything particularly helpful. One wants to know how to "implement" or "operationalize" such general notions. I cannot tell, from Elliott's text, whether "clinicians" know how to do this or whether they, like us, stumble in the dark a lot.

Second, I am not yet convinced that personality disorders do not yield exemptions from responsibility. The basic fact that in cases involving personality disorders the connection between action and agent is preserved seems somehow beside the point, and this is so even when this point is supplemented with Elliott's further points that judgments of moral responsibility are "one-shot affairs," that is, they are "judgments about single actions" (65) and not judgments about character or even judgments about whether the action was good or bad (66). Suppose *J* is a chronic risk taker and is now about to test his new parachute with the special large holes in it by performing a jump. Our judgment that his ensuing jump is responsible (because the connection between it and his agency is preserved) is simply unacceptable *as* a judgment about responsibility—*unless J* "being responsible" means nothing more normatively than that "*J* jumped." Clearly, the *J* in the case sketched is a person who has to be saved from himself (i.e., from his chronic risk-taking personality disorder), and if we do not act accordingly, we should be blamed. But we do not approach him, in my view, as a person who is *responsible* for what he does when he jumps (nor, in this case, as a person who is merely "being foolish"). My thought is that the notion of responsibility is, as it were, logically stubborn: it resists being reduced to "agency." Perhaps ascriptions of responsibility entail ascriptions of agency, and thus volitional disorders cancel responsibility by canceling agency. It does not follow that ascriptions of agency are or imply ascriptions of responsibility: personality disorders may well allow agency but still (in certain cases) cancel responsibility.

Finally, let me comment on the lack of discussion by Elliott of what I call a third level. Why should responsibility exemptions (for those "inside" our moral community) be limited to what can be analyzed in terms of "ignorance" and "compulsion"? Perhaps they should be limited in this way, but, philosophically, one wants to ask why. Constitutional shyness is neither a volitional disorder of the ignorance or compulsion sort (I think), nor is it what Elliott would classify as personality disorder (I think), yet it can paralyze its sufferer in ordinary life and is surely responsibility exempting in certain contexts. I cannot discuss other candidates here, though it would be necessary to do so in a full commentary. Why not simply allow that responsibility exemptions are provided by *whatever* condition (genuinely) blocks an exercise of will under principles relevant to the agent's situation and then approach candidate conditions with as empirically open a mind as one can muster? Clearly, agency can be "stuck" or "distorted" in many different ways, given unevenness and difference in the results of nature's lottery and social contingency.[15] Elliott's discussion is not self-critical enough about its own acceptance of the Aristotelian base for understanding exemptions from responsibility.

I suppose the simple thing to say, after this much discussion of Elliott's views on mental illness and responsibility, is that mental illness and the episodic moral indifference of ordinary decent people are not related.

Mental illness may cause a person to be indifferent to morality (or, in very extreme cases, indifferent to most everything). But it would be far-fetched, I think, to "reduce" the troubling indifference to "volitional disorders" or "personality disorders." My own thought is that the indifference I want to call attention to is something that we are "stuck" with—it is, as it were, a natural part of moral personality—but it is not a sort of illness.

It might help to elaborate slightly. If *J*'s child just died, and *J* is absorbed with grief, morality (surely) *understands*—and does not press on *J* (right then) his responsibility for others or much in the way of other moral imperatives. That much seems obvious. But if *J*'s lawnmower broke, and this irritates him, morality may "understand" the irritation—but it does not suspend pressing on *J* his responsibility for others or any other imperatives of morality.

Suppose *J*'s child dies, and years pass, and *J* does not take up again his responsibilities. He remains (as it were) *stuck* in grieving. We may feel sorry for him, urge him to get counseling, and push him to "bounce back" and "get on with his life." But is this just "us" doing the urging from our concern for *J*, or does *morality* do this urging and pushing as well? Does morality teach that *J ought* to get on with his life (and his responsibilities) as a matter of *duty*? If *J* does *not* do so and remains stuck in his grief, does morality *criticize* him or even condemn him?

Our responses (as real persons) may be mixed. Some of us may be saddened by *J*'s plight and try to give him support and urge him on—but be patient with him if he cannot move on (yet). Others of us, after a "reasonable time," may become impatient—even angry—with *J*. We (these others of us) may suspect *J* of self-pity and soon find ourselves thinking that *J* "has no right" to withdraw from life, to "isolate," to fail (refuse) to do his part for himself and for others. One has, after all, but one life to live. Of course, if *J* is *really* stuck in his grief—if he is absorbed, paralyzed, victimized by it—the impatience of "you have no right" claims of those others of us will seem like *moralizing* to *J* and perhaps to others as well.

What is "moralizing" anyway? Well, in the type of case I am concerned with here, I guess moralizing involves one pressing *J* to do *x*, as what *J* ought to do, when it seems plain to *J* that he *cannot* do *x*, just as *J* recognizes that the moralizer believes that *J* can do *x*. To be the recipient of moralizing is to be treated unfairly. The one who moralizes would, of course, object to that characterization (moralizing) of what he or she says.

It is worth adding, though, that moralizing is not necessarily bad, wrong, or unjustified.[16] In some cases moralizing a person is in the service of exhortation or encouragement, and when the victim meets the terms thus imposed (if he or she is able), even he or she grants that a good thing has happened. It may be, too, that moralizing is a necessary part of certain one-to-one relational practices, for example, parenting, mentoring, or friendship. But this is not to immunize moralizing in these settings from criticism; parents, children, mentors, those mentored, and friends can all report instances of unjustified moralizing.

Is the ordinary occasional moral indifference of decent people *like J*'s grief—so that morality may ring the changes on it in the fashion "we" do when J's grief is prolonged? J's grief is not illness, and yet morality "exempts" J from life for a time on its account—even though at some point we and morality both get impatient with J being stuck in it, and we (if not morality) may moralize at J (and be uneasy with ourselves for doing so, should we recognize our moralizing for what it is). Whatever the precise dynamics of our responses to grief, I am inclined to say that we are not *patient* with moral indifference in others or ourselves in the way we are with grief in another's life. Even though we may recognize that we, too, experience moral indifference from time to time, we do not tolerate it.

INDIFFERENCE WITH A POINT

Perhaps the most colorful account of our episodic moral indifference is that of Dostoevsky. In *Notes from Underground*,[17] Dostoevsky is concerned with *freedom*. But he is interested in it in a special way. Consider these two questions: (1) As a metaphysical doctrine: are we (in fact) free? (2) As a moral-psychological doctrine: what kind of beings are we? In his discussion Dostoevsky constantly runs these two questions together.

My perhaps flip way of understanding Dostoevsky's position is that we are condemned by our nature to be free—*and* it is a misfortune to be free—*and* it is our glory to be free. More elaborately, Dostoevsky wants to suggest that (a) in the metaphysical issue of freedom versus determinism, freedom is true; (b) the popular received conception of human beings as *rational calculators* in their own *interests* is importantly wrong; and (c) what is ultimately important to us is the freedom that conditions "personality" and "individuality."

What persuades Dostoevsky that we are free? Well, in the first instance (and interestingly), two things—"spite" and "perversity":

> Shower upon him every earthly blessing, drown him in a sea of happiness, so that nothing but bubbles of bliss can be seen on the surface; give him economic prosperity, such that he should have nothing else to do but sleep, eat cakes and busy himself with the continuation of his species, and even then out of sheer ingratitude, sheer spite, man would play you some nasty trick.[18]

What is to be done with the millions of facts that bear witness that men, *consciously*, that is, fully understanding their real interests, have left them in the background and have rushed headlong on another path, to meet peril and danger, compelled to this course by nobody and by nothing, but, as it were, simply disliking the beaten track, and have obstinately, willfully, struck out another difficult, absurd way, seeking it almost in the darkness.[19]

The argument, then, so far as the issue of freedom versus determinism goes, is really very simple: any prediction of my behavior can be thwarted as long as I know about it. The determinist's explanations are, so far as first-person sensibility is concerned, simply irrelevant. As a matter of practical fact, if one lets me know what one expects or predicts that I will do, then I *might* (or might not) do the opposite. We are not "rational calculators" in our own interests. We are not only capable of "perversity"—we are driven by it.

All this is interesting and provocative, of course. But I find myself most intrigued by Dostoevsky's doctrine of what persons, down deep, are like. He holds, apparently, that we are all (down deep) "underground folk."[20] We are not only free in the sense of being unpredictable; we are also *deeply* perverse. And this is no mere "streak of perversity": "Choice can, of course, if it chooses, be in agreement with reason. But *very often*, and even most often, choice is utterly and stubbornly opposed to reason . . . and . . . and . . . do you know that that, too, is profitable, sometimes even praiseworthy?"[21]

Why is it that choice "most often" opposes reason, and how is it that this is "profitable" and sometimes "praiseworthy," that is, a good thing? The answer goes as follows:

Of course, this very stupid thing, this caprice of ours, may be in reality . . . more advantageous for us than anything else on earth, especially in certain cases. And in particular it may be more advantageous than any advantage even when it does us obvious harm, and contradicts the soundest conclusions of our reason concerning our advantage—for in any circumstances it preserves for us what is most precious and most important—that is, our personality, our individuality.[22]

So freedom is, as it were, a two-sided coin for Dostoevsky: on the down side we get the risk of meaninglessness, the experience of alienation and perhaps despair, and a certain trivialization of our pursuits; but on the up side we get, through choice, the chance to make for ourselves our own personalities, our own individualities: "Yet I think man will never renounce real suffering, that is, destruction and chaos. Why, suffering is the sole origin of consciousness. Though I did lay it down at the beginning that consciousness is the greatest misfortune for man, yet I know man prizes it and would not give it up for any satisfaction."[23] We pay a certain price for the choice that allows us to develop personality and individuality: "Suffering means doubt, negation";[24] "The direct legitimate fruit of consciousness is inertia, that is, conscious sitting-with-the-hands-folded"; "To begin to act, you know, you must first have your mind completely at ease and no trace of doubt left in it. Why, how am I, for example, to set my mind at rest? . . . Where are my foundations? Where am I to get them from?"[25]

My impression of this colorful doctrine is that while it certainly provides, through its notion that perversity is a "built-in" of human nature, an account of a *sort* of indifference to morality, what is for Dostoevsky a reflection of spite and perversity is not the moral indifference that I suggest morally good people are vulnerable to and troubled by as part of their moral-emotional nature. This is not to say that Dostoevsky's view is wrong or not insightful. It is rather to say that its exotic negativity about human nature probably runs away with more modest facts (insofar as we are all supposed to be "underground folk," according to Dostoevsky). One way of indicating how Dostoevsky's account misses the point I want to make, or simply makes some other point, is to say that Dostoevskian moral indifference, rooted in perversity and spite, is indifference with a point. That is, the account points to something we can (indeed) do, namely, the "opposite" whenever something is predicted of us, and then it dresses up that small capacity in a defiant language of freedom and individuality. This is fine—and it makes for stirring reading. I am all for freedom and individuality (though I am not much of a fan of belligerence or defiance as a mode for the expression of these good things). But, again, the peculiar twist or tone Dostoevsky gives to his celebration of freedom and individuality is not what I think of as the troubling episodic indifference to morality known to decent people.

INDIFFERENCE WITH NO POINT

Perhaps the forms of moral indifference I have reviewed, together with my responses or reactions to them, are enough to suggest something of the nature of the indifference to morality that I wish to characterize. This indifference is not, and is not parasitic on, "self-interest," I think. And it is not really "cynicism" either. Nor is it (mere) academic moral skepticism, cognitively surfacing at the odd moment.[26] The moral indifference I have in mind is not as directed or "active" in its makeup as self-interest or cynicism. It is, as it were, "flat" in affective character. It is a sort of "uninterest" rather than "disinterest" (the latter, again, is too directed and active). It is a kind of "passing" on a given moral imperative—not because one is busy with something else, too tired or stressed, or taken by a competing imperative. One is *just* "unmoved" by the moral demand. There is no "because" behind or beneath it. At the same time we are usually quite aware of our indifference or uninterest. And this makes it troubling to us because it flies in the face of our moral goodness, constituted as it is by a commitment to taking morality seriously. It appears that the goodness we strive to realize is frustrated (from time to time) by a vulnerability to an uninterest that is itself a part of the moral-emotional nature by which we take morality seriously. It is as if we have a "nature" that is not fully up to the aspirations of our finest capacities. If Dostoevsky finds perversity and spite in our nature, redeemed as they are in his account by their relation to our freedom and individuality, our trouble is that we find in our nature an indifference *without point*. The uninterest I call attention to here has no redemption in something so dramatic as freedom and individuality. It just sits there, in us, and takes away from our moral aspirations, our efforts to be decent persons.

RECONCILIATION?

Rawls's book, *A Theory of Justice,* offers "the conception of justice as fairness," a view that teaches that if a society pursues justice on its terms, it will be able to *reconcile* itself to certain natural facts about the human condition.[27] My "shared-fate individualism" brings this notion of reconciliation down to the level of individual responsibility:[28] if *J* follows shared-fate individualism, he or she will reconcile him- or herself to the human condition. The "modularity thesis" in my *Living with One's Past: Personal Fates and Moral Pain* is also a ground of sorts for another reconciliation problem.[29] It allows one to reconcile oneself to the unevenness in human agency and thus make allowances for others when they do not (or do) what they ought to do.

In all these cases the facts one gets reconciled to are "givens" of one sort or other. They are not "of one's own making." But can we "reconcile" to the fact that we do not do what we know we ought to do and that we sometimes act in this way from, as it were, "unmotivation" or *indifference*? In this case what we must live with are certain facts that seem to be uncaused. They seem to be without grounds in external conditions, illness, cognitive failures, or even Dostoevsky's perversity. The unmotivation does not seem to be the result of Rawlsian "social contingency" or the "natural lottery," as these are usually construed. My "passing" on this or that moral imperative—my being indifferent to its pressures—does not seem a result of something else, such that it might be "fixed" by appropriate action directed to that something else. Indeed, it seems conceptually to be a curious sort of constitutive part of moral-emotional nature itself. If we are to be reconciled to it, the reconciliation could not have the same logic as that afforded by the Rawlsian conception of justice or the shared-fate individualism or modularity thesis I have supported.

Is there a conceptual vehicle—a way of thinking—that allows one to *live with* this indifference to morality—this fact that one's moral nature itself has, so to speak, a dark, and unredeemable, side? When I say "live with" this indifference, I mean to avoid the sorts of rationalization of it that lead on to weakening, dismissing, or somehow jettisoning our capacity to take morality seriously. We have those moments, too, when we find ourselves "stupid" or "foolish" for taking morality seriously and perhaps resentful of those who clearly do not. But, for most decent people, these are moments of embarrassment. In any case it is not clear that decent people *can* jettison their respect for morality.

Certain familiar ploys for living with this come to mind, but they have similar or analogous defects. If one recommends (in some form) *self-for-giveness*, then one wants, as it were, to be careful: one does not in this case want to make living with it too easy, for what is at stake here is the seriousness itself of our regard for morality. Presumably, in people who take morality seriously, the vulnerability to indifference to morality must be resisted. Similarly, if one attempts to view the vulnerability to indifference as, so to speak, a kind of *relief mechanism*, which allows us some breathers from the pressures of the imperatives of morality in a (very) imperfect world,[30] then again one must be careful: to "gloss" the indifference in this way is to excuse it—and that is precisely what the aspiration to take morality seriously wants us to resist. Similarly again, if one recommends (in some form) *generosity* toward oneself, or perhaps the tolerance of *resignation* toward oneself, then one again must be careful: one must not be too quick to "tolerate" *this* aspect of oneself. Yet, again, if I am right this flat episodic uninterest is built into our moral nature. We cannot drum it out or make it go away. It will arise in us from time to time—and perhaps in some cases it will last far too long or occur at the wrong time, and then we experience anger with ourselves.

Perhaps taking morality seriously here reaches a sort of internal limit or boundary. We have the moral nature we do. It equips us to take morality seriously. But it is not competent to sustain that seriousness. Our moral-emotional nature is a positive thing—Kant calls it a "jewel in its own right"[31]—but it has a negativity (a weakness) built into it that may seem curious or strange. I refer here not to a capacity for "evil," and I am certainly not claiming that decent people are all potentially moral monsters. Instead, we will find ourselves indifferent to morality from time to time, and this must be resisted. We cannot succeed in such resistance; we will from time to time not care about morality; there is no way to evade or ameliorate or explain away our vulnerability to moral indifference. The only "reconciliation" available to us, I think, is a realization about the metaphysics of moral agency. Being stuck with moral indifference makes us take the project of taking morality seriously all the more seriously. Our episodic indifference contributes to the moral life being an achievement of sorts. It is a challenge for us—and we are not guaranteed success at the seriousness to which we are, by our moral natures, committed.

Appendix A

Space for Motivation

MODELS

In what follows I wish not to offer a general theory of action but merely to distinguish two sorts of human actions. My thought is that the distinction I draw is important to understanding the distinction that I say at the beginning I want to take seriously in this book, namely, the distinction between one knowing the right thing to do and one being moved to do the right thing—though in this appendix my concern is not so much for the importance of these distinctions for ordinary moral thought or even moral theory. What is at stake here is the characterization of a sort of logical space that opens up in our attempt to understand why people do the things they do, such that there can be a distinction between knowing the right and being moved to do the right.

To make the point I have in mind I will follow the lead of many philosophers of action and discuss briefly how far the notion of *game* provides a "model" for understanding different sorts of human action—though, again, my aim in doing so is not to provide an account that is general for all sorts of human action. Consider, then, games. We distinguish among kinds of games, such as games of chance, games of skill or strategy, or puzzles; we separate more physical (sometimes violent) games, such as football or hockey, from sedentary ones, for example, chess or poker; we have outdoor sports, such as badminton or tennis, or drawing-room games, such as bridge, checkers, or monopoly. Many games serve the ends of amusement or recreation, yet others, such as Russian or ordinary roulette, have or can have serious stakes. Philosophers have puzzled over whether there is something essential to games, that is, something they all have in common. Many candidate commonalities bring to mind possible counterexamples when one reflects on the variety of items called or considered to be games. For example, one might suggest "competition" as a characteristic of all games; but such a feature, in any full sense requiring two players, is not a part of, say, solitaire, or a requirement for working out crossword puzzles. Still, competition may point to something that is surely a part of a great many games, namely, that they can be, in one way or other, "won." Without bothering further in this discussion with the essentialist question, let us notice that when one or more persons are playing a game, they typically have an aim, a goal to be reached—something counts as winning. This modest claim is enough for my purpose in this discussion, which is to distinguish two sorts of action so that we can see the logical space that allows the distinction between knowing the right and being moved to do the right to be real.

An important part of games being winnable is a structure within which the effort to win is carried on. The structure of a game is in fact a system of rules (principles and policies) serving to define a form of activity as the game it is. Such a system defines a game insofar as it specifies the terms of positions or player roles, establishes possible rewards or penalties, and, most important, characterizes the scope or bounds of permitted game moves. The part of the system of rules that outlines moves in a game often circumscribes players in making their moves but does not determine their moves for them. Given an actual game situation, the rules that apply commonly delimit the scope of alternative moves but do not dictate the outcome of the situation. Such rules may figure more prominently in games of strategy than games of chance. At any rate, many rules assume this delimiting role by specifying only what is forbidden, given certain game circumstances, but not what is permitted. After the deal and first round of betting in five-card poker one is not (usually) permitted to discard more than three cards, though one may discard fewer cards or none at all.

Finally, it is worth noticing that the facts that games are winnable and that they are defined by systems of rules make possible different sorts of evaluative judgments of the moves made by players of games. Learners (and sometimes experienced players) make mistakes that consist chiefly of their making moves falling outside the permitted zones of alternatives. The system of rules making up a game forms a sufficient condition for the possibility of right and wrong moves being made by a person engaging in that game. What should be said, though, of judgments to the effect that a given move is "better" or "more strategic" than another? Roughly, such judgments point up how adequately a player met certain standards in handling a game's more or less complex system of rules or perhaps how insightful a player was in foreseeing consequences of moves relative to the complexity made possible by the game's system of rules. A person may play a better game of chess than another, given the complexity of that game's system of rules and certain standards prevailing in it being applied, whereas we would not ordinarily consider someone a better player of roulette in the same sense. In the latter case, anyhow, winners usually are described as "lucky" rather than "better." Both games of strategy and games of chance, in virtue of being winnable at all, have systems of rules outlining procedures of play. But games of strategy commonly have a large proportion of delimiting rules affording a variety of options in many game situations, which rules are for the most part lacking in games of chance. Thus, the standards to be met in applying rules in strategy games will differ from those met with in games of chance. There are, of course, many fascinating games located on the thick boundary between games of strategy and games of chance: one can, for example, be a skillful poker player as well as a lucky one.

ACTIVITIES AND CONSTITUENT ACTIONS

Games, then, are (a) winnable and (b) structured according to systems of rules, and, through those systems of rules, they (c) allow for evaluative judgments of moves in games. I want now to say that the notions of "game" and "move in a game" may serve as models for two kinds of human action. One of these I shall call *activities* (or "enterprises"), and the other I shall call *constituent actions,* thereby intending to emphasize that actions of this latter kind have their place within or as *parts* of larger activities structured by systems of rules.

More specifically, I want to say that constituent actions are like moves in games in the ways we can evaluate them and that actions that can be so evaluated, like moves in games, presuppose systems of rules. Such actions, like moves in games, are parts of winnable enterprises. I suggest further that, just as moves in a game can be made intelligible by reference to the game's defining system of rules, so constituent actions illuminable by reference to, say, an agent's reasons for acting are so because such reasons cite, in effect, relevant portions of the system of rules defining the activity of which the constituent action in question is a part. Thus, reasons that explain constituent actions, the intentions with which actions of the constituent sort were done, the purposes for or motives from which such actions were done—all these operate to make clear different aspects of the system of rules giving structure to an activity and thereby to any constituent part of that activity.[1]

Most important, insofar as our ultimate aim in this discussion is to understand what I refer to as "space for motivation," a system of rules defining an enterprise is logically prior to the constituent actions it renders intelligible, and it being so is a condition of the possibility of it rendering such actions intelligible.[2] An explanation utilizing such reasons consists of placing the action in question within the scope of an activity given its structure by a system of rules. Any moves *in* chess are explainable in terms of the system of rules specifying what it is to play chess, and insofar as this is the case, the system of rules of chess is logically prior to any particular chess move. One may only call an event a move in chess by reference to the game of chess, and the game of chess is what it is in virtue of it being structured by a certain system of rules.[3]

But the notions we employ to account for persons engaging in activities are not logically prior to their activities in the way rule-based reasons are prior to the constituent actions they explain. One's reasons for playing five-card poker may vary from week to week, though when one does play, one's reasons for dealing five cards to each of one's associates do not vary. Sometimes indeed we do not want to say we have "reasons" at all for the activities we engage in or pursue, though we can typically give some basis for what we thereby do, even if this only amounts to saying that we "just wanted to" or "just felt like it." But the point of importance (here) is that such grounds for activities, whatever their manner of operating may be, are not logically prior to particular activities in the way in which an activity's system of rules is logically prior to any constituent actions of that activity.

It becomes clear, then, that the models of action suggested by games do not help us to understand the workings of reasons people have for engaging in activities. More carefully put, those models leave logical space for there to *be* motivational factors for activities, but they do not fill in that space in the way they fill in the workings of reasons for constituent actions. When a call for explanation concerns an action as part of an activity, an answer in terms of reasons operates as does an answer in terms of a game's system of rules to a why question about a move in that game. But an explanatory or justificatory request about the activity itself, for example, an inquiry that in fact makes participation in the game itself the object of the why question, cannot be answered in terms of the rules of the game. The rules of table tennis do not justify playing table tennis, and the rules of music composition do not account for anyone composing music. Yet persons do, of course, have and give reasons for playing table tennis and composing music.

So reasons for engaging in activities must be of a different sort than reasons for actions that are parts of those activities. This is not to claim that activities have no court of appeal or that we do what we do (activities) "for no reason." It is rather the claim that the appeal, when made, is not similar in form to consulting the rule book of a game. And it is of course true that activities, even ones that take considerable time, energy, and resources, for example, pursuing higher education, may be parts of still larger enterprises, such as pleasing the family; and in these cases they can be accounted for in terms of whatever passes for being the system of rules defining the larger enterprise.

I have not claimed that the distinction I have suggested provides a general classification of human actions. Classification in philosophy, as elsewhere, depends on our aims. I have offered, in effect, two ways of regarding what a person has done, given that he or she has applied rules in doing it: namely, as an activity or as a constituent action within an activity. But these ways of regarding actions are mutually exclusive for any one description of action: under a certain description a person either engaged in an activity or performed a constituent action of some other activity. We may regard what *J* has done under a certain description (e.g., "painting the ceiling") as itself an enterprise having constituent actions ("setting up a ladder," "finding some rags," "stirring up the paint"); or we may regard what he or she has done under that description as part of some other enterprise (e.g., "redecorating the house"). But we cannot regard what *J* has done under some one description as at once an enterprise and a constituent action of the same enterprise. "Redecorating the house," when used to describe an activity, does not describe a move in the game of "redecorating the house." It is true that "painting the ceiling" may describe an essential part of the activity of painting the ceiling, but when it does so it describes a constituent action of the latter and not the latter itself.

Further, I do not claim that dividing human actions into "activities" and "constituent actions" is internally complete, for it would surely be possible to discriminate in various ways further sorts of human action. However, it is not clear that there is any other way of regarding what a person has done, given that he or she has applied rules in doing it, which stands alongside these categories. That is, it appears that classifying actions in this way is exhaustive, given the basis for the classification. The warrant for distinguishing kinds of action as I have is that agents apply rules in what they do. And so long as a person is in fact applying rules in what he or she does, he or she is both engaging in an activity (because the rules he or she applies constitute a system defining what it is to engage in an activity) and performing a constituent action of an activity (because the rules he or she applies also specify how one may carry through some activity)—though not both of these under the same description.

GROUNDS FOR ACTIVITIES

Given the distinction between activities and constituent actions, let us turn
to the matter of the logic of explanations of activities and explanations of
constituent actions. Notice first that explanatory accounts of constituent
actions must be "internal" explanations in a way that activity accounts are
not. That is, insofar as constituent actions have a place as parts of enterprises, the explanatory elements we employ to illuminate them will function to exhibit portions of the structure of the enterprises of which they
are parts. But when we regard what someone has done as itself an enterprise, we cannot offer an account of its structure as an explanation of a
person engaging in it, for to do so would be merely to describe in some
detail the nature of the enterprise but not to explain *why* it took place. An
account explaining why an activity took place at all is "external" inasmuch
as it refers beyond (in some sense) the activity itself to show why it took
place.[4]

This "reference beyond" that we encounter in activity explanations is
not unfamiliar. We distinguish "having a taste for an apple" from "snatch-
ing one off the vendor's cart" or "disliking the politician's views" from
"heckling him during his public speeches." We want to say that "liking a
book" need not insure "writing a favorable review of it"; nor will "having great respect for a candidate" guarantee "voting for her in the election." In general we notice that there is a gap of sorts between *reasons* or
motives and engaging in what I call "activities" such that one cannot "de-
duce" the participation in the activities from reasons or motives even
though those reasons or motives *are* used effectively to explain instances
of participating or engaging in activities.[5] We voted for a certain candidate because we had great respect for her, or we heckled a speaker because we disliked his views. Yet, if we can set apart these explanatory
items from the activities we cite them to explain, in the sense that one may
have an opinion, motive, reason, or liking (or disliking) regarding something or other but not necessarily act on it, how do such items account
for the activities we cite them to explain?

Notice first that, regardless of the evident variety among such explanatory notions, they evince at least one common property. No matter how
such notions may vary in specific content, their explanatory force requires
that they be predicable of the agent engaged in the activity in question.
One may not be able to see any similarity in content among, say, one's
ambitions, one's bonds of loyalty, one's family feelings, and one's patrio-
tism. But the fact of logical importance is that, insofar as such notions may
figure in accounts of one's activities, they are considered to belong or

attach to the persons to whom the activities in question are ascribed. An ambition or bond of loyalty may have a role to play in an account of my participation or engagement in a certain activity insofar as it is *my* ambition or bond of loyalty.

We must, then, distinguish *what*, for example, a motive is from the *having* of a motive. It is an agent's *having* such-and-such a motive, hope, or reason that explains his or her engaging in a certain enterprise, not merely *what* that motive, hope, or reason may be. It is not just that the politician's motive happened to be an ambition to dominate the foreign affairs policy making in his party but that the politician *had* such a motive that is alleged to account for him campaigning against his rival.

In this account, then, an explanation of a person participating in a certain activity that cites a motive, hope, reason, and so forth, does not operate simply to characterize or redescribe the activity in question.[6] The explanation does not work just by virtue of the characterization of what was done offered in the "content" of the motive, reason, or hope. It works in virtue of the notion of a person *having* a motive with such content. My thought is that to discuss the features of motive contents is not to discuss the question of how someone having a motive accomplishes the business of explaining what he or she has done.

This is not to deny that describing what someone has done may be very illuminating in its own right or that descriptions (or characterizations or redescriptions) may be called explanations. But it is to deny that the illumination provided is of the same order. More precisely, it is to deny that the business of activity accounts is to describe activities in the sense in which to do so is to answer, or primarily answer, the question, "What is *J* doing?"

It might be suggested that we acknowledge two aspects of the explanatory power of an activity account containing an ascription of, for example, a motive to an agent: on the one side, the characterization of *what* the agent did that it affords and, on the other, its claim that the agent *had* such-and-such a motive, the content of which provides this characterization. But it remains that these are not both parts of an answer to a why question directed to an activity, and in that sense they are not both parts of the "explanatory power" of an activity account. For the characterization involved in a motive ascription is logically an answer to the question, "What did *J* do?" not, "Why did *J* do it?" Of course, our practice of accounting for someone's activity may, on occasion, involve our characterizing or redescribing what he or she has done, but this is not to say that we have thereby explained why he or she so acted.

Suppose we attempt to account for something that has taken place under the following description: "The mayor took a kickback on a city contract." Now, we may venture explanations of this in terms of the mayor's greed, or alternatively his need for money to pay personal debts, or alternatively his private desire to endow a chair in philosophy at the municipal university, or still different terms. These, we might say, are competing explanations of what the mayor has done. But these accounts can only be *in* competition if they concern the same thing. That is, in order for these explanations to compete with one another there must be some (logically) prior agreement on *what* they are alleged to explain. But this prior agreement can only be achieved on the condition that it is possible to establish a description of what the mayor has done which is itself independent of any of the proffered explanations. Thus, the possibility of our giving competing explanatory accounts of what someone has done is predicated on the condition that we are able to establish, independently, some description of what was done. And, of course, to say that a description is established independently of such competing explanations is precisely to say that it is not itself an explanation. The description is, then, not something that becomes an explanation when it is replaced by a redescription; the redescription may afford a better account of what was done, but it still stands as what an explanation needs to illuminate.

In general, understanding a description consists of our seeing, perhaps with varying degrees of accuracy, "how the world is." When we understand a description, we gain a version of what the world (or a portion of it) is like from at least the describer's point of view. But our understanding of an explanation of what a person has done is something different from this. What we achieve in this case is intelligibility of a different order from "how the world is." Briefly, we see a connection of some sort between what a person has done, which is the object of a description, and something *other* than what he or she has done: we gain access to something beyond the person's activity, something that illuminates the person's engagement in the activity even though we cannot infer deductively the engagement from that "something." What we employ in this case to account for a person's activity is not the same object as the object of the description of his or her activity.

Once we distinguish between the kinds of actions I called "activities" and "constituent actions," we could not explain someone's performance of a constituent action or engagement in an activity merely by redescribing his or her actions, no matter how imaginatively or accurately we did this. For in the case of a constituent action, giving a description of the activity of which this action is part is evidently the main burden of the explanatory task. And in cases of human activities, what performs this task is often, I think, a description of a psychological fact about the agent, such as a motive he or she may have had. In neither case do we account for an action merely by redescribing *it*. Our account may indeed contain descriptions, but these will not only be answers to the question, "What did *J* do?" Explanations of activities make reference beyond what was done.

Appendix B

Hidden Reasons

REASONS AND MY REASONS

We sometimes make the distinction between understanding the principles of right action and being moved to obey or rise to such principles in our actions in the language of "reasons." Thus, in some cases we acknowledge that there are or can be a plurality of reasons for doing *x*, but then we worry or wonder about which of these several reasons "really" operated to move a person (oneself or another) into action. We appear to recognize a distinction, then, between *a* reason for action and a reason that actually moved the person to do what he or she did.

It will be convenient for this discussion to approach this familiar distinction in, so to speak, the first person. Thus, I ask, When is a reason for action such that it is *my* reason for action? That is, what conditions must be satisfied for one or several reasons for doing a certain thing to qualify as my reason or reasons for doing that thing, that is, to be what moved me to so act? My interest in this discussion extends to how this distinction operates in psychoanalytic contexts (in therapy or in ordinary life) in which one may be puzzled about whether a reason that is "hidden" from one, in the manner of psychoanalytic reasons as popularly understood, can be one's actual reason for doing a certain thing. Can a hidden reason be *my* reason for action?

By *psychoanalytic reason* I do not mean just a reason that might be given by a psychoanalyst in the course of treating a patient. Rather, a psychoanalytic reason is one of which the agent to whom it is ascribed may say, "I did not suspect that I had that reason for what I did." And, if an agent

159

accepts an explanation involving psychoanalytic reasons, he or she might typically say, "Now I see what the reasons must have been on which I acted, though I did not suspect so." Thus, a mother who continually remarks on the culinary procedures of her daughter-in-law, only to help, might not suspect that she criticizes out of jealousy or a desire to control. Or a person who volunteers to teach reading to children doing poorly in school, but finds him- or herself too tired to keep up the commitment, might not suspect that what moves him or her to renege is prejudice against the minority children he or she encounters. It requires little imagination to step off from these to other examples in which explanations involve such unsuspected reasons as fear of one's father, a death wish, or repressed homosexual tendencies.

AVOWING REASONS

It might be suggested that r is not my reason for what I have done unless I can recognize r as the reason that in fact influenced my behavior, that is, unless I can recall having *had* the reason r.[1] Accordingly, it might then be claimed that psychoanalytic reasons cannot be my reasons, for they are not reasons I can recognize as those that in fact influenced my behavior. I cannot recall having had them.

But it can be countersuggested that though there are reasons of the sort I am calling "psychoanalytic," it is plausible to think that such reasons can be my reasons for what I have done.[2] For one might question whether the notion of recognizing r as a reason that in fact influenced my behavior must mean that for a reason to be my reason I must somehow be able to find it among my private mental possessions, that is, that my reason for what I have done is a reason I can discover having "had in mind." One might object that reasons need not be interpreted in this way for the language of recognizing them to apply: for I might recognize a reason in the sense of seeing a pattern in my actions that I did not suspect, and this form of recognition involves no reference to private mental property. At any rate, it has been claimed as part of the countersuggestion that for a reason to be my reason "it does not need to be an item I can locate among my private possessions; it is mine in the sense that ultimately I must be the one to *avow* it."[3] And in this sense of "my reason," psychoanalytic reasons can be my reasons, for, as has been further suggested, it is part of a correct psychoanalytic account of a person's behavior that he or she "will—at least ideally—come to agree with it in the long run."[4]

In what follows I ask whether avowability is a condition of a reason being my reason for action. I find it difficult to attach a sense to avowability as such a condition. And I argue for a distinction between my reasons and psychoanalytic reasons in support of the view that there is a sense in which psychoanalytic reasons cannot be my reasons.

Notice first that my avowability of *r* is not a sufficient condition of *r* being a *reason* for doing a certain thing. For *r* may be avowable by me without being a reason for doing anything at all. I may avow in court that I went to a concert last month without "going to a concert last month" having been a reason for doing something or anything else. My avowability of *r* is a condition of *r* being my reason for doing a certain thing only together with at least this further condition: that *r* be a reason for action. But *r* cannot be merely a reason to act, as when facts about famine in distant or nearby parts of the world make one want to do "something," but it is not clear what. We must require, I think, that *r* be a reason for doing something of the type to which the particular thing I have done belongs. But I will not stop to examine the notion of "types of action" here, for this would take us too far away from our main subject. Perhaps it will suffice to illustrate the notion as follows: if *J* redecorates his or her house, *J* engages in an action type, namely, "redecorating one's house." "Redecorating one's house" is a type or form of activity in which not only *J* may engage and in which not only *J* may have reasons for engaging. When we are interested in formulating a condition of a reason being my reason, we are interested in understanding when a reason for doing something of type *K* is my reason for having done a thing of that type. The task of stating requirements for my reasons is generated on the assumption that there are reasons that may but may not be my reasons for what I have done, that is, that there are reasons for engaging in a form of activity that agents may but may not "have." In sum, the problem is one of specifying what conditions must be satisfied for a reason for doing something of type *K*, which I may but may not "have," to be my reason for having done a certain thing of that type. It is this problem that the reference to *avowing* a reason for doing something of that type is intended to solve.

It we accept these minor patches, we may formulate the view in question as the claim that it is a complex condition of *r* being *my* reason for having done a thing of type *K* that (1) *r* be a reason for doing something of type *K* and (2) *r* be ultimately avowed by me. Now we may ask what could be intended by the words "*r* be ultimately avowed by me."

Suppose we take our lead from the remark above that, if a psychoanalytic account of my behavior is correct, it may be expected that I will (at least ideally) "come to agree with it in the long run." We might then interpret (a) "*r* be ultimately avowed by me" as (b) "*r* be ultimately agreed to by me." But this will not do, for in certain circumstances I may be brought to agree to most anything that was a reason (and perhaps some

Appendix B

things that were not) for doing something of the kind I did. I might agree willingly to any reason someone might be pushing, perhaps just to end an exhausting session of analysis or, in other circumstances, to boost someone's professional ego. The same difficulty appears if we interpret statement a as (c) "*r* be ultimately admitted by me," (d) "*r* be ultimately confessed to by me," or (e) "*r* be ultimately acknowledged by me."

One might propose that we simply rule out ad hoc agreement or admission. We might require that agreement or admission be *sincere* agreement or *genuine* admission, where the force of "sincere" or "genuine" is at least that one not have such ulterior motives for agreeing or confessing to *r* as wanting to end a session of analysis or boost someone's ego. Thus, we might try to reformulate, say, statement b as (f) "*r* be ultimately agreed to by me, without any hidden reasons for doing so." But interpreting "sincere" in this way is not helpful, for how are we to understand the words "without any hidden reasons"? It seems that we can only understand them in terms of a prior understanding of what it is for me to have reasons. That is, it would appear to be a condition of our understanding one not having hidden reasons that we understand one having reasons. But it is precisely this latter notion that is in question: we are asking what the conditions are for a reason being the reason I had. I do not see that we answer this question if our answer involves a reference to not having hidden reasons, for this latter notion requires understanding in terms of the notion it is proffered to explain.

It might be suggested that "sincere agreement" is meant to be descriptive not of a person merely going through the motions of agreeing to *r* but doing so, or ultimately doing so, in a certain frame of mind. But this will not do either, for any *r* that is a reason for doing something of the kind I have done is an *r* that I may not only go through the motions of agreeing to but also go through the motions of agreeing to in a certain frame of mind. To hold this version of avowability as a condition for my reasons, one must require additionally that there be correlations of some checkable sort obtaining between certain reasons for action and certain of my frames of mind, such that whenever (or almost whenever) I find myself in that frame of mind, the reasons I then agree to are my reasons for having done what I have. I doubt whether there are such correlations or whether, in general, being in a certain frame of mind is any key to what my reasons were for what I did.

THE STRUCTURE OF REASONS

Consider this question: is there any *r* such that *r* is a reason for doing something of type *K* but is not capable ideally of being avowed (agreed to, admitted, confessed to, acknowledged) by me? Perhaps the following is such a case: to help a candidate win an election is a reason for having campaigned on his behalf, but this cannot ultimately be avowed by me because I know that candidate C, for whom I campaigned, could not, in the circumstances, have won the election. I think we would say here that the proffered reason was not really a reason for doing something of the type "campaigning for C." That is, we would deny that winning the election could have been a reason for campaigning for C, though it might well have been a reason for campaigning for other candidates. And, if we are to understand a reference to avowability as descriptive of a certain frame of mind, the problem remains that whatever is a reason for campaigning for C is a reason that can be avowed ultimately by me, that is, a reason toward which I can have, or be induced to adopt, the characteristic frame of mind. If this is so, then the avowability requirement does not distinguish any reason for doing something of type K from any other reason for doing something of type K. So, as a possible condition of a reason being my reason, avowability would be, in a word, superfluous.

In any view of the sort I am considering, it seems to be assumed that one must "add" something to a reason for action to make it my reason for what I have done. Given this assumption, it is perhaps natural to think that what is added is something "mental" and that what is required for a reason to be or become my reason is the presence or addition of this mental something. In such a view, an avowal of a reason is a report on oneself as being in a certain frame of mind respecting that reason.

But consider the shape that is typical of an avowal of a reason. Suppose I have done m, which is an action of type K, and someone suggests that r was my reason for doing m. I reply, "Yes, you're right; r was my reason." Surely I do not have to be in any special frame of mind to say this and mean it; so the function of my avowal is not to describe myself as being in a certain frame of mind respecting r. And surely, again, when I avow r, my avowal is not itself what is "added" to r to make r my reason. For consider what I do respecting a reason for action, when on someone's suggestion of that reason, I say, "You're right." What is that suggestion? It is not merely a presentation of a reason for action or indeed of a reason for my action. It is a characterization of a reason *as* my reason for action. So, when I say, "You're right," I do not make that reason my reason *by* what I say, for what I am saying that the person is right about is that a certain reason is my reason. Thus, a reason being my reason for what I have done is prior to my avowal of it as my reason and cannot be made my reason by my avowal of it.

To generalize these points, I do not think we can construe the difference between a reason and my reason for what I have done as the difference between a reason and a reason plus some such thing as a frame of mind or an act of avowal. My reason for what I have done is not of the form "a reason plus x."

REASONS AS PERSUADERS

How, then, are we to understand the difference between a reason and my reason for what I have done? And what do I do when I reply, "You're right," and mean it, to someone's suggestion that a certain reason is my reason for what I have done?

Consider the idea of a reason for doing something of type K. I have not said what may count as an instance of this idea, for example, whether emotions and feelings, as well as motives, intentions, and purpose, may be regarded as *reasons* for action. But however questions of this sort may be settled, it is an essential part of something being a reason for an action of a certain type that it be something in light of which someone in some circumstances may be convinced that an action of that type should be performed. Put another way, if r is a reason for doing something of type K, then r has the property of being persuasive to someone in some circumstances that a thing of type K must be done. If gaining power is a reason for running for political office, then it may be construed as persuasive to someone somewhere that he or she must run for political office. A reason need not be the only reason for doing something of a certain type for it to be convincing in this way. Doubtless it is rarely the case that forms of activity have solitary reasons for being engaged in. And I do not suggest that whatever may persuade someone to do something of a certain type is a reason for doing something of that type. This would be to define *reason* in such a way as to settle by fiat questions as to whether feelings and emotions may count as reasons. And, though it is plain that one's feelings can persuade one to do certain things, it is not plain that one's feelings are thereby describable as reasons.

What is at stake is a basic conceptual point about reasons: namely, that they are persuaders. Such a point cannot be rejected by reciting psychological or sociological facts. It does not defeat the claim that reasons are persuaders to produce a reason that, as a matter of fact, has not been convincing to anyone that he or she should do a thing of a certain type. One would have to produce an r of which it was true that r could not persuade anyone in any circumstances to do something of that type. But such an r could not be a reason for doing a thing of type K: an r for which we could not construct a set of circumstances in which we could envisage someone being convinced by r that he or she must do a thing of type K is not a reason *for* doing a thing of that sort.

This is not to suggest that any reason for doing a thing of the sort I have done can be convincing to me. A candidate's promises of political favors would hardly suffice to persuade me that I must support him or her (I think). The actual persuasiveness of reasons for action is a separate matter. A reason being convincing to me on some occasion would appear to depend on my evaluation of my circumstances, my understanding of the consequences of what I might do, my current stock of more or less trusted principles of action, and similarly complex matters. I am inclined to think that the actual persuasiveness of reasons is a matter of degree, that is, that reasons may be more or less convincing to me; but all this is compatible with the conceptual point that the idea of a reason for action is the idea of what may be persuasive to someone in some circumstances that he or she must do a certain thing.

I do not think a general account describing when a reason is actually persuasive to an agent can be given, and this is so because general conditions sufficient for a reason to be actually persuasive cannot be specified. This is not to say that reasons are never convincing to persons. It is to say that their actual persuasiveness rests essentially on the particular case in such a way that before-the-fact criteria for persuasiveness cannot be given. I would view it as a hopeless task to specify a priori the conditions for a reason actually convincing me or someone else that something of a certain type must be done.

VIEW

These remarks afford a sketch of the difference between a reason and my reason for what I have done. Roughly, my reason is a reason that convinced me, as I saw my situation, that a thing of the type I have done had to be done. When I avow or am prepared to avow a reason, I claim or am prepared to claim that a certain reason is my reason for what I have done, and to claim this is to express the fact that it was that reason that persuaded me to do something of the type I did. It is to say that a certain reason, in light of my understanding an evaluation of my situation, persuaded me that I must do what I did.

This yields the view, then, that r having been my reason for what I have done is a sufficient condition for (1) r having been a reason for doing something of type K, (2) what I have done having been something of type K, and (3) r having been anyhow highly convincing to me, given my understanding and evaluation of my situation, that something of type K must be done. And I have said that my avowal of a reason is not descriptive of, and is not itself, something that is somehow "added" to that reason to make it my reason. Rather, my avowal of a certain reason is logically posterior to that reason being my reason, and my avowal is an expression of the fact that that reason is what convinced me in those circumstances that something of type K must be done.

The form of this claim is that r being my reason is a sufficient condition of the three items just mentioned. But to make this claim is not to put down requirements for my reasons. For example, it is not to require that I somehow add "convincingness" to a reason for action to make it my reason for what I have done. It follows from my avowal of a certain reason as my reason that the reason was what persuaded me, given my understanding of my situation, that I must act as I did. But this is not to say that I have made any reason my reason or that any reason has become my reason, by, say, the addition of certain mental ingredients. The items that follow from r being my reason do not form a complex sufficient condition for r being my reason, for they may all obtain without r being my reason. Thus, there may be another reason, s, even more convincing to me than r, or r, albeit highly persuasive, may not yet be persuasive enough to me that I must do a thing of a certain type.

A NOTE ON PSYCHOANALYTIC REASONS

Although a priori requirements cannot be given that reasons for action must satisfy to count as my reasons, what I have suggested follows from a reason being my reason will suffice to allow some final remarks about the prospects for a psychoanalytic reason being my reason for what I have done.

The claim that psychoanalytic reasons can be my reasons comes to the claim that a reason of which I can say, "I did not suspect that I had that reason for what I did," may be a reason for what I have done which was highly convincing to me, given my understanding and evaluation of my situation, that something of type K must be done. But a psychoanalytic reason cannot be a reason of this sort. That is, a proffered reason that I did not suspect I had for what I did cannot be a reason that had been highly persuasive to me, given my understanding of my situation, that I must do a certain thing. I could not avow such a reason in the sense I have described: I could not express the fact that r was the reason that persuaded me to act as I did if r is a reason I did not suspect I had. To hold that psychoanalytic reasons cannot be my reasons for what I have done is at least to hold that there are certain reasons that were not what convinced me that I must do a certain thing, though they may be reasons for doing something of the type I did.

Consider what would have to be so for psychoanalytic reasons to be my reasons. It would not be enough to show me that, given the circumstances in which I acted, they were the reasons on which I acted. Rather, I must be shown that, in light of my understanding and evaluation of my situation, they were reasons that convinced me that a thing of a certain type should be done. But the point is that I cannot be *shown* this. Indeed, someone must come to me for this. It might be open to psychoanalytic explanation to carry through the former of these tasks: that is, it seems possible that a person could be shown that certain reasons were the reasons on which he or she acted. But I cannot see that the latter task is open to psychoanalytic explanation: that is, it does not seem possible that a person could be shown what reasons persuaded him or her, as he or she understood the situation, that he or she must do a thing of a certain kind.

Doubtless these two tasks are often run together. But we may separate them if we recognize that the notions of reason, my reason, and psychoanalytic reason carry such implications as these: *r* being any reason for action implies that it also be a reason for doing something of a certain type which I may but may not have, that is, *r* having the property of being convincing to someone in some circumstances that he or she must do a thing of that type; *r* being my reason for what I have done implies that it was highly convincing to me in my circumstances that I must do something of the type I have done; and *r* being a psychoanalytic reason for what I have done implies that it is a reason I did not suspect I had. In this discussion I have assumed that both my reasons and psychoanalytic reasons may count as reasons for action and have argued in light of their implications that psychoanalytic reasons cannot be my reasons for what I have done.

It may be asked, Is either my reason or a psychoanalytic reason *the* reason for what I have done? At this point the best reply to this question is, I think, that the notion of *the* reason for my action is simply a separate matter. So far as I have characterized these notions, *r* being either my reason or a psychoanalytic reason is neither necessary nor sufficient for *r* to be *the* reason for what I have done. To hold otherwise is perhaps to propose a definition in light of one's appraisal of a theory allowing that unsuspected reasons may be operative in human action. But I shall not begin to discuss such a definition or theory here.

Notes

PREFACE

1. *A Sand County Almanac* (1949) (New York: Ballantine Books, 1970), 197.
2. This is one aim of John Rawls's *A Theory of Justice* (Cambridge, Mass.: Belknap Press of Harvard University Press, 1971).
3. This is my aim in *On Sharing Fate* (Philadelphia: Temple University Press, 1987) and in *Living with One's Past: Personal Fates and Moral Pain* (Lanham, Md.: Rowman & Littlefield, 1996).
4. This encyclopedia is a project of the American Psychological Association; it is to be published by Oxford University Press.

CHAPTER 1

1. I discuss "hidden reasons" in appendix B.
2. Kant, *Foundations of the Metaphysics of Morals* (1785), trans. and introduction by Lewis White Beck (Indianapolis: Bobbs-Merrill, 1959), 23.
3. Cf. Kant's discussion in section 2 of *Foundations of the Metaphysics of Morals*.
4. Here I follow Aristotle's advice whereby one cannot discuss ethics with those who have no moral experience; see *The Nicomachean Ethics*, ed. W. D. Ross (London: Oxford University Press, 1980), book 1, chs. 3–4.
5. Cf. Bernard Williams's discussion in "Moral Luck," in *Moral Luck* (Cambridge: Cambridge University Press, 1981). Kant's view was that, with respect to kinds of value, moral value trumps all other sorts: "To duty every other motive

must give place, because duty is the condition of a will good in itself, whose worth transcends everything" (*Foundations of the Metaphysics of Morals*, 20). Williams's account challenges the Kantian view, as does Susan Wolf's discussion in "Moral Saints" (*The Journal of Philosophy* 79 [August 1982]).

6. The contemporary philosophical literature on motivation in some ways starts from R. S. Peters's *The Concept of Motivation* (London: Routledge and Kegan Paul, 1958). Relative to issues in moral theory, I find helpful Samuel Scheffler's *Human Morality* (New York: Oxford University Press, 1992) and especially the writings of Alfred R. Mele, in, for example, *Springs of Action* (New York: Oxford University Press, 1992) and "Motivation: Essentially Motivation-Constituting Attitudes" (*The Philosophical Review* 104, no. 3 [July 1995]).

7. What follows is based loosely on my *On Sharing Fate* (Philadelphia: Temple University Press, 1987), 103–06.

8. David Hume, *An Enquiry Concerning the Principles of Morals* (1777), in *Hume's Enquiries*, ed. L. A. Selby-Bigge (Oxford: Clarendon Press, 1962), section 9, 283.

9. See Williams, *Moral Luck*, especially the chapters titled "Persons, Character, and Morality" and "Moral Luck."

10. See Kant, *Foundations of the Metaphysics of Morals*, section 1, 17 (n. 2).

11. Henry Sidgwick, *The Methods of Ethics* (1907), 7th edition (New York: Dover, 1966), 262.

12. "The Schizophrenia of Modern Ethical Theories," *The Journal of Philosophy* 73, no. 14 (12 August 1976). For an earlier discussion of the sort of point the Stocker example suggests, see the inaugural lecture titled "Moral Integrity" by Peter Winch (Oxford: Basil Blackwell, 1968). My thanks go to Jeffrie G. Murphy for this reference.

13. This is in effect to ask whether Aristotle is right when he claims that morality involves, among many things, "feeling rightly" (see *The Nicomachean Ethics*, book 2, ch. 6, 38). In *Utilitarianism* (1863) (ed. George Sher [Indianapolis: Hackett, 1979], ch. 2), John Stuart Mill appears to separate "motive" and "action" and to claim that morality is, as it were, mainly interested in right action, the agent's motive being what it may. The motive may bear on "the worth of the agent" but not the assessment of the action as morally right or wrong.

14. Aristotle, *The Nicomachean Ethics*, book 2, ch. 9, 45.

15. Aristotle, *The Nicomachean Ethics*, book 2, ch. 9, 45. Aristotle also writes, "But up to what point and to what extent a man must deviate before he becomes blameworthy it is not easy to determine by reasoning, any more than anything else that is perceived by the senses; such things depend on particular facts, and the decision rests with perception" (book 2, ch. 9, 47). But this, it should be noted, does not turn Aristotle to an "anything goes" ethicist: "So much, then, is plain, that the intermediate state is in all things to be praised, but that we must incline sometimes towards the excess, sometimes towards the deficiency; for so shall we most easily hit the mean and what is right" (book 2, ch. 9, 47).

16. Actually, the four examples Kant gives to illustrate what it is to universalize maxims reduce to two: there are two cases (maxims enjoining suicide and false promising) in which the universalizing runs into "contradiction in thought" and two cases (maxims refusing self-realization and service to others) in which

the universalizing runs the agent into "conflict in the will." See the discussion in *Foundations of the Metaphysics of Morals*, section 2, 39–42.

17. Though I do not know that Mill actually does acknowledge this, in *Utilitarianism*.

18. Aristotle, *The Nicomachean Ethics*, book 2, ch. 6, 38.

19. Of course, "reason" and "inclination" can coincide in their instructions in particular cases for Kant.

20. See Kant, *Foundations of the Metaphysics of Morality*, section 2, 29–31.

21. The discussion of this point is in ch. 3 of Mill's *Utilitarianism*. Mill does not claim that this elementary other-regarding "sentiment" must be as strong in one as the self-regarding sentiment.

22. See Mill, *Utilitarianism*, ch. 3, 33.

23. In ch. 5 of *Utilitarianism*, Mill separates "the social sympathies" and the criterion of right (i.e., the principle of utility). The social sympathies are a condition of the possibility of morality and are to be cultivated, but they do not themselves necessarily lead to right action for Mill.

24. I have heard snatches of conversation in which decent people characterize themselves as "stupid" for not being more calculating or self-interested in what they do. Even decent people can be irritated with good character, when it does not pay off.

25. I approach other aspects of this subject in my *Living with One's Past: Personal Fates and Moral Pain* (Lanham, Md.: Rowman & Littlefield, 1996).

26. I will, though, touch lightly on "alienation," mental illness, and Dostoevskian "perversity" in ch. 7.

27. Percy, *The Moviegoer* (1960, 1961) (New York: Vintage, 1998), 220–27.

28. These remarks do not suggest that there is no such thing as "justified indifference." There may be circumstances in which the demands of morality are too constant and too strenuous. Episodic indifference might be recommended as relief. Apart, though, from how far episodic indifference might be justified, for discussions of the notion that morality can be too strenuous, see, for example, James S. Fishkin, *The Limits of Obligation* (New Haven, Conn.: Yale University Press, 1982); Peter Railton, "Alienation, Consequentialism, and the Demands of Morality," *Philosophy and Public Affairs* 13 (spring 1984); and Shelly Kagan, *The Limits of Morality* (Oxford: Clarendon Press, 1989).

29. I love, in this connection, the florid expression of this point by Paul Dietrichson: "My only partially self-transparent complex rational and sensuously conditioned nature being what it is, I am not likely to come to believe and remain believing in full honesty that I on some occasion strived to the very limit of my capacity to develop purity of heart" ("What Does Kant Mean by 'Acting from Duty'?" in *Kant*, ed. Robert Paul Wolff [Garden City, N.Y.: Anchor Books, 1967], 324).

CHAPTER 2

1. Cambridge, Mass.: Belknap Press of Harvard University Press, 1971.

2. Lawrence A. Blum's *Moral Perception and Particularity* (Cambridge: Cambridge University Press, 1994) is helpful on this point.

3. Cf. W. D. Falk, "Morality, Self, and Others," in *Morality and the Language of Conduct*, ed. Hector-Neri Castaneda and George Nakhnikian (Detroit: Wayne State University Press, 1963).

4. Cf. ch. 1 in my *Living with One's Past: Personal Fates and Moral Pain* (Lanham, Md.: Rowman & Littlefield, 1996).

5. In ch. 3 below I consider a particular recovery strategy in some detail. In my *Living with One's Past: Personal Fates and Moral Pain*, I discuss in much detail the twelve-step program of Alcoholics Anonymous as a recovery strategy.

6. I discuss integrity in ch. 3 below. The wider notion of self-respect is discussed in ch. 4.

7. *Living with One's Past*, especially ch. 5.

8. AA, of course, is well aware of this issue. By and large, it sees the main motivation for *undertaking* the twelve-step program to be the intensity and extreme character of the "bottom" suffered by the alcoholic. In the short discussion of the first step of the twelve-step program ("We admitted we were powerless over alcohol, and our lives had become unmanageable") in *Twelve Steps and Twelve Traditions* (New York: Alcoholics Anonymous World Services, Inc., 1953), there are five references to death.

9. It is a metaphor accessible, I trust, to even the most unnerd-like persons among us.

10. For the latter point, see Harry G. Frankfurt's discussion of "unthinkables" in *The Importance of What We Care About* (Cambridge: Cambridge University Press, 1988), ch. 13.

11. *The Myth of Sisyphus*, trans. Justin O'Brien (New York: Vintage Books, 1955).

12. James, *The Will to Believe* (New York: Dover, 1956); and *The Varieties of Religious Experience* (New York: Penguin, 1982).

13. Wilson discusses the influence of James on him in ch. 2 of *Alcoholics Anonymous Comes of Age* (New York: Alcoholics Anonymous World Services, Inc., 1957), especially 64 ff.

14. Camus, *The Myth of Sisyphus*, 41.

15. See, for example, ch. 1 of *The Will to Believe*.

16. James, *The Will to Believe*, 82–83, 88, 171; see, too, 100–01.

17. *The Will to Believe*, 56–57.

18. *The Will to Believe*, 52.

19. *The Will to Believe*, 56–57.

20. Here I suspect that Camus himself commits the "philosophical suicide" he warns us against. For his view rests on the "positive" claim that life *is* meaningless, a claim that is ideological in the context of discussion that he provides. Camus goes beyond the agnostic's notion that whether life has meaning is unknown.

21. Cf. James, *The Will to Believe*, 100–01.

22. Cf. Bernard Williams's remarks about the function of "categorical desire," in "Persons, Character, and Morality," in *Moral Luck* (Cambridge: Cambridge University Press, 1981).

23. Camus, *The Myth of Sisyphus*, 40–41.
24. Camus, *The Myth of Sisyphus*, 51.
25. "Personality and Personality Disorders—Part II," *The Harvard Medical School Mental Health Letter* 4, no. 4 (October 1987), 4.
26. "William James and the Case of the Epileptic Patient," *The New York Review of Books*, 17 December 1998, 93.
27. Susan Sontag's famous essays—"Illness as Metaphor" (1978) and "AIDS and Its Metaphors" (1989)—argue that illness in some cases comes to be glossed by metaphorical spins that can be punitive and, in fact, increase the suffering of victims (in *Illness as Metaphor and AIDS and Its Metaphors* [New York: Doubleday, 1990]). My thought is that this can happen in the matter of whether or not basic attitudes are objects of choice.

CHAPTER 3

1. I am intrigued by the moral ranking by Maureen Dowd of President Clinton and "the unforgiving and hypocritical behavior of Henry Hyde, Bob Barr and their lynch mob," namely, that "it is worse to refuse to forgive than to need forgiveness" ("The Great Empath Basks in the Glow," *The [Cleveland] Plain Dealer*, 28 January 1999, 11-B).
2. John Rawls claims that self-respect has as one of its bases the respect of, as it were, selected others—in particular, "finding our person and deeds appreciated and confirmed by others who are likewise esteemed and their association enjoyed" (*A Theory of Justice* [Cambridge, Mass.: Belknap Press of Harvard University Press, 1971], 440). I discuss self-respect in ch. 4 below.
3. For discussion of the connections between forgiveness and repentance, see Jeffrie G. Murphy's essay, "Forgiveness and Resentment" (in *Forgiveness and Mercy*, Jeffrie G. Murphy and Jean Hampton [Cambridge: Cambridge University Press, 1988]), and Joram Graf Haber's *Forgiveness* (Savage, Md.: Rowman & Littlefield, 1991), especially the introduction and ch. 5.
4. New York: Schocken Books, 1966.
5. The letter itself was never given to the father, as I understand the history, but one suspects the father was aware of the unforgiveness.
6. *The Confessions*, trans. J. M. Cohen (Harmondsworth, U.K.: Penguin Books, 1954), book 2, 86–89. *The Reveries of the Solitary Walker*, trans., preface, notes, and interpretive essay by Charles E. Butterworth (New York: Harper Colophon, 1982), "Fourth Walk," 43–44.
7. I have benefited from a manuscript titled "Morally Managing Medical Mistakes" by Martin L. Smith and Heidi Forster (forthcoming in *Cambridge Quarterly of Healthcare Ethics*). How "medical mistakes" are dealt with is, of course, a problem for institutions (e.g., hospitals, medical schools, insurance companies) as well as for individual physicians. In my discussion I do not venture into the policy issues for institutions, but the paper by Smith and Forster does, as does Charles L. Bosk's *Forgive and Remember* (Chicago: University of Chicago Press, 1977).
8. New York: Simon and Schuster, 1994, 177–84.

9. I make use of the modularity thesis about the makeup of the self in *Living with One's Past: Personal Fates and Moral Pain* (Lanham, Md.: Rowman & Littlefield, 1996), especially chs. 3–5.

10. I suggest a "general structure" for "recovery strategies" in ch. 2 above (in the section titled "Ethical Theory and Recovery"). What follows assumes that account and does not modify it.

11. *The Unnatural Lottery* (Philadelphia: Temple University Press, 1996), ch. 2: "Responsibility and Moral Luck."

12. I think physicians ought to have exercises in self-knowledge built into their medical education—though I will not try to suggest here how such forms of education could or ought to be constructed.

13. There is an interesting issue lurking here that I will note but not be able to explore: if one does wrong or makes a serious mistake, and one suffers negative emotional pain, for how long must one endure such pain? In most cases punishments for legal wrongs have limits. Are there limits on moral-emotional suffering? Can one suffer moral-emotional pain for too long? Is one blameworthy if one's moral-emotional suffering ends "too soon"?

14. In a way that seems to me appropriate to the notion of generosity, Bill Wilson, the cofounder of Alcoholics Anonymous, writes in his powerful commentary on the twelve–step program, "Finally, we begin to see that all people, including ourselves, are to some extent emotionally ill as well as frequently wrong, and then we approach true tolerance and see what real love for our fellows actually means" (in *Twelve Steps and Twelve Traditions* [New York: Alcoholics Anonymous World Services, Inc., 1953], 92).

15. The numbers in parentheses are page references to the chapter titled "Responsibility and Moral Luck" in Card's *The Unnatural Lottery*.

16. For an early discussion distinguishing these different perspectives on our moral life, see Stuart Hampshire's "Fallacies in Moral Philosophy," in *Contemporary Ethical Theory*, ed. Joseph Margolis (New York: Random House, 1966) (first published in *Mind* 58 [1949]).

17. The helpful term *background stories* is used in Gary Watson's "Responsibility and the Limits of Evil: Variations on a Strawsonian Theme" (in *Responsibility, Character, and the Emotions*, ed. Ferdinand Schoeman [Cambridge: Cambridge University Press, 1987]).

18. "Integrity," *Ethics* 98 (October 1987).

19. For Card, the integrity project for victims of abuse or oppression may involve "constructing identity." William F. May's book in medical ethics, *The Patient's Ordeal* (Bloomington: Indiana University Press, 1991), concerns recovery from catastrophic or devastating illness (for example, for a burn victim). For May, recovery in cases of this extreme kind may also involve the construction—or, indeed, reconstruction—of identity.

20. Cf. some remarks in Card's lengthy review of *Women and Moral Theory*, edited by Eva Feder Kittay and Diana T. Meyers (Totowa, N.J.: Rowman & Littlefield, 1987) (*Ethics* 99 [October 1988], 130).

21. Card adds at this point, "To determine whether it is justifiable to hold an agent responsible, we may also need to know how that agent's luck compares

with that of those who would hold the agent responsible" (*The Unnatural Lottery,* 33).

22. See Harry G. Frankfurt's discussion of "necessities of the will" in the final essay, "Rationality and the Unthinkable," in *The Importance of What We Care About* (Cambridge: Cambridge University Press, 1988).

23. *The Will to Believe* (New York: Dover, 1956), 82–83, 88, 171; see, too, 100–01.

24. I do not wish to exaggerate the powers of such evidence, but I am charmed by Jeffrie G. Murphy's remarks about invoking experience: "I do not know what other test to apply. . . . I do not see how one can profitably discuss these issues in the abstract," ("Jean Hampton on Immorality, Self-Hatred, and Self-Forgiveness," *Philosophical Studies* 89 [1998]).

25. *Heavy Drinking* (Berkeley: University of California Press, 1988).

26. I discuss how one is to "live with others" when this epistemological difficulty is taken into account in ch. 4 of *Living with One's Past: Personal Fates and Moral Pain.*

CHAPTER 4

1. Cambridge, Mass.: Belknap Press of Harvard University Press, 1971. Rawls's theory of justice is, in part, a working out of Kantian ethics in political philosophy. Kant writes, "If legal justice perishes then it is no longer worthwhile for men to remain alive on this earth" (*The Metaphysical Elements of Justice* [1797], trans. John Ladd [Indianapolis: Bobbs-Merrill, 1965], 100).

2. See Rawls's discussion of self-respect in *A Theory of Justice,* 440 ff.

3. I have thought that paradigmatic examples of items having intrinsic value are activities one can be *absorbed* in "for their own sake," apart from any "benefits" they can lead to that are themselves valuable in some way. Think of being caught up in puzzling something out or listening to music so that one is absorbed in the activity but not profited by it, entertained by it, or made famous by it. The activity draws one into it, even if it is not particularly pleasant. Whatever the valuational character of self-respect, it is not of that sort. One can see how, philosophically, the notion of intrinsic value would be difficult to analyze. I will settle, again, for attempting to show how certain forms of self-respect "work." It does not follow from the fact that I am unclear whether there is a sense in which self-respect is an intrinsic value that, in fact, it is not an intrinsic value.

4. Immanuel Kant, *Lectures on Ethics,* trans. Louis Infield, foreword by Lewis White Beck (New York: Harper Torchbooks, 1963), 121.

5. Rawls, *A Theory of Justice,* 440.

6. Rawls, *A Theory of Justice,* 536.

7. "Servility and Self-Respect" (1973), in *Autonomy and Self-Respect,* Thomas E. Hill Jr. (Cambridge: Cambridge University Press, 1991) (first published in *The Monist*). Numbers in parentheses in this section are page references to this book.

8. Doubtless there are more.

9. Cf. Sharon Bishop Hill, "Self-Determination and Autonomy," in *Today's*

Moral Problems, 3rd edition, ed. Richard A. Wasserstrom (New York: Macmillan, 1985).

10. A full treatment of "dirty hands" problems, with emphasis on politics, is given in Michael Walzer's "Political Action: The Problem of Dirty Hands" (*Philosophy and Public Affairs* 2, no. 2 [winter 1973]). See, too, Thomas Nagel, "Ruthlessness in Public Life," in *Mortal Questions* (Cambridge: Cambridge University Press, 1979); and Bernard Williams, "Politics and Moral Character," in *Moral Luck* (Cambridge: Cambridge University Press, 1981).

11. Here I follow Thomas E. Hill Jr., "Self-Respect Reconsidered," in *Respect for Persons,* ed. O. H. Green (New Orleans: Tulane University, 1982), 132, 134, 137.

12. In my *Living with One's Past: Personal Fates and Moral Pain* (Lanham, Md.: Rowman & Littlefield, 1996), I discuss "personal moral absolutes" as ingredients of *integrity* (172–73). Cf. Lynne McFall, "Integrity," *Ethics* 98 (October 1987).

13. There have been many commentaries on American culture that criticize an apparent trend in social or popular morality emphasizing emotion and feeling over logic and "thought." My favorite short piece in this connection is Richard Stengel's "The Republic of Feeling," which I found on the Internet at <http://www.msnbc.com/news/247101.asp.html> (8 March 1999). I hope it is clear that my treatment of self-respect does not reduce it to "feeling good about oneself."

14. In *A Theory of Justice,* Rawls regularly distinguishes features of our nature that are results of "nature's lottery" from features that flow from "social contingency" (see 12, 15, 18, 74–75).

15. I discuss "membership in the moral community" in ch. 3 of my *On Sharing Fate* (Philadelphia: Temple University Press, 1987).

16. I call such thinking "persona moralism" in ch. 2 of my *Living with One's Past: Personal Fates and Moral Pain.*

17. I am not the first one to think of the moral community as in some sense "transcending" local and national communities. The notion is present in Locke's *Second Treatise* (in *Locke's Two Treatises of Government,* ed. Peter Laslett [Cambridge: Cambridge University Press, 1963]) and certainly in Kant's ethics (wherein moral agents form a "realm of ends" distinct from any particularized local or national community). I am moved by the words of Vaclav Havel in a recent speech:

> I have often asked myself why human beings have any rights at all. I always come to the conclusion that human rights, human freedoms, and human dignity have their deepest roots somewhere outside the perceptible world. These values are as powerful as they are because, under certain circumstances, people accept them without compulsion and are willing to die for them, and they make sense only in the perspective of the infinite and the eternal. . . . [W]hile the state is a human creation, human beings are the creation of God. ["Kosovo and the End of the Nation-State," *The New York Review of Books,* 10 June 1999, 6]

I join in the view that the moral community is "transcendent," but I would keep my interpretation of that notion quite secular (as in ch. 3 of my *On Sharing Fate*).

18. As I suggest above, I do not want the notion of "local and national communities" to be narrow. Let it include, for example, the "communities" one belongs to or aspires to belong to relative to one's work (the scientific community, the art world, etc.). The notion of "local community" need not be geographical, and it may transcend generations as well. (Einstein, for example, had membership in the same community as Newton and Aristotle; similarly, Descartes, Hume, and Kant had membership in a [different] community of inquirers.)

19. What follows might fit as well in an account of how "self-realization" is to be understood. I discuss self-realization in ch. 8 of my *On Sharing Fate*. What I offer here complements that earlier account.

20. Rawls, *A Theory of Justice*, 15, 72.

21. These elements seem built into the notion of rationality in Rawls's account in *A Theory of Justice*: a plan of life is that one that would be chosen by a person "with full deliberative rationality, that is, with full awareness of the relevant facts and after a careful consideration of the consequences" (408). Needless to say (perhaps), *full* awareness of *all* relevant facts is hard to come by. See my discussion of this matter in ch. 4 of *On Sharing Fate*.

22. Rawls refers to this as the "Aristotelian Principle," which he characterizes in *A Theory of Justice* as "a basic principle of motivation" (424):

> Other things equal, human beings enjoy the exercise of their realized capacities (their innate or trained abilities), and this enjoyment increases the more the capacity is realized, or the greater its complexity. The intuitive idea here is that human beings take more pleasure in doing something as they become more proficient at it, and of two activities they do equally well, they prefer the one calling on a larger repertoire of more intricate and subtle discriminations. [426]

23. Rawls comments, "Unless our endeavors are appreciated by our associates it is impossible for us to maintain the conviction that they are worthwhile" (*A Theory of Justice*, 441).

24. Here again I find useful the essay by Sharon Bishop Hill: "Self-Determination and Autonomy."

25. Rawls's account is compatible with these points. In one place Rawls suggests that a rational plan of life is a series of "subplans suitably arranged in a hierarchy, the broad features of the plan allowing for the more permanent aims and interests that complement one another" (*A Theory of Justice*, 411). I have to say that this is perhaps too tidy a characterization for application to the de facto plans of life of real people. Interestingly, Rawls makes use of the notion of plan of life to provide a gloss on human *happiness*: a person may be said to be happy "when he is more or less successfully in the way of carrying out this plan" (*A Theory of Justice*, 93).

26. This way of thinking about the rights people have in a just society is found in Locke, Kant, and Rawls. The view that the rights people have *in* a just society are to be thought of as logically prior to actual social institutions and practices is expressed most powerfully in Ronald Dworkin's writings, for example, *Taking*

Rights Seriously (Cambridge, Mass.: Harvard University Press, 1978), especially chs. 4, 7, 12, 13. See, too, Dworkin's *A Matter of Principle* (Cambridge, Mass.: Harvard University Press, 1985), *Law's Empire* (Cambridge, Mass.: Belknap Press of Harvard University Press, 1986), and *Life's Dominion* (New York: Random House [Vintage], 1994).

27. I discuss "self-realization" briefly in the next chapter and more fully in ch. 8 of *Living with One's Past: Personal Fates and Moral Pain*.

CHAPTER 5

1. See Ralph Miliband, *The State in Capitalist Society* (London: Weidenfeld and Nicolson, 1969), for a characteristic socialist critique of capitalist democracy in which this claim is basic.

2. Michael Harrington, *Toward a Democratic Left* (New York: Macmillan Co., 1968), 56. Harrington describes such a recommendation as at least "radical"—if neither "revolutionary" nor "socialist"—when the decision in question is arrived at through the democratic process.

3. One full treatment is given in David Braybrooke's *Meeting Needs* (Princeton, N.J.: Princeton University Press, 1987).

4. W. G. Runciman argues for such a priority in *Relative Deprivation and Social Justice* (London: Routledge and Kegan Paul, 1966), especially part 4.

5. For present purposes, to say of *r* that it has independent justificatory force is to say that *r* is a *reason* for action that is, so to speak, *complete* unto itself; in other words, its provision of "reason to act" is not dependent on related or further facts.

6. Brian Barry, *Political Argument* (London: Routledge and Kegan Paul, 1965), especially 48–49.

7. Barry, *Political Argument*, 48.

8. Barry, *Political Argument*, 49 (emphasis added).

9. This follows the first passage from Barry's text quoted above.

10. Cf. Joel Feinberg's remark that "we don't think of every desire or even every need as a claim, but important needs are another matter. They 'cry out,' we say, for satisfaction" ("Duties, Rights, and Claims," *American Philosophical Quarterly* 3 [1966], 142).

11. Daniel Callahan has argued in recent books that even needs for medical care may not be such that we should "spare no expense": see *Setting Limits: Medical Goals in an Aging Society* (New York: Simon and Schuster, 1987) and *What Kind of Life: The Limits of Medical Progress* (New York: Simon and Schuster, 1990).

12. Barry, *Political Argument*, 49.

13. I discuss this in "Hidden Reasons" in appendix B.

14. Something rather close to this view is suggested by George Schrader's remark, "It is the sheer *fact* of the other's existence in all its concreteness that constitutes the initial ground of our obligation to him" ("Autonomy, Heteronomy, and Moral Imperatives," *The Journal of Philosophy* 60, no. 3 [1963], 74).

15. My view here seems to me to parallel P. F. Strawson's argument for the

"practical inconceivability" of determinism from the "human commitment to participation in ordinary inter-personal relationships" in "Freedom and Resentment" (*Proceedings of the British Academy* 48 [1962]). See, too, H. L. A. Hart's notion of "natural necessity" (*The Concept of Law* [London: Clarendon Press, 1961], 195).

16. *Utilitarianism* (1863), ed. George Sher (Indianapolis: Hackett, 1979), ch. 3.

17. I am moved by Michael Ignatieff's remark, "Being human is a second nature which history taught us, and which terror and deprivation can batter us into forgetting" (*The Needs of Strangers* [New York: Viking Penguin, 1984], 142). I suspect that what I call "moral-emotional nature" is part of Ignatieff's "second nature."

18. These remarks summarize some themes from my book, *On Sharing Fate* (Philadelphia: Temple University Press, 1987), which concerns the nature and character of individual responsibility in a world of the sort we find ourselves in.

19. Onora O'Neill, *Faces of Hunger* (London: Allen and Unwin, 1986).

20. *A Discourse on the Origin of Inequality* (1755), in *The Social Contract and Discourses*, trans. and introduction by G. D. H. Cole (New York: Everyman, 1950), 271–72.

21. *Ground projects* is Bernard Williams's term, in "Persons, Character, and Morality," in *Moral Luck* (Cambridge: Cambridge University Press, 1981).

22. "How the Figures Add Up," *The Guardian*, 23 April 1984.

23. "The Art World," *The New Yorker*, 21 March 1983, 95.

24. Cf. Leo N. Tolstoy, *What Is Art?* (1896), trans. Almyer Maude, introduction by Vincent Tomas (Indianapolis: Bobbs-Merrill, 1960).

25. "Toward a Redefinition of Public Sculpture," paper presented at the U.S./Japan Symposium on Urban Life and Culture, 1–4 October 1982.

26. Statement made available by the artist.

27. Tompkins, "The Art World," 92.

28. "Out of Order: The Public Art Machine," *Art Forum* (December 1988), 96.

29. See Lucy Lippard, *Athena Tacha: Massacre Memorials and Other Public Projects*, exhibition essay, Max Hutchinson Gallery, New York, 25 October–17 November 1984.

30. Carrie Rickey, "The Writing on the Wall," *Art in America* (May 1981), 54–55.

31. The following remarks draw on my discussion of self-realization in ch. 8 of *On Sharing Fate*.

32. *The German Ideology*, in *The Marx–Engels Reader*, ed. Robert C. Tucker (New York: Norton, 1972), 124.

33. *Foundations of the Metaphysics of Morals* (1785), trans. and introduction by Lewis White Beck (Indianapolis: Bobbs-Merrill, 1959), section 2, 40.

34. *The World Viewed: Reflections on the Ontology of Film*, enlarged edition (Cambridge, Mass.: Harvard University Press, 1971), 32.

35. Cf. Kendall L. Walton, "Categories of Art," *The Philosophical Review* 79 (1970).

36. *Diary* (1909), in *The Diaries of Paul Klee, 1898–1918* (Berkeley: University of California Press, 1964).

37. Clement Greenberg, "After Abstract Expressionism" (1962), in *Aesthetics,* ed. George Dickie and Richard J. Sclafani (New York: St. Martin's Press, 1977). Cf. Michael Fried, *Three American Painters* (Cambridge, Mass.: Fogg Art Museum, Harvard University, 1965).

38. Paul Griffiths, *Cage* (London: Oxford University Press, 1981), 44.

39. John Cage, "Experimental Music: Doctrine" (1955, 1958), reprinted from *Silence* (1961) in *Modern Culture and the Arts,* ed. James B. Hall and Barry Ulanov (New York: McGraw-Hill, 1967), 89.

40. Cage, "Experimental Music: Doctrine," 89.

41. Cage, "Experimental Music: Doctrine," 89.

42. Griffiths, *Cage,* 44.

43. Cage, "Experimental Music: Doctrine," 89.

44. Cage, "Experimental Music: Doctrine," 91.

45. Cage, "Experimental Music: Doctrine," 89.

46. Cage, "Experimental Music: Doctrine," 93.

47. Cage, "Experimental Music: Doctrine," 91.

48. Cage, "Experimental Music: Doctrine," 91.

49. John Cage, *Empty Words* (Middletown, Conn.: Wesleyan University Press, 1974–79), 3.

50. "A Very Real Obscenity" (editorial), *The (Cleveland) Plain Dealer,* 15 November 1990, 8-B.

51. "A Very Real Obscenity," 8-B.

CHAPTER 6

Acknowledgments. For help with earlier drafts of the novel ideas part of this chapter, I am grateful to David Orr, Ernest Partridge, Barbara Care, Daniel Merrill, George Rainbolt, Rudd Crawford, Steven Volk, and Phyllis Morris.

1. My thoughts on what it is to be an "independent policy maker for a free society" put together features from, for example, the position of the Supreme Court justice, the tenured professor with academic freedom and research time, and the Rawlsian parties to the original position. But the position of the independent policy maker in a free society is not identical to any of these. In rough terms, the independent policy maker is the "participant" in an "agreement group" engaged in the "strong participation" discussed in ch. 4 of my *On Sharing Fate* (Philadelphia: Temple University Press, 1987), but the "free society" here is not necessarily the "moral community."

2. Here I think of the words of A. M. Honoré: "Moral duties are pitched at a point where the conformity of the ordinary man can reasonably be expected" ("Law, Morals, and Rescue," in *Philosophy of Law,* 2nd edition, ed. Joel Feinberg and Hyman Gross [Belmont, Calif.: Wadsworth, 1980], 441).

3. The phrase is Robert L. Heilbroner's, in *An Inquiry into the Human Prospect* (New York: Norton, 1975, 1974), 114.

4. This is the theme of Christopher Lasch's *The Culture of Narcissism* (New York: Norton, 1979).

5. This supposition is not meant to deny either that morality requires other things as well, for example, policies that address destitution among *current* people, or even that these latter policies are more urgent or important than policies regarding our legacy for the world of the future. The "motivation problem" I discuss in this chapter is independent of this priority issue. See, too, the last paragraph of the next section.

6. See David Hume, *An Enquiry Concerning the Principles of Morals* (1777), in *Hume's Enquiries,* ed. L. A. Selby-Bigge (Oxford: Clarendon, 1962), section 9.

7. See *On Sharing Fate*, ch. 4, especially section 5.

8. See John Rawls, *A Theory of Justice* (Cambridge, Mass.: Belknap Press of Harvard University Press, 1971), 145, 176–77, 423, for discussion of "the strains of commitment." Rawls writes,

> The general facts of human psychology and the principles of moral learning are relevant matters for the parties to examine. If a conception of justice is unlikely to generate its own support, or lacks stability, this fact must not be overlooked. . . . [T]hey will not enter into agreements they know they cannot keep, or can do so only with great difficulty. Along with other considerations, they count the strains of commitment. [145]

By way of examples of what is meant, Rawls argues that agreements that have the parties acquiescing in a loss of freedom over a lifetime for the sake of the greater good of others "exceed the capacity of human nature" (176) and that the parties "cannot agree to a conception of justice if the consequences of applying it may lead to self-reproach should the least happy possibilities be realized. They should strive to be free from such regrets" (423). Rawls adds, though, that if the only possible candidate conceptions of justice all involved risks that similarly exceed the capacity of human nature, then "the problem of the strains of commitment would have to be waived" (177).

9. Perhaps, though, it is difficult to feel much toward persons in large numbers. Henry Sidgwick remarks that "one cannot easily sympathize with each individual in a multitude" (*Methods of Ethics*, 7th edition [1907] [New York: Dover, 1966], 251).

10. Heilbroner, *An Inquiry into the Human Prospect*, 114–15.

11. Heilbroner, *An Inquiry into the Human Prospect*, 131, 132, 135–36.

12. Heilbroner's pessimistic motivational claim may be controversial, of course. Cf. Joel Feinberg's remarks: "I shall assume . . . that it is psychologically possible for us to care about our remote descendants, that many of us do in fact care, and indeed that we ought to care" ("The Rights of Animals and Unborn Generations," in *Today's Moral Problems*, 2nd edition, ed. Richard A. Wasserstrom [New York: Macmillan, 1979], 581).

13. Feinberg, "The Rights of Animals and Unborn Generations," 598.

14. The equal opportunity maxim is discussed by Brian Barry in "Circumstances of Justice and Future Generations," in *Obligations to Future Generations*, ed. R. I. Sikora and Brian Barry (Philadelphia: Temple University Press, 1978),

242–44; the custody maxim is endorsed though not discussed by Barry in "Justice between Generations," in *Law, Morality and Society*, ed. P. M. S. Hacker and Joseph Raz (Oxford: Clarendon Press, 1977), 284. (Barry remarks at the end of the latter essay that these maxims might form the minimum content of the "new ethics" that some theorists call for regarding our obligations to future people.) The equal opportunity maxim is characterized as a "global extension" of a principle for families that have wealth to pass on, namely, "Keep the capital intact" ("Circumstances of Justice and Future Generations," 243–44). One might ask, Why don't our intuitions pick out a "global extension" of the principle that immigrants to a new nation promising great opportunity and material improvement have been known to follow regarding their own level of sacrifice for their children, namely, "Your lot better than mine"? I can think of two things that bear on why the immigrants' principle does not seem right for the world of the future, even though they do not settle this matter: (1) the facelessness and impersonality of future people such that their fate does not arouse our ambition, or even our concern, in the way the fate of our own children may; and (2) the sense we have— perhaps itself a recent development among us—that our resources are now strained, so that we could not do better than pass the world along "intact" without excessive sacrifice. Barry discusses the appropriateness of "equal opportunity justice" for future generations further in "Intergenerational Justice in Energy Policy," in *Energy and the Future*, ed. Douglas MacLean and Peter G. Brown (Totowa, N.J.: Rowman & Littlefield, 1983).

15. See Immanuel Kant, *Foundations of the Metaphysics of Morals* (1785), trans. and introduction by Lewis White Beck (Indianapolis: Bobbs-Merrill, 1959), section 2. Kant writes,

> If reason of itself does not sufficiently determine the will . . . , in a word, if the will is not of itself in complete accord with reason (the actual case of men), then the actions which are recognized as objectively necessary are subjectively contingent, and the determination of such a will according to objective laws is constraint. That is, the relation of objective laws to a will which is not completely good is conceived as the determination of the will of a rational being by principles of reason to which this will is not by nature necessarily obedient. [section 2]

16. Such accounts include, for example, Kant's theory of the categorical imperative or Mill's utilitarianism.

17. Cf. H. L. A. Hart, *The Concept of Law* (Oxford: Clarendon Press, 1961), 189–95. Hart writes,

> It is a truth of some importance that for the adequate description not only of law but of many other social institutions, a place must be reserved, besides definitions and ordinary statements of fact, for a third category of statements: those the truth of which is contingent on human beings and the world they live in retaining the salient characteristics which they have. [195]

18. Again, this follows Feinberg in "The Rights of Animals and Unborn Generations":

> It is important to reemphasize here that the questions of whether fetuses [in our case, future people] do or ought to have rights are substantive questions of law and morals open to argument and decision. The prior question of whether fetuses [in our case, future people] are the kind of beings that can have rights, however, is a conceptual, not a moral question, amenable only to what is called "logical analysis," and irrelevant to moral judgment. The correct answer to the conceptual question, I believe, is that unborn children [in our case, future people] are among the sorts of beings of whom possession of rights can meaningfully be predicated, even though they are (temporarily) incapable of having interests, because their future interests can be protected now, and it does make sense to protect a potential interest even before it has grown into actuality. [587]

One must add, though, that how far our protection of the interests of future people is effective depends "on the behavior of the intervening generations, whom we have no way of binding" (Barry, "Justice between Generations," 276).

19. Rawls writes, "We acquire attachments to persons and institutions according to how we perceive our good to be affected by them. The basic idea is one of reciprocity, a tendency to answer in kind. Now this tendency is a deep psychological fact. Without it our nature would be very different and fruitful social cooperation fragile if not impossible" (*A Theory of Justice*, 494–95).

20. Perhaps it is already known that these are not thought of highly as motivational bases relative to the world of the present either. As Barrington Moore Jr. puts it, "By itself, love, sympathetic identification, empathy, or whatever one chooses to call this elusive emotion or series of emotions, is nowhere near enough to hold together any large human society and make it run. Under certain conditions it can be very powerful. But it won't get food and water into the cities and garbage off the streets" (*Injustice: The Social Bases of Obedience and Revolt* [White Plains, N.Y.: Sharpe, 1978], 99).

21. Here I am following the advice in the quotation from Feinberg at the beginning of note 18.

22. Cf. Rawls, in *A Theory of Justice*, who writes, "Individuals in their role as citizens with a full understanding of the content of the principles of justice may be moved to act upon them largely because of their bonds to particular persons and an attachment to their own society" (475).

23. For helpful studies of the moral emotions, see Herbert Morris, *On Guilt and Innocence* (Berkeley: University of California Press, 1976).

24. How this arousal works, that is, what its mechanisms are, I do not know. Its characterization is a problem for psychology.

25. Apparently, we are positioned so as to have unilateral power over future people. Some might argue that because we have power over the fate of future people, but they have no power over our fate, we can have no *obligations* to them.

But I do not hold that obligations require reciprocal power relations. Nor do I think that the absence of reciprocation qua exchange of ideas and interpretations of ends eliminates the possibility of morality requiring something of us relative to future people. Cf. Barry, "Justice between Generations," 269–70.

26. Rawls, *A Theory of Justice*, 475.

27. It may be that this "appropriate conception of what morality requires" is what Rawls calls "the conception of justice as fairness"; but it is not my aim here to make a case for this claim. In ch. 7 of *On Sharing Fate* I discuss the compatibility of shared-fate individualism as a moral conception for individual responsibility with the Rawlsian conception of justice as fairness for the basic structure of society.

28. Cf. ch. 4, "Participation and Policy," in *On Sharing Fate*, especially section 5.

29. Feinberg, "The Rights of Animals and Unborn Generations," 599.

30. Rawls, *A Theory of Justice*, 491.

31. It is not clear to me whether the form of motivation I call "extended shared-fate motivation" is what Rawls calls "the sense of justice." Perhaps there is a certain ambiguity in Rawls's work on this point. Much of his discussion is conducted under the assumption that the subject of justice is the basic structure of the nation-state: "The relevant systems here, of course, are the basic structures of the well-ordered societies corresponding to the different conceptions of justice. . . . Now I assume that the boundaries of these schemes are given by the notion of a self-contained national community" (*A Theory of Justice*, 458). But the shared-fate motivation requisite to the nation-state is hardly "extended" at all when contrasted with the extended shared-fate motivation needed to support policies implementing what morality requires for the world of the future. The latter, I have suggested, is linked to the idea of a community *without* "boundaries" in any familiar sense. In certain parts of Rawls's discussion, though, it seems clear that his sense of justice is something like the more "extreme" extended shared-fate motivation that I have in mind (see, for example, 587). Cf. Barry, "Circumstances of Justice and Future Generations," especially 235–37.

32. Cf. David Gauthier, "The Social Contract as Ideology," *Philosophy and Public Affairs* 6 (winter 1977).

33. Here I should note that my discussion is limited. I have not, for example, canvassed all the forms of motivation that might operate on behalf of what Ernest Partridge has called "self-transcendence," in "Why Care about the Future?" in *Responsibilities to Future Generations*, ed. Ernest Partridge (Buffalo, N.Y.: Prometheus Press, 1981). It is not part of my view in any case that ordinary people are locked into their present lives in a narrow way. We do make provision for our children, our reputations, and the projects we care about, well into the future. But the special problem for my imagined "independent policy makes for a free society," sketched at the beginning of the discussion, should be recalled. It is not at all clear to me that, in the circumstances there imagined, the familiar motivational bases of "ordinary" self-transcendence are "available and reliable" to support policies of serious sacrifice as they may be required by morality for the world of the future. And, as I have suggested (though with little elaboration),

the form of motivation that might be directly serviceable in this connection, namely, extended shared-fate motivation, is hardly *cultivated* by our current social institutions and moral ideology.

34. I hope this "motivation problem" is of interest to philosophy. It might also be of interest to advertising, propaganda, politics, and even education.

35. I discuss this in "Environmental Crisis and Morality" (1989), a reading program prepared for the Ohio Humanities Council (P. O. Box 06354, Columbus, Ohio 42306) for use in public libraries.

36. *Walden* (1854), introduction by Norman Holmes Pearson (New York: Rinehart, 1948).

37. Thoreau, *Walden*, 274.

38. Thoreau, *Walden*, 74.

39. Thoreau, *Walden*, 173.

40. Thoreau, *Walden*, 277.

41. Thoreau, *Walden*, 275.

42. *A Sand County Almanac* (1949) (New York: Ballantine Books, 1970), xviii.

43. Leopold, *A Sand County Almanac*, xviii–xix.

44. *Philosophy Gone Wild* (Buffalo, N.Y.: Prometheus Books, 1986); *Environmental Ethics* (Philadelphia: Temple University Press, 1988).

45. Rolston, *Environmental Ethics*, 73.

46. This is so, too, in the case of the "radical reconceptualization" in John Cage's work, discussed above in ch. 5, whereby the contrast between sound and silence is abolished, thereby letting silence be considered sound (and "sitting quietly listening" be considered "producing" sound and possibly music).

47. This could include sound, in the case of Cage's view.

48. Even in Cage's view there is a normative element beyond the conceptual maneuvering. It is what I refer to in ch. 5 as an "ethics of sound": alongside the move in Cage's conception whereby we think differently about silence, the normative proposal urges us to adopt a new attitude, namely, the attitude of respect, toward the environmental items (in this case items we have in auditory sensation) that the novel conception of sound is "about." Sounds (too) are worthy of respect, in this interpretation of Cage's conception, even the ones we used to call "silence."

49. That is, I do not think the question is outside the ken of philosophy.

50. In *The Social Contract and Discourses*, trans. and introduction by G. D. H. Cole (New York: Everyman, 1950).

51. So I argue in *On Sharing Fate*.

52. Leopold, *A Sand County Almanac*, 197.

53. I offer explanation and discussion in *Living with One's Past: Personal Fates and Moral Pain* (Lanham, Md.: Rowman & Littlefield, 1996), especially ch. 5.

CHAPTER 7

1. Cf. H. L. A. Hart, *The Concept of Law* (Oxford: Clarendon, 1961), chs. 7 and 9, especially 160.

2. This might be one way to understand the doctrine of "natural sympathy" in the tradition of utilitarianism. Cf., for example, John Stuart Mill, *Utilitarianism* (1863), ed. George Sher (Indianapolis: Hackett, 1979), ch. 3.

3. I suppose one might ask, Are there very many "morally good people"? I have not made an empirical count and, in fact, would not know how to go about making one. For whatever it may be worth, my sense of the situation is that, despite what I go on to discuss in this final chapter, most people are "morally good people." I do not take myself as writing about a small number of people. Even morally good people suffer "lapses," of course—which is part of what this chapter is about.

4. In *Karl Marx: Early Writings*, ed. T. B. Bottomore (New York: McGraw-Hill, 1964).

5. In *A Theory of Justice* (Cambridge, Mass.: Belknap Press of Harvard University Press, 1971).

6. The famous restructuring maxim, "abolish private property," is expressed by Marx and Engels in *The Communist Manifesto* (1848), introduction by Martin Malia (New York: Penguin [Signet Classic], 1998).

7. I think Marx's theory of alienation cannot be reduced to an effort to describe psychological phenomena. The four forms of alienation are variations on a relation that I understand to require analysis in terms of the notions of *independence* and *usability*. To be alienated, as I interpret Marx, is not necessarily to feel alienated.

8. In *Foundations of the Metaphysics of Morals* (1785), trans. and introduction by Lewis White Beck (Indianapolis: Bobbs-Merrill, 1959); especially section 2.

9. This ideal is not compatible even with a just liberal capitalism of the sort, for example, that Rawls outlines in *A Theory of Justice*.

10. Certain questions are prompted by this characterization of the fault in capitalism. One of these is whether that fault, as specified, is a necessary truth about capitalism or a contingent (though perhaps general and prevailing) fact about it. The distinction between "necessary" and "contingent" here may make a large difference to the question of the extent to which the radical social prescription can be considered supported. And it is useful to remember that while the feature in question may be a necessary truth about capitalism, that is, about the way of organizing economic life that employs the institution of private property, it may not on that account be necessarily a *pervasive* feature of a liberal society, that is, that complex of practices and institutions of which certain structures form an economic "sector." A further important question is whether it can be argued that the fault—even if it is a necessary feature of capitalism—can be, in at least some circumstances, morally tolerable.

11. Certain contemporary "communitarian" conceptions of the self object to the independence of the self characteristic of the Kantian view. In my *On Sharing Fate* (Philadelphia: Temple University Press, 1987), I discuss the communitarian views of Michael Sandel in *Liberalism and the Limits of Justice* (Cambridge: Cambridge University Press, 1982) and Bernard Williams in *Moral Luck* (Cambridge: Cambridge University Press, 1981).

12. *Entail* seems the correct term here, for Marx. When a society is capitalist

in its economic life, it *follows*, for Marx, that the people in it—all of them—are alienated in the manner described above. Accordingly, if a society were to "change" (perhaps through revolution) from capitalism to some other organizational mode of economic life, then the people in it would not be alienated—though, indeed, the new form of society might have difficulties of other kinds.

13. Albany: State University of New York Press, 1996. Numbers in parentheses in this section are page references to this book.

14. Cf. "Problematic Agency," in my *Living with One's Past: Personal Fates and Moral Pain* (Lanham, Md.: Rowman & Littlefield, 1996), ch. 3.

15. So I argue in *Living with One's Past: Personal Fates and Moral Pain*.

16. This paragraph draws on n. 4 of "Personal Moralism," in *Living with One's Past: Personal Fates and Moral Pain*, ch. 2, 163.

17. In *Classics of Modern Fiction*, ed. Irving Howe (New York: Harcourt Brace Jovanovich, 1968, 1972). My discussion focuses on part 1 of this work by Dostoevsky.

18. Dostoevsky, *Notes from Underground*, 34.

19. Dostoevsky, *Notes from Underground*, 27.

20. Dostoevsky, *Notes from Underground*, 39.

21. Dostoevsky, *Notes from Underground*, 33.

22. Dostoevsky, *Notes from Underground*, 33.

23. Dostoevsky, *Notes from Underground*, 37.

24. Dostoevsky, *Notes from Underground*, 37.

25. Dostoevsky, *Notes from Underground*, 24.

26. At the end of editor's introduction to the collection titled *Challenges to Morality* (New York: Macmillan, 1993), Jonathan Harrison writes, "I do not myself know what the academic justification of moral beliefs is. . . . Moral beliefs resemble neither factual statements about the world nor the truths of mathematics and logic. They do not seem to fit into any known pigeon hole of justification" (40). That view might point toward a sort of moral indifference—though in any case Harrison himself goes on to say,

> But if one turns one's attention from the academic problem of justifying moral *beliefs* to that of finding reasons for having moral *rules*, it is not difficult to justify morality—up to a point, at any rate. We have morality because we need it. Having its members keep their promises; pay their debts; bring up their children; cooperate with one another; be honest, kind, moderately nonaggressive, truthful, and reliable are qualities that for rather obvious reasons benefit a community. . . . [T]he belief that they are obligations or duties does reinforce them. [40]

27. Rawls writes in *A Theory of Justice*, "The conception of justice, should it be truly effective and publicly recognized as such, seems more likely than its rivals to transform our perspective on the social world and to reconcile us to the dispositions of the natural order and the conditions of human life" (512).

28. See my discussion in ch. 5 above and, more fully, in *On Sharing Fate*.

29. This is also invoked in ch. 4 above.

30. I think here of recent discussions that warn that morality can be interpreted in a way that makes it too "strenuous," in which case we suffer what Peter Railton has called "alienation" from morality itself; see Railton, "Alienation, Consequentialism, and the Demands of Morality," *Philosophy and Public Affairs* 13 (spring 1984).

31. See Kant's characterization of "good will," in *Foundations of the Metaphysics of Morals*, 10.

APPENDIX A

1. This may be a slight overstatement. One thinks of certain sorts of non-system-of-rules elements that may be involved in explaining moves in games or constituent actions in some cases. Thus, the psychology of the mean or nasty player (or agent) may be a factor in the performance of certain moves in games or constituent actions—moves or actions that are permitted by the system of rules but would be especially hard on opponents or competitors.

2. Cf. John Rawls, "Two Concepts of Rules," *The Philosophical Review* 64 (1955), 3–32.

3. Cf. Ludwig Wittgenstein, *Philosophical Investigations*, trans. G. E. M. Anscombe (New York: Macmillan, 1953), para. 205 ff.

4. This is the first part of the meaning of the "logical space" metaphor I use above.

5. This is the second part of the meaning of the "logical space" metaphor.

6. This view that motive explanations are to be understood as characterizations or redescriptions of actions is held by G. E. M. Anscombe in *Intention* (Oxford: Blackwell, 1957), 21; and also by A. I. Melden in *Free Action* (London: Routledge and Kegan Paul, 1961), 88.

APPENDIX B

1. Peter Alexander, "Rational Behaviour and Psychoanalytic Explanation," *Mind* 71 (July 1962), 326–41; especially 328–39 and 337.

2. Theodore Mischel, "Concerning Rational Behaviour and Psychoanalytic Explanation," *Mind* 74 (January 1965), 71–78; especially 76–77.

3. Mischel, "Concerning Rational Behaviour and Psychoanalytic Explanation," 77 (emphasis added).

4. Mischel, "Concerning Rational Behaviour and Psychoanalytic Explanation," 77.

Works Cited

Alcoholics Anonymous Comes of Age. New York: Alcoholics Anonymous World Services, Inc., 1957.

Alexander, Peter. "Rational Behaviour and Psychoanalytic Explanations." *Mind* 71 (July 1962).

Anscombe, G. E. M. *Intention*. Oxford: Blackwell, 1957.

Aristotle. *The Nicomachean Ethics*. Ed. W. D. Ross. London: Oxford University Press, 1980.

Barry, Brian. *Political Argument*. London: Routledge and Kegan Paul, 1965.

———. "Justice between Generations." In *Law, Morality and Society*, ed. P. M. S. Hacker and Joseph Raz. Oxford: Clarendon Press, 1977.

———. "Circumstances of Justice and Future Generations." In *Obligations to Future Generations*, ed. R. I. Sikora and Brian Barry. Philadelphia: Temple University Press, 1978.

———. "Intergenerational Justice in Energy Policy." In *Energy and the Future*, ed. Douglas MacLean and Peter G. Brown. Totowa, N.J.: Rowman & Littlefield, 1983.

Blum, Lawrence A. *Moral Perception and Particularity*. Cambridge: Cambridge University Press, 1994.

Bosk, Charles L. *Forgive and Remember*. Chicago: University of Chicago Press, 1977.

Braybrooke, David. *Meeting Needs*. Princeton, N.J.: Princeton University Press, 1987.

Cage, John. "Experimental Music: Doctrine" (1955, 1958). Reprinted from *Silence* (1961) in *Modern Culture and the Arts*, ed. James B. Hall and Barry Ulanov. New York: McGraw-Hill, 1967.

———. *Empty Words*. Middletown, Conn.: Wesleyan University Press, 1974–79.

Callahan, Daniel. *Setting Limits: Medical Goals in an Aging Society*. New York: Simon and Schuster, 1987.

189

———. *What Kind of Life: The Limits of Medical Progress*. New York: Simon and Schuster, 1990.

Camus, Albert. *The Myth of Sisyphus*. Trans. Justin O'Brien. New York: Vintage Books, 1955.

Card, Claudia. "Review of *Women and Moral Theory*, ed. Eva Feder Kittay and Diana T. Meyers." *Ethics* 99 (October 1988).

———. *The Unnatural Lottery*. Philadelphia: Temple University Press, 1996.

Care, Norman S. *On Sharing Fate*. Philadelphia: Temple University Press, 1987.

———. "Environmental Crisis and Morality." 1989. A reading program prepared for the Ohio Humanities Council (P. O. Box 06354, Columbus, Ohio 42306) for use in public libraries.

———. *Living with One's Past: Personal Fates and Moral Pain*. Lanham, Md.: Rowman & Littlefield, 1996.

Cavell, Stanley. *The World Viewed: Reflections on the Ontology of Film*, enlarged edition. Cambridge, Mass.: Harvard University Press, 1971.

Dietrichson, Paul. "What Does Kant Mean by 'Acting from Duty'?" In *Kant*, ed. Robert Paul Wolff. Garden City, N.Y.: Anchor Books,1967.

Dostoevsky, Fyodor. *Notes from Underground*. In *Classics of Modern Fiction*, ed. Irving Howe. New York: Harcourt Brace Jovanovich, 1968, 1972.

Dowd, Maureen. "The Great Empath Basks in the Glow." *The (Cleveland) Plain Dealer*, 28 January 1999.

Dworkin, Ronald. *Taking Rights Seriously*. Cambridge, Mass.: Harvard University Press, 1978.

———. *A Matter of Principle*. Cambridge, Mass.: Harvard University Press, 1985.

———. *Law's Empire*. Cambridge, Mass.: Belknap Press of Harvard University Press, 1986.

———. *Life's Dominion*. New York: Random House (Vintage), 1994.

Elliott, Carl. *The Rules of Insanity: Moral Responsibility and the Mentally Ill Offender*. Albany: State University of New York Press, 1996.

Falk, W. D. "Morality, Self, and Others." In *Morality and the Language of Conduct*, ed. Hector-Neri Castaneda and George Nakhnikian. Detroit: Wayne State University Press, 1963.

Feinberg, Joel. "Duties, Rights, and Claims." *American Philosophical Quarterly* 3 (1966).

———. "The Rights of Animals and Unborn Generations." In *Today's Moral Problems*, 2nd edition, ed. Richard A. Wasserstrom. New York: Macmillan, 1979.

Fingarette, Herbert. *Heavy Drinking*. Berkeley: University of California Press, 1988.

Fishkin, James S. *The Limits of Obligation*. New Haven, Conn.: Yale University Press, 1982.

Frankfurt, Harry G. *The Importance of What We Care About*. Cambridge: Cambridge University Press, 1988.

Fried, Michael. *Three American Painters*. Cambridge, Mass.: Fogg Art Museum, Harvard University, 1965.

Gauthier, David. "The Social Contract as Ideology." *Philosophy and Public Affairs* 6 (winter 1977).

Greenberg, Clement. "After Abstract Expressionism" (1962). In *Aesthetics*, ed. George Dickie and Richard J. Sclafani. New York: St. Martin's Press, 1977.

Griffiths, Paul. *Cage*. London: Oxford University Press, 1981.

Haber, Joram Graf. *Forgiveness*. Savage, Md.: Rowman & Littlefield, 1991.

Hampshire, Stuart. "Fallacies in Moral Philosophy" (1949). In *Contemporary Ethical Theory*, ed. Joseph Margolis. New York: Random House, 1966.

Harrington, Michael. *Toward a Democratic Left*. New York: Macmillan Co., 1968.

Harris, Dale. "How the Figures Add Up." *The Guardian*, 23 April 1984.

Harrison, Jonathan. "Introduction." In *Challenges to Morality*, ed. Jonathan Harrison. New York: Macmillan, 1993.

Hart, H. L. A. *The Concept of Law*. Oxford: Clarendon Press, 1961.

Havel, Vaclev. "Kosovo and the End of the Nation-State." *The New York Review of Books*, 10 June 1999.

Heilbroner, Robert L. *An Inquiry into the Human Prospect*. New York: Norton, 1974, 1975.

Hill, Sharon Bishop. "Self-Determination and Autonomy." In *Today's Moral Problems*, 3rd edition, ed. Richard A. Wasserstrom. New York: Macmillan, 1985.

Hill, Thomas E., Jr. "Servility and Self-Respect" (1973). In *Autonomy and Self-Respect*, Thomas E. Hill Jr. Cambridge: Cambridge University Press, 1991.

———. "Self-Respect Reconsidered." In *Respect for Persons*, ed. O. H. Green. Tulane Studies in Philosophy, 31. New Orleans: Tulane University, 1982. (Also published in Thomas E. Hill Jr., *Autonomy and Self-Respect* [Cambridge: Cambridge University Press, 1991].)

Honore, A. M. "Law, Morals, and Rescue." In *Philosophy of Law*, 2nd edition, ed. Joel Feinberg and Hyman Gross. Belmont, Calif.: Wadsworth, 1980.

Hume, David. *An Enquiry Concerning the Principles of Morals* (1777). In *Hume's Enquiries*, ed. L. A. Selby-Bigge. Oxford: Clarendon Press, 1962.

Ignatieff, Michael. *The Needs of Strangers*. New York: Viking Penguin, 1984.

James, William. *The Will to Believe*. New York: Dover, 1956.

———. *The Varieties of Religious Experience*. New York: Penguin, 1982.

Kafka, Franz. *Letter to His Father*. New York: Schocken Books, 1966.

Kagan, Shelly. *The Limits of Morality*. Oxford: Clarendon Press, 1989.

Kant, Immanuel. *Foundations of the Metaphysics of Morals* (1785). Trans. and introduction by Lewis White Beck. Indianapolis: Bobbs-Merrill, 1959.

———. *Lectures on Ethics*. Trans. Louis Infield, foreword by Lewis White Beck. New York: Harper Torchbooks, 1963.

———. *The Metaphysical Elements of Justice* (1797). Trans. John Ladd. Indianapolis: Bobbs-Merrill, 1965.

Klee, Paul. *Diary (1909): The Diaries of Paul Klee, 1898–1918*. Berkeley: University of California Press, 1964.

Lasch, Christopher. *The Culture of Narcissism*. New York: Norton, 1979.

Leopold, Aldo. *A Sand County Almanac* (1949). New York: Ballantine Books, 1970.

Lippard, Lucy. *Athena Tacha: Massacre Memorials and Other Public Projects*. Exhibition essay, Max Hutchinson Gallery, New York, 25 October–17 November 1984.

Locke, John. *The Second Treatise of Government*. In *Locke's Two Treatises of Government*, ed. Peter Laslett. Cambridge: Cambridge University Press, 1963.

Marx, Karl. "Alienated Labor." In *Karl Marx: Early Writings*, ed. T. B. Bottomore. New York: McGraw-Hill, 1964.

———. *The German Ideology*. In *The Marx–Engels Reader*, ed. Robert C. Tucker. New York: Norton, 1972.

Marx, Karl, and Friedrich Engels. *The Communist Manifesto* (1848). Introduction by Martin Malia. New York: Penguin (Signet Classic), 1998.

May, William F. *The Patient's Ordeal*. Bloomington: Indiana University Press, 1991.

McFall, Lynne. "Integrity." *Ethics* 98 (October 1987).

Melden, A. I. *Free Action*. London: Routledge and Kegan Paul, 1961.

Mele, Alfred R. *Springs of Action*. New York: Oxford University Press,1992.

———. "Motivation: Essentially Motivation-Constituting Attitudes." *The Philosophical Review* 104, no. 3 (July 1995).

Menand, Louis. "William James and the Case of the Epileptic Patient." *The New York Review of Books*, 17 December 1998.

Miliband, Ralph. *The State in Capitalist Society*. London: Weidenfeld and Nicolson, 1969.

Mill, John Stuart. *Utilitarianism* (1863). Ed. George Sher. Indianapolis: Hackett, 1979.

Mischel, Theodore. "Concerning Rational Behaviour and Psychoanalytic Explanation." *Mind* 74 (January 1965).

Miss, Mary. "Toward a Redefinition of Public Sculpture." Paper prepared for the U.S./Japan Symposium on Urban Life and Culture, 1–4 October 1982.

Moore, Barrington, Jr. *Injustice: The Social Bases of Obedience and Revolt*. White Plains, N.Y.: Sharpe, 1978.

Morris, Herbert. *On Guilt and Innocence*. Berkeley: University of California Press, 1976.

Murphy, Jeffrie G. "Forgiveness and Resentment." In *Forgiveness and Mercy*, Jeffrie G. Murphy and Jean Hampton. Cambridge: Cambridge University Press, 1988.

———. "Jean Hampton on Immorality, Self-Hatred, and Self-Forgiveness." *Philosophical Studies* 89 (1998).

Nagel. Thomas. "Ruthlessness in Public Life." In *Mortal Questions*, Thomas Nagel. Cambridge: Cambridge University Press, 1979.

O'Neill, Onora. *Faces of Hunger*. London: Allen and Unwin, 1986.

Partridge, Ernest. "Why Care about the Future?" In *Responsibilities to Future Generations*, ed. Ernest Partridge. Buffalo, N.Y.: Prometheus Press, 1981.

Percy, Walker. *The Moviegoer* (1960, 1961). New York: Vintage, 1998.

"Personality and Personality Disorders—Part II." *The Harvard Medical School Mental Health Letter* 4, no.4 (October 1987).

Peters, R. S. *The Concept of Motivation*. London: Routledge and Kegan Paul, 1958.

Phillips, Patricia C. "Out of Order: The Public Art Machine." *Art Forum* (December 1988).

Railton, Peter. "Alienation, Consequentialism, and the Demands of Morality." *Philosophy and Public Affairs* 13 (spring 1984).

Rawls, John. "Two Concepts of Rules." *The Philosophical Review* 64 (1955).

Works Cited 193

————. *A Theory of Justice.* Cambridge, Mass.: Belknap Press of Harvard University Press, 1971.

Rickey, Carrie. "The Writing on the Wall." *Art in America* (May 1981).

Rolston, Holmes, III. *Philosophy Gone Wild.* Buffalo, N.Y.: Prometheus Books, 1986.

————. *Environmental Ethics.* Philadelphia: Temple University Press, 1988.

Rousseau, Jean-Jacques. *A Discourse on the Origin of Inequality* (1755). In *The Social Contract and Discourses,* trans. and introduction by G. D. H. Cole. New York: Everyman, 1950.

————. *The Confessions.* Trans. J. M. Cohen. Harmondsworth, U.K.: Penguin Books, 1954.

————. *The Reveries of the Solitary Walker.* Trans., preface, notes, and interpretive essay by Charles E. Butterworth. New York: Harper Colophon, 1982.

Runciman, W. G. *Relative Deprivation and Social Justice.* London: Routledge and Kegan Paul, 1966.

Sandel, Michael. *Liberalism and the Limits of Justice.* Cambridge: Cambridge University Press, 1982.

Scheffler, Samuel. *Human Morality.* New York: Oxford University Press, 1992.

Schrader, George. "Autonomy, Heteronomy, and Moral Imperatives." *The Journal of Philosophy* 60, no. 3 (1963).

Sidgwick, Henry. *The Methods of Ethics* (1907), 7th edition. New York: Dover, 1966.

Smith, Martin L., and Heidi Forster. "Morally Managing Medical Mistakes." *Cambridge Quarterly of Healthcare Ethics* (forthcoming).

Sontag, Susan. *Illness as Metaphor and AIDS and Its Metaphors.* New York: Doubleday (Anchor edition), 1990.

Stengel, Richard. "The Republic of Feeling." <http://www.msnbc.com/news/247101.asp.html>, 8 March 1999.

Stocker, Michael. 1976. "The Schizophrenia of Modern Ethical Theories." *The Journal of Philosophy* 73, no. 14 (12 August 1976).

Strawson, P. F. "Freedom and Resentment." *Proceedings of the British Academy* 48 (1962).

Tacha, Athena. 1980. Statement from an interview, made available by the artist.

Thoreau, Henry David. *Walden* (1854). Introduction by Norman Holmes Pearson. New York: Rinehart, 1948.

Tolstoy, Leo N. *What Is Art?* (1896). Trans. Almyer Maude, introduction by Vincent Tomas. Indianapolis: Bobbs-Merrill, 1960.

Tomkins, Calvin. "The Art World." *The New Yorker,* 21 March 1983.

Twelve Steps and Twelve Traditions. New York: Alcoholics Anonymous World Services, Inc., 1953.

Verghese, Abraham. *My Own Country.* New York: Simon and Schuster, 1994.

"A Very Real Obscenity" (editorial). *The (Cleveland) Plain Dealer,* 15 November 1990.

Walton, Kendall L. "Categories of Art." *The Philosophical Review* 79 (1970).

Walzer, Michael. "Political Action: The Problem of Dirty Hands." *Philosophy and Public Affairs* 2, no. 2 (winter 1973).

Watson, Gary. "Responsibility and the Limits of Evil: Variations on a Strawsonian

Works Cited

Theme." In *Responsibility, Character, and the Emotions,* ed. Ferdinand Schoeman. Cambridge: Cambridge University Press, 1987.

Williams, Bernard. *Moral Luck.* Cambridge: Cambridge University Press, 1981.

Winch, Peter. "Moral Integrity." Oxford: Basil Blackwell, 1968.

Wittgenstein, Ludwig. *Philosophical Investigations.* Trans. G. E. M. Anscombe. New York: Macmillan, 1953.

Wolf, Susan. "Moral Saints." *The Journal of Philosophy* 79 (August 1982).

Index

195

Murphy, Jeffrie G., 170n12, 175n24
my reasons, 160–67

natural sympathy, 11, 81–82, 132,
186n2
needs, 13, 67–101, 131; awareness of,
76–78; critique of an analytic
account of, 69–76; immediate and
urgent, 74
negative moral emotion, 5, 17, 21–
23, 46, 48, 58, 84–85, 131
neutral facts, 79–83
Nietzsche, Friedrich, 44
normative facts, 68, 76, 78–83
novel ideas, the motivational power
of, 13, 120–29

O'Neill, Onora, 179n19
optimism (William James's view),
25–32

particularity about persons, 110–11
Partridge, Ernest, 184n33
peace of mind, 23, 33–34, 49, 58
Percy, Walker, 13
perversity (Dostoevsky's view), 143–
45
Phillips, Patricia C., 89, 99
plans of life, 61–62
political oppression, 42–44, 47
psychoanalytic (hidden) reasons,
159–67
public art, 87–90

radical conceptualization, 93–99
Railton, Peter, 188n30
Rawls, John, 19, 53, 60–61, 63, 105,
113, 115, 133, 145, 173n2, 175n1,
177nn21–23, 177nn25–26, 181n8,
183n19, 183n22, 184n27, 184n31,
187n27, 188n2
reasons, 159–67
reciprocation, 111–13, 183n25
reconciliation problem, 132, 145–47
recovery of agency, 12–13, 20, 24,
33–42, 125–26
recovery strategy, 3, 21–23, 40, 42–49

relationships, 19–20, 43
resignation, 136–37, 146
respect for principles, 1–2, 4–13, 17,
23, 125
responding and reacting to persons,
79–83
responsibility exemptions, 138–42
responsible agency, 139–40
Rickey, Carrie, 89, 179n30
Rolston, Holmes, III, 123
Rousseau, Jean-Jacques, 36, 84–85,
125
Runciman, W. G., 178n4

sacrifice (for future generations),
108, 132
Sandel, Michael, 186n11
Schoenberg, Arnold, 92–93
Schrader, George, 178n14
self-knowledge, 41, 174n12
self-realization, 65, 86, 90–99, 135
self-respect, 13, 34, 51–65, 131; four
conceptions of, 63–65; general
idea of, 59–62; threats and
challenges to, 52–59
sense of justice, 115
service to others, 86–99
servility, 55–58
shared-fate individualism, 85–99,
145
Smith, Martin L., 173n7
Sontag, Susan, 173n27
Stocker, Michael, 9
Strawson, P. F., 178n15

Tacha, Athena, 88–89, 99
therapy, 2–3
Thoreau, Henry David, 97, 101, 122–
23
Tolstoy, Leo N., 88
Tomkins, Calvin, 88–89

utilitarianism, 3, 10–12, 15, 18–21,
25, 27–29, 31, 68, 137, 182n16,
186n2

value in nature, 123

About the Author

Norman S. Care is professor of philosophy at Oberlin College. He was educated in music at Indiana University and in philosophy at the University of Kansas, Yale University, and Oxford University. His areas of interest in teaching and writing are moral theory, moral psychology, political philosophy, environmental ethics, and philosophy of art. He is the author of *On Sharing Fate* (1987) and *Living with One's Past: Personal Fates and Moral Pain* (1996), and coeditor of a number of collections; he has published essays and reviews in journals in philosophy, law, and education, and in magazines of social comment. In 1991 professor Care received a Teaching Excellence and Campus Leadership Award from the Sears-Roebuck Foundation, and in 2000 he received a Distinguished Teaching award from Oberlin College. His research and writings have been supported over the years by a Fulbright Fellowship and grants from the American Council of Learned Societies, the National Endowment for the Humanities, and Oberlin College.